MUSIC EDUCATION IN ENGLAND, 1950–2010

*In memory of Edwin Newland Finney, young schoolmaster killed
on 19 May 1917 in the Battle of the Somme*

Music Education in England, 1950–2010

1950–2010

The Child-Centred Progressive Tradition

JOHN FINNEY
University of Cambridge, UK

ASHGATE

Published by
Ashgate Publishing Limited
Wey Court East
Union Road
Farnham
Surrey, GU9 7PT
England

Ashgate Publishing Company
Suite 420
101 Cherry Street
Burlington
VT 05401-4405
USA

www.ashgate.com

British Library Cataloguing in Publication Data
Finney, John.
  Music education in England, 1950–2010: the child-centred progressive tradition.
  1. Music–Instruction and study–England–History–20th century.
  I. Title
  780.7'1042-dc22

Library of Congress Cataloging-in-Publication Data
Finney, John, 1944–
  Music education in England, 1950-2010 : the child-centred progressive tradition / John Finney.
    p. cm.
  Includes bibliographical references and index.
  ISBN 978-1-4094-1076-8 (hardcover) – ISBN 978-1-4094-1946-4
  (ebook) 1. School music–Instruction and study–England–History–20th century. 2. School music–Instruction and study–England–History–21st century. I. Title.
  MT3.G7F56 2010
  780.71'042–dc22

2010024209

ISBN 9781409410768 (hbk)
ISBN 9781409419464 (ebk)

Printed and bound in Great Britain by
TJ International Ltd, Padstow, Cornwall.

Contents

Preface

Writing an account of music education in England from 1950 to the present time is bound to involve this writer in a form of autobiography, for the period covers the time during which I progressed from childhood to secondary school music teacher, then to music teacher educator and now commentator on contemporary policy and practice. It is the time in which I have lived music education. It was in the 1950s as an inquisitive child hearing from my primary school teacher, Mr Blanchard, about his Second World War exploits that music began to grow in my mind as a way of understanding who I was and what I might become. In due course as a secondary school music teacher I became aware that I was part of an ever-changing milieu of music educational thought and practice, and that there was a long-running conversation with which to engage. Whose music should I teach? Was I teaching a subject or teaching a child? To what extent should I listen to the mind of the child? What authority did I have to declare a child's musical needs? To what extent was it my responsibility to infer these needs and might the child be expected to express a different set of needs? Could children be seen as artists uniquely expressing their thoughts and feelings? Were the products of their imaginations *sui generis*? Whose music education was this? These were not new questions. However, it was the discovery of child-centred progressive practice and its tradition manifest in the privileging of children's expressive thoughts and feelings that brought about a change in my own identity as a music teacher and which in due course called for serious reflection. This story of personal awakening and reflection runs quietly throughout what follows.

While the study offers a fresh viewing point from which to evaluate ideas and practices evolving during the past 60 years within English music education, there is another task to accomplish; a critique of the present, exposing the dangers lurking in our unrelenting pursuit of future gains and market values which are thought to serve the making and sustaining of the social order. Problems of the present are much in mind as the story of the past 60 years unfolds.

To speak of music education in the present time draws in a great deal more than the idea of music in the school, for music education is widely recognized as existing in a vast range of regulated and unregulated settings, and altogether more out of school than in. However, music remains a part of the idea of the school, involving a relationship between music teachers and their students. It is this species of music education that is worked with in what follows. The reader will find a story which draws in major debates of the period covered, along with their protagonists, counterpointed by the voices of teachers and pupils. At the same time the voices of policy and governance are found becoming ever louder as we reach the present time. Here is a contextualized account of music education: social, cultural and political matters have an important role to play.

In telling the story the labels 'children', 'young people', 'pupils' and 'students' will be used as the context requires. These of course tell something of the ways in which the young are regarded. The first two recognize the existence of a 'person' living both within and beyond the school and potentially free from tutelage, while there is no such freedom afforded by the terms 'pupil' and 'student'. There is still one more label, recently in use: the child is a 'learner', but this is now an identity for all, adult and child alike.

In bringing the project to fruition I must first recall and in particular thank amongst my teachers Henry George, Ian Carswell, Gordon Cox and Tony Kemp, who listened and encouraged. I am thankful too for the support and stimulation of colleagues I have worked with in secondary schools; Alex Mitchell, Cliff Lancaster, Peter Kendall, Frank Mason, Audrey Atter, Ian Muir and a great many more. Again, it was their encouraging friendship and frequent forbearance that sustained thought about what were the challenges of the daily meeting with our classes in our efforts to educate. There is much gratitude too to express to my current colleagues in the Faculty of Education in Cambridge, who meet each day as an early morning coffee collective. The group's spontaneous agenda continues to give space to the sociological mind of John Beck, Mary Earl's quest to better conceptualize Religious Education, Richard Hickman's steady grasp of matters artistic and aesthetic and Anne Sinkinson's redoubtable realism. Together these provide a strong source of intellectual stimulation and rootedness. It was Gabrielle Cliff-Hodges who one morning asked whether I knew of Sybil Marshall's *An Experiment in Education*, of her Symphonic Method and the Beethoven term. My discovery of this text gave impetus to the whole. For this I am very grateful.

Important too were times spent during the first half of 2008 in the company of characters close to the story being told. Long conversations with Jill Cafferky telling of Sybil Marshall's schoolroom of the 1950s and a day spent with Sybil Marshall's daughter Pru and husband Tony were immensely rewarding times. Likewise days spent first with Malcolm Ross and then John Paynter proved to be important. But too must be acknowledged those who have supported the project through ongoing discussions and through reading of the text: Gordon Cox, Kristen Eglinton, John Hopkins, Tim Cain, Jennie Francis and Felicity Laurence for their close readings and critique; Louise Cooper, Ruth Wright, Gabrielle Cliff-Hodges, Emily Finney and Mary Finney for reading and commenting on individual chapters; Alan Morgan, a long time mentor in my use of the English language, for his sympathetic and detailed attention to the text, its meanings, idiosyncratic spellings, ambiguities and confusions and for never discouraging a tendency towards the poetic; Katherine Shaw for her astute and dedicated support in preparing the final text for publication; Heidi Bishop and colleagues at Ashgate for their gentle encouragement and splendid support. For the final text I must of course take full responsibility. The work was substantially carried out during two sabbatical terms granted by the University of Cambridge for which I am grateful and likewise to Roger Green and Rob Lepley for covering aspects of my teaching.

Finally I am grateful for the permissions granted to include extracts from previously published work. Chapter 4 draws from the paper 'Music Education as Aesthetic Education: a re-think' in the *British Journal of Music Education* (Vol. 19, No. 3) with permission granted by Cambridge University Press, and likewise elements of 'The rights and wrongs of school music: considering the expressivist argument and its existential component' in the *British Journal of Music Education* (Vol. 16, No. 3) and used in Chapters 5 and 8. Chapter 6 contains the previously published Chapter 5 of *Rebuilding Engagement through the Arts: Responding to disaffected students* (2005) and is reproduced by kind permission from Pearson Publishing Ltd. Elsewhere there are small amounts of material taken from the article 'From Resentment to Enchantment: what a class of 13-year-olds and their music teacher tell about a musical education', *International Journal of Education and the Arts* (Vol. 4, No. 6) and from Routledge the following extracts: in *Learning to Teach Music in the Secondary School* edited by Chris Philpott and Gary Spruce (2007) the section on page 5 'A Moral and Political Question' and the section 'Concession and Change' on pages 6 to 8; from Chapter 3 of *A Practical Guide to Teaching Music in the Secondary School* the section on page 29 'Why teach the Blues?' and the section 'Finding cultural depth' on page 30. For all these permissions I am grateful.

John Finney
Cambridge, May 2010

Dorothy recalls the Silent Band of school days, circa 1930

There was Margaret, the clever one, Sheila – very sweet and good, and me, always on the look out for a bit of fun. The game started when we reached the back lane, a long narrow lane where we never saw any one, and of course, no one ever saw us. Each one chose an instrument – 'I'll play the drum, I'm going to play the trombone, I'll play the violin.' We line up, and one, two, three we're off, marching in line, arms waving and not a single sound. Then laughter overcomes us, we are doubled up, rolling about with laughter. Then 'what did you play?' – Land of Hope and Glory. 'What did you play?' – Polly Wolly Doodle – 'What did you play?' Red Sails in the Sunset – Right – off again. Usually we managed three goes, then we had reached the end of the lane. Coats smoothed down, hats straightened, back to normal once more. Game over until tomorrow.

(Written communication, 2006)

Chapter 1

Introduction

The future of class music! There was one, but what was it to be? This was the question that concentrated the minds of delegates attending the Music Advisors' National Conference at Saffron Walden in the last days of June 1977. The source of provocation had been the book *Music in Education: A Point of View* by Arnold Bentley (Bentley 1975). To Bentley many contemporary practices were trivial, for he deemed that music in school should focus on music listening, singing, playing classroom instruments, and music reading and writing. Bentley's was a reaction against 'progressive tendencies' of the time. In the July/August 1977 edition of the popular publication *Music in Education*, feature space is given over to a discussion recorded shortly before the conference. The protagonists are Bentley himself, head of the music education centre at Reading University, and Hamish Preston, music advisor for Berkshire. Severe tensions are brought to the surface between a long-standing commitment to the mastery of the techniques and disciplines expected of a music education and the problems presented by reluctant teenagers rejecting what music teachers had to offer (Music in Education 1977). The discussion bore the title 'The future of class music' which reflected a controversy that was emblematic of the time. Preston alludes to John Paynter's notion of creative work, thinking and feeling like a composer and children gaining greater insight into music, while Bentley defers to traditional practices that are tried and tested. For Preston what is important is the musical engagement of young people, artistic values and a humanizing education. For Bentley there is commitment to the integrity of a well ordered and balanced curriculum which he concedes may not be appropriate for all beyond early adolescence.

Bentley was swimming against the tide of progressive ideas, for the child-centred progressive educational movement had grown in force in the decades following the Second World War. The child could be viewed as playful, curious, insightful and with an impulse to create and make, and the school could become more open and responsive to the interests of its pupils. It was such ideas that were to yield a vast array of possibilities that would change the nature of classrooms, how knowledge, culture and authority were to be thought about and the kind of relationships that were possible between teacher and pupil and what was being learnt. The impact upon music education and education in general was to be long lasting. The crudely formed distinction between traditional and progressive approaches was to become one way of framing political, social and cultural contestations within a shifting educational landscape. Indeed, it was to serve as a focus for arguments about the moral purpose of education. As Moore points out: 'The traditional versus progressive debate has been conducted as a conflict about society itself, as reflecting a tension between social order and change, respect for tradition versus "permissiveness"' (Moore 2004: 147–8).

Justification

If Moore is right then there are good reasons for a study of music education in England from 1950 to the present day seen through the lens of those child-centred progressive ideas that gained momentum in the post-war period. The enquiry draws together developments of the period in a unique way, yielding fresh insights into the place of music in education. It becomes possible to view social, political and cultural changes of the period in a particular light and to uncover new relationships between those ideas that have been most influential in the development of music in schools.

Beyond justifying the study as offering a fresh perspective on music education of the recent past, there is a pressing case for understanding this in the context of the present, where the place of the child in making a music education is framed by a contradictory rhetoric. No longer is a 'child-centred' education promoted. The idea is both *passé* and politically inept. Instead, there is talk of an education that is 'learner-centred', and where there is 'personalized learning' addressing the needs of the child as a consumer and producer of education. Indeed, the notion of 'personalization' proposes that education, like other services, should be designed, co-produced and co-delivered involving 'intimate consultation' and 'expanded choice' (Leadbeater 2005). The child is indeed the centre of attention. Hartley notes 'the strong semantic accord between the terms "personalization" and "child-centred education"', pointing out how the government's denial of association between the two serves to 'adapt education further to a consumerist society ...' (Hartley 2009: 423). The roots of the 'personalization' concept lie within marketing theory and with an attachment to neo-liberal doctrine.

The neo-liberal present sees education as a state investment from which there needs to be tangible economic dividends. It must be ever more efficient and economically productive. State education in England now works as a quasi-market where schools must compete as well as children (Ball 2007, 2008). Children take centre place as consumer-learner-citizens with entrepreneurial potential. The neo-liberal way is seen as liberating enterprise where the individual finds greater freedom, exercising unlimited choice and autonomy. Children are expected to be not just enterprising but to become members of an enterprise culture, and to ensure themselves that they are not only employable but marketable too. Neo-liberalism assumes that people are driven by private interest, that they are best served by market competition, that seeking equality of opportunity is misguided and doomed to failure and that greed is a source of social progress (Lauder et al. 2006: 26; see also Harvey 2005). What is private is necessarily good and what is public is necessarily bad, or at least suspect, and investment in education allows the nation to successfully compete, for the world is intensely competitive. In Gordon Brown's phrase, 'there is a skills race' and this is reason for 'pushing ahead' with reforms to the education system – 'the challenge is now to unlock the talents of all people' to take part in a 'global skills race' (Brown 2008: 27). The vision advances the notion of 'opportunity for all' and the need to 'personalize these services so they meet the distinct and unique needs of individuals'. This requires that we 'nurture and develop creativity, interpersonal skills and technical abilities, as well as analytic intelligence' (ibid). Education becomes a commodity.

This neo-liberal present exists in stark contrast to the benevolent workings of a liberal state supporting education in 1950 where the protected child was embedded in traditional forms of community and institutional order. At the beginning of the new millennium the child is no longer situated within a set of traditional values. And there are no institutions stable enough to provide ease, comfort and secure identity. Identity is no longer a given but a 'task' to perform, a process of 'obligatory self determination' (Bauman 2008, xv). While child-centred progressive educators of earlier times were offering children new freedoms within the secure bounds of an established order, children today *are* what Beck and Beck-Gernsheim (2008) define as 'freedom's children'. Not identity but freedom is a given as they 'practise a seeking, experimenting morality that ties together things that seem to be mutually exclusive: egoism and altruism, self-realization and active compassion' (Beck and Beck Gernsheim 2008: 159). In this view we have to accept children as members of the 'me' generation, and as an inevitable product of democratic evolution and the source of new values. Freedom has arrived and in school children will be looking for something other than the routines and disciplines of former times, seeking space to develop their own biography, and at the same time a worthy pack of credentials.

In English schools the introduction of non-negotiable standards, assessment regimes with high stake testing and league tables, and with a proclivity for certain kinds of knowledge having greater currency than others, sets the rules of the official game. Learning objectives narrow, outcomes become entirely predictable accompanied by the closure of 'open engagement that allows for expression of values, beliefs and interpretations' (Doddington and Hilton 2007: 117). Beyond this there is increasing concern about the loss of depth and quality in learning and about the enforced dedication of schools to an input-output model of education embedded within a 'culture of pragmatism and compliance' (Alexander 2008: 79). Education is very clearly future-orientated, market-orientated and bereft of history.

In February 2009 Ofsted, the schools' inspection body, published a 78-page report 'Making more of music' based on evidence from inspections in a range of maintained schools in England between 2005 and 2008 (Ofsted 2009). Quite unlike the Ministry of Education's 'Music in School' report of 1956 there is no engagement with the past (HMSO 1956). In the 1956 report a substantial chapter is devoted to the historical context in which the way ahead is located. There is respectful and carefully measured critical comment on the long revolution that effected the development of music in schools. There is a conversation between what has been and what might be. Now there is only the matter of raising standards. If education has become overwhelmingly future-orientated the case for more history of education is compelling. Without it criticism of the present as well as hope for the future is diminished.

The Lure of History

In providing a 'usable past' for music educators, Gordon Cox argues for the need to 'engage with the real concerns of policy makers, administrators, and practitioners in music classrooms' (Cox 2002: 145–6). What follows will need to make sense for music teachers, teachers of music teachers and curriculum innovators too. It must explain and clarify the problems, confusions and errors in the thinking and practices of the present as well as the past. It must cause reflection as it shapes ambition and hope. It must draw forth human sympathy and the empathic imagination if it is to contribute to better understanding of the present, a love of the past and trust in the future.

For myself the value of a historical perspective was a slow burning process and first came through reading the first chapter of *Music in the Secondary School Curriculum* written by John Paynter in 1982, in which is related the development of music as a subject within a general education with a concern to reach all pupils. The fact that what I did as a secondary school music teacher at the time was without a sense of history became a matter of interest. In 1987, and now a student of music education, Anthony Kemp at Reading University presented the proposition that there might be enduring principles of music education to consider. Music educators of the past such as John Curwen and Emile Jacques-Dalcroze still had much to teach provided that principles underlying their methods were grasped. That there were key individuals, sometimes iconoclasts, having considerable effect on the formulation of policy and influencing practice as demonstrated in Gordon Cox's 1993 study *A History of Music Education in England 1872–1928*, in due course became of interest too. People, ideas, values embedded in philosophies were what counted. There was no science of music education and indeed, as Allan Hewitt points out in reviewing *Music in Educational Thought and Practice* (Rainbow with Cox 2006) … 'the structure and content of school music education is inevitably (and perhaps regrettably) driven by values rather than empirical evidence …' (Hewitt 2008: 132). Values, beliefs and ideologies are what we subscribe to and what leads us on.

Perhaps unsurprisingly, I read Stephanie Pitts's *A Century of Change in Music Education: Historical Perspectives on Contemporary Practice in British Secondary School Music* in one day (Pitts 2000). I missed no word and read quickly. It was a story that was important to me. There was a compelling narrative and in the second half of what was revealed I was deeply implicated, first as a child in school and subsequently as a music teacher, and finally teacher of music teachers. In part what follows is autobiography, part a story of others who were convinced about the creative potentials of the child, part too an account of living realities in classrooms and schools and part philosophical enquiry, seeking to better understand the distinction between a music education as self-realization and a music education for musical understanding unburdened by the self. It is the tensions arising between a music education as self-understanding and a music education as a cognitive discipline that seeks resolution in an acceptance of a form of understanding that recognizes 'being in the world' and 'being in the world with others'. In this way musical understanding takes on a particular depth and ethical significance. Music education seeks out a 'humanistic conscience' (Fromm 1941/2007).

Child-centred and Progressive Traditions

The notion of child-centredness has little currency or meaning at the present time. It is a thing of the past and in discussing child-centredness Pring (2004) reminds us that the idea arises from different traditions.

> Put crudely, the distinction is between, on the one hand, those who emphasize the individual nature of growth – the gradual development of potential that is there waiting to be recognized, fertilized, watered, or just allowed to grow (the horticultural metaphor is popular among the followers of Froebel and Pestalozzi) – and, on the other hand, those who stress the social context of development.
>
> (Pring 2004: 82)

It is the latter that is associated with the work of John Dewey and the former with the legacy of Rousseau and John Locke, the educational freedom thinkers of the Enlightenment. In the case of Dewey there is a commitment to a socialized intelligence, the development of participatory democracy with the school as the site where this is first experienced and progressively learnt. Education is life itself and not merely a preparation for life, a lived present with a 'potent instrumentality for the future' (Dewey 1938/1971: 23). Subject matter is important. Subjects need to be socially relevant, problematical in a way that makes the present alive with human interest. For Dewey this idea was some distance from a child-centred education that leads to the 'relativizing of authority that quickly degenerated into authoritarianism' (Woodford 2005). In the case of the arts the child-centred tradition had an easily discernable lineage found within the expressivism of early nineteenth-century Romanticism, leading to ideas of the child as artist and the child as individually and uniquely expressive. However, the overlapping and intersecting of ideas from both child-centred and progressive traditions is considerable and in any case, in the period investigated, the notion of child-centredness is sustained and invigorated by ideas emerging from wide-ranging sources as its proponents sought out fresh authority and compelling witnesses in support of their case. Branches of psychology, existential philosophy, expressivist theories of art, modernism and contemporary artistic practices, for example, were all to make contributions. The child-centredness of which I write can have no pure form and is best referred to as a child-centred progressive tradition.

Within this frame of reference I do have in mind a particular kind of relationship between teacher, pupil and what is being learnt, for it involves fundamentally the negotiation of beliefs and values. The relationship is more than a functional one. In school it is within this tradition that relationships come to be thought of as personal rather than instrumental. In the relationships formed there will be some revealing of selves, and what we are teaching and learning will be an interpersonal matter and come to be of mutual interest. There will be a 'clearing' created between those engaged … 'a *clear* space is created that allows and even calls each person to articulate his or her own values and beliefs' (Doddington and Hilton 2007: 89). And in this are implied principles of democracy. It is this dedication to creating a climate of exchange that the notion of the 'whole child' can be best made sense of. Childhood is viewed as a distinctive time, and it is the state of children's 'here and now' existence that matters most, for 'childhood is a *time in itself*' (ibid: 55). In this way of thinking, the school, the music lesson can be thought of as a way-of-life, as something apart and largely free from necessity. Of course, if this way-of-life is non-authoritarian where democratic ideals are practised, there may well arise a life-long love of learning and the possibility of making a contribution to a better future for all. But the music lesson needs to make sense now. Music teachers will be listening to those they teach, to see each child as being unique. The teacher will be able to respond to each child and enter into a conversation that discerns and nurtures the musicality and humanity of each. So how shall we proceed?

The Project: Structure and Method

The argument presented works through a series of six episodes, each seeking to capture the spirit and fervour characteristic of a particular phase within the period studied. The first episode (Chapter 2) is a portrait of Sybil Marshall, a woman of the immediate post-war period, independent in mind and spirit, a 'liberal romantic', whose class of children aged five to eleven learnt to imagine and to express their understanding of the world through artistic outpourings and through music in song, dance and famously through coming to know a whole symphony. Sybil Marshall was a woman of the 1950s attuned to the criticisms of an unduly conformist society, an overbearing rational order where there was repression of feeling and spontaneity and lack of individuality. It was Sybil's free-spirited enterprise in unique circumstances that was to become a source of inspiration for several generations of primary school teachers, and which was to chime well with the Plowden Report of 1967 and the official reshaping of the primary school. What was emerging was 'the age of authenticity' leading to the contemporary demand for an 'expressive individualism', a search for sources of the authentic self (Taylor 2007).

The first episode sets out to be a compelling narrative drawing upon Sybil Marshall's writings both educational and literary, interviews with pupils from her class of the 1950s, examination of their art work and poetry still preserved, the voice of Sybil as archived radio broadcast material, my own reflections on being in primary school and teacher training, and all this set in the context of an HMI report of the time calling for fewer large group musical performance activities and more attention to individual musical development. The chapter is an 'experiment in portraiture' serving Sybil Marshall's own 'experiment in education'. The art of portraiture demands that 'the boundaries of aesthetics and empiricism are blurred in an effort to capture the complexity, dynamics, and subtlety of human experience and organizational life' (Lawrence-Lightfoot 1997: xv).

Sybil Marshall's robust resistance to authoritarian models of the past and her reaching out for intellectual stimulus from the progressive thinking of artist educators such as David Holbrook and Wilfred Mellers, served as a precursor to the more widespread distaste expressed by the young for what seemed mechanical and all that smothered creativity, individuality, the body and the possibility of informal organic ties in place of traditional communities of order. Thus, the second episode (Chapter 3) examines the 1960s and 1970s and the impact of egalitarian ideals, focusing on a bold response to the changing expectations of adolescents and their rejection of the canons of good taste. Why did reason dominate feeling, why was play marginalized by work and why was school so different from 'not school'? Could not the authentic self of the adolescent be present in school? The radical thought and practice of Robert Witkin and Malcolm Ross, like that of Sybil Marshall, bring to the fore the dialogic character of the teacher-pupil relationship and how to know the medium of musical expression was to know self and to learn a respect for subjectivity. At the same time the clash of educational ideologies brought into play by the rejection of traditional values and creeping cultural relativities saw the emergence of a highly partisan political positioning that was to establish a 'new right' educational voice of great force. Culture was now contestable and at the heart of politics. Quite unlike the portrait of Sybil Marshall, this episode explores complex theoretical ideas that were posited in the name of self-expression, where the arts would have a common purpose and the adolescent first and foremost would have a life of feeling.

This prepares the way for considering the response to changing circumstances and a major crisis of confidence within music education through the perspective of the thought and practice of composer and music educator John Paynter. Concurrent with the turbulence caused by Witkin and Ross, episode three (Chapter 4) uses the text *Sound and Silence* as the starting point for understanding how the idea of creative music and creative music making worked to reconfigure what it meant to know music and to be musical. This was conceived as a part of a liberal education in which music education would need to find underpinnings in philosophical debate about what it meant to 'know music', what was distinctive about music and the arts and just whose music was to be a source of education. This coincided with my own most formative phase of experience in the classroom, where an

ideological shift of some significance led to innovative practice and being drawn
to find further and better explanations for what I was experiencing.

In considering the upheavals of the 1960s and 1970s and the more circumspect
1980s, the reader will be taken into classrooms and become acquainted with
particular pupils and my own progress as a music teacher in secondary schools.
It is now time to hear the voices of youth through an ethnographic study yielding
better understanding of ways in which the young are, in Paul Willis's phrase,
'culturally energized'. In episode four (Chapter 5) a group of four adolescent boys,
engaged in managing their own music education, present what must *ipso facto*
constitute a child-centred progressive view of how music is learnt and the kind
of values that come to be attached to the creative process. In this way theoretical
concepts previously developed are brought down to earth and developed further.
This gives rise to more questions about music's social and cultural significance
and the inadequacy of a model over-reliant on music as an expression of the self.
And this coincides with the making of a National Curriculum, representing a call
to order leading to a centralization of policy making and the onset of bureaucratic
management and the surveillance of music in school. With 'new era values' comes
the closure of practices celebrating the authority of the child as artist.

By the new millennium the official curriculum had repositioned the child as
a 'learner' amongst a dazzling rhetoric surrounding the notion of 'learning'. Out
of all this had come 'pupil voice', a fresh attempt to place children at the centre
of the educational process and promote their full participation in the life of the
school. The fifth episode (Chapter 6) presents the story of a class of 13-year-olds
and their teacher in a school striving to improve following the educational reforms
of the 1990s. In particular it celebrates the agency of four of the class given voice
and authority to engage a class of 11- and 12-year-olds in their vernacular musical
practices. The chapter draws on ethnographic data as well as that gleaned through
action-research making full use of the pupils' voices as they create an image of a
school where, for a short time, they are seen differently and where a school might
be seen differently.

In the wake of a second crisis of confidence in music education and amidst the
hope of a music educational renaissance, the final episode (Chapter 7) is presented
as a critique of attempts to revive the fortunes of music in school at the start
of the new millennium. This is focused on two initiatives boldly setting out to
enliven music in the school. On the one hand there is offered a radical quasi child-
centred progressive curriculum in recognition that 'freedom's children' know how
to learn music through their consumption and production of music beyond the
school gates. On the other, there is a National Strategy intensifying the official
curriculum through the deployment of set procedures and templates of practice.
All this is placed in the context of New Labour's educational policies investing in
the future and the consumer-learner-citizen.

In the final chapter the unfolding narrative is reviewed and the idea of music
education as an ethical pursuit is proposed in which classroom relationships can be
thought of as playfully dialogic, where teacher and pupil remain curious, and where

attention is paid to what is to be taught and why. These pedagogic imperatives will always need to be negotiated to ensure the expressed and inferred needs of children work together to find a critical approach to what is being learnt.

The enquiry tells of a time through which music education in England has travelled with both abounding confidence and great uncertainty. It is an era during which two major crises of confidence have surfaced within music education and in each case been met by bold responses disruptive and contentious in equal measure of well-established orthodoxies. Throughout the period there have been child-centred progressive tendencies drawing on child-centred and progressive traditions that have emanated from the belief that a music education for the child and adolescent here and now should hold personal meaning and significance.

In what follows we must ask not so much what is the nature of music, although that will arise, but what are schools for, what is music in school for, what are music teachers for and what kind of relationship are music teachers to have with their pupils? What kind of pupils and what kind of schools do we want? What is the place of music in the school?

The Festival of Britain held in 1951, 100 years after the Great Exhibition of 1851, was an occasion of hope well expressed by King George VI on the steps of St Paul's Cathedral:

> Let us pray that by God's good grace the vast range of modern knowledge which is here shown may be turned from destructive to peaceful ends, so that all people, as the century goes on, may be lifted to greater happiness.
>
> (Kynaston, accessed 15 March 2009)

In that year I moved from the infant section of my primary school to Mr Burton's class numbering 48 children. I continued to drink the milk provided at morning break time and to ingest the statutory small red capsule that was cod liver oil. The social historian Eric Hobsbawm writes of the twentieth century as an 'Age of Extremes' and the 25 years that followed the Festival of Britain as a 'golden age', marked by rising prosperity and social contentment in which the welfare state did its work (Hobsbawm 1994). It was a time to construct fresh visions and potent realities and one such place was the Fenlands of Eastern England.

Chapter 2
A Whole Symphony in Your Head

> Perhaps we can never teach the child anything – we can only provide the materials, show him how to use the tools, surround him with a great many examples, and encourage him to learn, as Thomas Traherne wrote three centuries ago, 'for the double notion of interest and treasure'.
>
> (Sybil Marshall 1971: 37)

Ramsey Heights is close by the small town of Ramsey in the Fenlands of Eastern England, a town first coming to mind as a ten-year-old on a wet stay-indoors day during the summer holiday of 1954. My father had set me the task of calculating the populations of Huntingdonshire and Cambridgeshire, distant rural places to my way of thinking at the time, places waiting to be better imagined through my morning's work. My source would be an out of date Automobile Association Handbook providing the population figure for each place included. I wondered about the villages, hamlets and scattered dwellings not included in the Handbook and did anybody actually know the population of the whole of Cambridgeshire?

Ramsey Heights was one of those places unlikely to be accounted for in the Handbook. You have to go out of the way to find it and take care to distinguish it from Ramsey Mereside, Ramsey Hollow, Ramsey St Mary and Ramsey Forty Foot with its Forty Foot Bank and the reliable reports of its dyke claiming the careless motorist with some regularity. It is unnerving to drive alongside the bank from the town of Chatteris. The warning that 'speed kills' is sufficient to stifle any thought of whether the Fens are really a region of strange beauty, as they say (and as proposed by Charles Kingsley in his rambling tale of Hereward the Wake), or whether its relentlessly horizontal span, with hardly a tree, its miserable drains, rivers reluctant to move and sparse population, condemn it to be a backwater. There is the hope of seeing the cathedral at Ely stand up and there is the compelling advocacy of Charles Kingsley:

> Overhead the arch of heaven spread more ample than elsewhere, as over the open sea: and that vastness gave, and still gives, such cloudlands, such sunrises, such sunsets, as can be seen nowhere else within these isles.
>
> (Kingsley circa 1910: 15–16)

And, of course, the vastness still yields such things with cloudlands faithfully offering a poetic moment or two if you wish, while *Hereward the Wake* becomes ever more available from antiquarian online book sellers, and Ramsey Heights, apart from its causeways, sinks a little more deeply into the fen. Ramsey Heights is where Sybil Marshall absorbed knowledge of the world in the early years of the twentieth century. It was here she took in local custom, cherishing the rhymes, narratives and the metaphors of the moment, often spontaneous responses made to life in and around her family clan who had lived and worked the land of the Fens for six generations past (Marshall 1995).

At home Sybil encountered Dickens early, *Huckleberry Finn* was a favourite too and her *Children's Encyclopedia* had a much loved poetry section. By the age of ten a long list of poetry had come to be appreciated. William Cowper's 'The Nightingale and the Glowworm', Tennyson's 'Ulysses', Scott's 'Young Lochinvar' and the 'Ballade of Sir Partrick Spens', and much more lived in Sybil's imagination alongside the pleasures of country dancing and all that was expressed in rhyme and rhythm. In the village primary school music was a discrete lesson and beyond the store of National and Folk Songs there were the special times when 'Miss went a bit up-market, and taught us a new song such as 'My Mother Bids me Bind my Hair' – it hurt me somewhere in my diaphragm. I had never heard music like this. I loved it so much' (BBC *Desert Island Discs*, 11 November 1993).

There was hearty, full-blooded singing on Sunday evenings in the Chapel which overwhelmed the organ, quite unlike the polite Anglican version of singing overwhelmed by the organ in the other place of worship. Here was Sybil's very particular way of life that grew in intellectual stature in the local Grammar School where a formal music education faded into nothing much and was quickly overtaken by the making of music in the community and at home, where her love of dancing to popular music could be rehearsed in time with the piano playing of her elder sister and done for real within the community at every opportunity. In school the encounter with Shakespeare's *Julius Caesar* proved to be of enduring fascination and much of it learnt by heart. Learning Shakespeare by heart had been different from learning tables by rote as Sybil later reflected on her inability to grasp arithmetic principles. At age 18 family needs called rather than further study as the agricultural depression took hold. Sybil's work began as a primary school teacher (Marshall 1995).

A Schoolroom Remembered

Jill, the youngest of five, was born in 1948 in the village of Kingston eight miles west of Cambridge, no fenland here but a mild rising and falling of the land, a dew pond in the meadow behind the village school, trees that grow tall and Bourne Brook running fast towards the river Cam and Cambridge, where Sybil in mid-life was to fulfil a dream and gain her degree in English. At the crossroads in Kingston lies the village school, now the village hall, a village green and a cluster of houses. The bus to Cambridge glides past empty this cloudless sun-drenched mid-morning in February 2008 and a stately modern people-carrier creeps sedately from the drive of a local resident. My recent conversations with Jill have inspired her to arrange for me to meet with others from her class of the 1950s and to visit the schoolroom. This was Mrs Marshall's schoolroom and Mrs Marshall was their only teacher. But first a walk around the village past the house where Jill was born and where her mother ran the village post office. Jill talks of pennies earnt by picking fruit in the fields around and all the time 'do you remember' and 'I wonder what happened to?'

The church is locked and Philip points out the grave stones of his forbearers, chattering fast to tell his story of family and childhood. Inside what had been their village schoolroom, we are joined by Gay and David and they talk of how it all was in their time with Mrs Marshall. They tell of her throat clicking when she was concentrating hard, of her storytelling voice that enchanted, of her piano playing and of the way she kept the class busy, always absorbed and the memorable blending of what they were learning through the creative arts and especially through the making of collage, mosaic and mural. There is much 'do you remember the time when …' and they recall the coach trip to London to see their art work on display in the National Gallery as winners of the News Chronicle competition, with the visit to London Zoo to complete the day. The question as to whether Mrs Marshall ever got cross is met with puzzlement and Jill had already told me in my Cambridge-based conversations with her that:

> We were simply happy doing what we were doing … there was no standing in the corner or anything like that … she would clap her hands and call you to order. 'Right, come on now [claps] we need to sit down.' Never, ever can I remember her thumping the desk or anything like that. She would clap her hands. She had lovely hands, really nice hands. There was never a sign of aggression to command attention.

Jill had been drawn to taking her grandchildren to Kingston village fete the previous summer and had found a quiet moment to be alone and to revisit the schoolroom. It is recalled as a deeply strange experience:

> I could hear the voices of the past and even the piano playing. Very high ceiling … lots of pictures on the wall, always … and writings. The floor always smelled of scrubbed wood, the work of Lucy the school cleaner. Walking on the wooden floor produced a nice echo, good for singing and playing instruments. That's what you remember. We were all taught to write in italics. We copied short pieces of prose and rhymes from cards beautifully produced by Mrs Marshall. For reading practice there were reading books. You progressed through Books 1, 2 and 3 and so on. The school inspector would come at any time and you had to be seen to be … 'Oh, she's on Book 3, she's on Book 5'. And we read to each other, with older pupils teaching the younger ones. So of course the one listening to your reading was at the same time honing their skills as they put you right. And then every now and then Mrs Marshall would say, 'Well right, you come

and read it to me now', and she'd check that you were getting it right. The older ones helped the smaller ones in everything.

Sybil Marshall had come to the school during the Second World War, her third school, realizing her unspoken ambition of becoming a village school ma'am. Suspicious of doctrines and orthodoxies, she relished the freedom to experiment that lay before her. There was the challenge too of teaching a class of 30 or so listless children aged five to 11, some of whom were evacuees. This was in great contrast to her previous school which had been large and the headmaster an authoritarian who had made a rule about everything.

> He stalked the corridors on pussy-feet, with a cane concealed under the back of his jacket and the handle curled over his collar, peering through the glass pane in every door, on constant watch for naughty children or disobedient staff.
>
> (Marshall 1963: 11)

Sybil Marshall had in mind another way, with a different view of the purpose of education and of how children might learn. *An Experiment in Education* published in 1963 recounts Sybil's journey of discovery as the sole teacher at Kingston between 1943 and 1961 when the school closed. The work was to become a foundational text for those training to become primary teachers in the period immediately prior to and following the publication of the Plowden Report.

Rural Idyll

By age three Jill had become an under-aged regular in the village schoolroom with a plan in place for Jill to be slipped out through the back door should the school inspector arrive. Now 50 years on from the time it came for Jill to leave what became her primary school idyll, she again takes pleasure in the wood floor, the high windows and high ceiling, and there is a gentle debate with those of her classmates about just where Mrs Marshall's desk was placed, 'the piano was over there, and there was the library in the corner used by all the village', with Jill's mother as librarian on Tuesday evenings. There had been the tortoise stove which had dominated the room and alongside which the frozen milk of winter days would be placed. There were desks for arithmetic, reading and writing and then the space made where you did things together, where you sat on the floor and talked about things and where you could be doing and making, sometimes together and sometimes all alone, some activity through which you could express the ideas and feelings provoked by some memorable stimulus.

Painting, poetry, writing, needlework, smocking, singing, dancing, moving, the playing of instruments and the making of puppets were such activities that were offered as means of expression. One such stimulus was the Sixth Symphony of Beethoven, the Pastoral Symphony. Beethoven had written of the symphony that it was 'more a matter of feeling than of painting sounds' (record sleeve notes). Like Wordsworth in his Prelude, Beethoven had no interest in depictions and representations but rather with the ways in which the mind of each and the landscape of all communicated through the agency of feeling rather than reason. This was the romantic road to freedom.

Away from the schoolroom I sit with Jill as we listen to the symphony's first movement. Jill is unable to hold back the tears ... there was always singing; the performances in the church and Jill's 'O, Little Town of Bethlehem' solo; Jill as Oberon in the enactment of *A Midsummer Night's Dream*; the daily hymn, a rousing 'Let All the World in Every Corner Sing' was a favourite; the playing of recorders, percussion instruments and learning to pluck and bow the violinda. Then there were the weekly radio broadcasts. Jill wants to show me the *Singing Together* booklet bought in a jumble sale a few years past, and inside The Capstan Shanty 'The Drummer and Cook' taken from *The Shanty Book II*, the third song in Spring Term of 1951 heard on Mondays between 11.00 and 11.18 am (BBC 1951). The first verse of the song is presented with staff notation, words underlain and with tonic sol-fa written above.

> William Appleby was the man on the radio who sang and broke the song down. [sings] 'There was a little drummer and he loved a one-eyed cook'. And then he'd stop, and we'd all sing it, the whole school that is. And then we would work our way through it. We each had our *Singing Together* book. The alternative book, *Time and Tune*, was much more about rhythm and beat ... clap, clap, clap ... quavers and semi-quavers ... a rest and that sort of thing. It was all done quite slowly and systematically and each programme followed the preceding one, so the whole thing worked as a package. This was the formal music education that was offered. The line of the song, 'With one eye in the pot and the other up the chimney ...' caught our imagination and we actually used to tease my mother about the song. My mother had one eye. Well she had two eyes but she was blind in one.

Writing in her autobiographical sketch *A Pride of Tigers*, Sybil recalls music experienced as a child in her primary school in the years immediately following the First World War:

> Songs there were reserved for music lessons – each of which, for me, began with ten minutes or so of plain torture. I could not, and never did, catch on to what tonic sol-fa was all about. I still haven't – though as the voice, which though not musical, was at least able to sing in tune, has departed this life ahead of the rest of me, it doesn't matter much now that I could not produce a musical interval on command to save my life from extinction. But this is the one thing all my life has eluded me and defeated me ... What on earth was the purpose of it? Nobody ever explained it – though it seemed that everybody else knew and understood

... Now if only Miss had but once informed me what her queer monosyllables and extraordinary gestures meant. But she didn't. I could not guess, so this was 'a door to which I found no key'. I hated not being able to do things well. I suffered more in the ten minutes of tonic sol-fa than in any other event of my whole educational life.

(Marshall 1995: 228–9)

What *was* the purpose of tonic sol-fa and the hand signs that had become associated with it? I too had wondered that as a music teacher in training. Nobody had explained its principles to me either, although when observed teaching a song in a primary school I had been warmly congratulated for making use of it. Its dysfunctional practice, as experienced by Sybil, could only be matched by my own memory of a modulator resting unused on top of the upright piano in a hut with polished floor where country dancing and occasional class singing took place in the dreamy consciousness of my own primary school days. It was without tonic sol-fa that I learnt later to sight-sing.

Broadening the Music Curriculum

The latter years of the nineteenth century and first of the twentieth had seen great interest in the place of sight-singing within the school. While songs could be sung with spontaneity and enjoyment, it was a concern for pedagogic technique to provide a disciplined and structured means of enabling children to move between the natural and the cultured, for music in schools to make legitimate claims to the formality of instruction and schooled understandings, a disciplinary measure of sorts. '*The real problem in learning music* is how to get the outward eye and ear to act with the inward eye and ear, and to make, so to speak, one combined sense' had been written in Cassell's *New Popular Educator* published around 1880 (Cassell circa 1880: 31). Central here is the idea of ear training, aural knowledge and the co-ordination of ear, eye, voice and the reading of music in silence and in all its concreteness, essential to the training of the mind and what school inspector John Stainer referred to as 'musicianship of the mind' (see Cox 1993).

The belief that sight-singing had a principled place within children's musical schooling and that some kind of mnemonic device be used to aid musical thinking and feeling was orthodoxy in the first half of the twentieth century, and obligatory in the mind of Sybil's primary school teacher, and in Jill's *Singing Together – Rhythm and Melody* 40 years later. The Ministry of Education's Pamphlet of 1956, Music in Schools, sounds a note of realism on the matter, pointing out that 'unless the teacher thoroughly understands these devices ... the children will derive little benefit from them' (HMSO 1956: 13). Sybil's primary school teacher, Sybil herself, Jill and my Teacher Training College Lecturer shared in little or no understanding of the principles of tonic sol-fa.

The weekly radio broadcasts represented for Jill a formal training in music, an insistence that you listened to detail. This provided an example of how music might be taught as a singing-plus lesson. It was singing that formed the hub around which all else revolved. In singing lay opportunity to develop aural perception applicable to wider listening as well as instrumental playing. However, it was this over-reliance on massed musical performance on which the Ministry of Education pamphlet focused. Whereas there is a legacy to celebrate there is also scope for change allowing for greater pupil autonomy made possible through small group working. In this the greater use of instruments is recommended. The small group is set in contrast to the large and it is the large group percussion band lesson that is singled out as an example of inflexibility. Large group performance is insufficient and called to account. There is 'the music corner', 'experimental discovery' and the potential offered by the small interpersonal group (ibid: 14).

As a teacher in training in 1963 I had observed a class of eight-year-olds in rural Hampshire rehearse and perform as a percussion band. I recall the massed performance as being highly disciplined with each member of the class of 40 children assigned a notated part contributing to an orchestrated whole led by the teacher through accomplished piano playing. This performance of Sullivan's Overture to the *Pirates of Penzance* required the counting of rests, the individualization of parts through times of sparseness in textures as well as much trilling and temelandoing tutties calmly executed. In the previous decade and at the time of Jill's primary music education, this highly differentiated teacher-led whole class music making presenting a surface of mechanical behaviour was losing its lustre. The Ministry pamphlet, reprinted in 1960, offered no advice on ways in which large group performance work might be differentiated. Instead there is a turn towards the work of child-centred educators Rousseau, Petzalotsi and Froebel, noting their wisdom in understanding that children were children and not 'as adults in miniature', and recognizing their naturalness and propensity to learn through self-direction. In this the role of the teacher would be changed.

An Experiment in Education

This way of thinking mirrored a gathering of momentum in the progressive movement in primary schools, characterized by a reduction in teacher authority, alternatives to class lessons, dissolution of the formal timetable and a shift from the three Rs to more creative and expressive activities: individuality, freedom and growth were key ideas (Alexander 1995, Cunningham 1988).

Sybil Marshall tells of the freedom of spirit she herself exercised in coming to terms with her teaching during the 1950s; of how on the one hand she satisfied the demands of the Cambridgeshire Education Authority by submitting schemes of work, only for these to be consigned to the drawer of her desk, rather than following the recommendation from the Authority that these be framed and hung on the wall of her classroom. She tells of her circumspection towards the authority of the Local Authority organizers and of her independence of mind in searching out what would be of meaning and value to her children. Writing about the Local Authority's organizers she notes:

> The terminology applied to these worthy people damns their work from the start; but in the eyes of the ordinary teacher they have even greater faults. It is true that most of them have been teachers themselves, but the very nature of their jobs lifts them to a position of some authority, and in doing so usually magnifies for them the importance of the subjects to which they, personally, are attached. In turn they visit every school (and in districts such as ours there are almost as many types of school as there are schools), giving advice which is unsought and, what is worse, not understood anyway, tactfully refraining from either praise or candid criticism, but leaving behind them when the door closes the impression that they will expect to see a great improvement in their particular subject by the time of their next visit.
>
> (Marshall 1963: 19)

But such Local Authority influence did play a part in Sybil's developing understanding of the arts in education. The Cambridgeshire art organizer Nan Youngman, for example, was to teach Sybil a great deal through an evening class for teachers, and the schoolroom's piano was a welcome arrival made possible by the county music organizer, Ludovic Stuart. Indeed, it was Ludovic who had opened up opportunities for the children of Kingston to make music in county festivals and who had supplied the school with violindas for the whole school to learn together.

If there was now some questioning of the reliance on massed musical performance activity, there had been for some time suspicion about the role of the gramophone in the classroom. Would a concession to the mechanical reproduction of music further instil a passive, uncritical approach taking pupils away from active participation in music? This had been a not uncommon call from official pronouncements (Pitts 2000; Rainbow 1989).

The participatory character of music education is clearly set out in the 14 plates at the centre of The Ministry of Education Pamphlet of 1956. There are large and small performing ensembles with pride of place given to the National Youth Orchestra. Smaller group work is represented through a group of children with recorders clustered around a music stand engaged in discussing what might be a point of interpretation and there is a group of five children tending a gramophone. The teacher is not present.

For Jill and fellow pupils at Kingston the arrival of what was referred to as a record player by Sybil and as a gramophone by Jill was a matter of great interest.

> The gramophone was a gift from a family who lived in Barrington and the mum was a GP. Father was a scientific inventor, so they were affluent and lived in a big, beautiful house. The boys were driven to school. Eversden had its own

school but they were choosing this school and this type of education. The gramophone was a thank you gift when the boys left school. It was Beethoven's Pastoral Symphony that we first heard played on it. And that absorbed us for quite a long time. We're not talking about something that happened and was forgotten the next week. We looked at it from every angle. This piece of music totally consumed us. It was a magic thing taking us beyond *Time and Tune*.

For Sybil the record player immediately provided the starting point for her most celebrated project that was to crystallize her thinking and to lead to the establishment of a method. The gramophone provided the means whereby her own appreciation of classical music could be shared with her pupils. What could be more appropriate for the children of Kingston than to hear the Pastoral Symphony of Beethoven as they entered the classroom at the beginning of the summer term 1959, a term blessed by long spells of sunshine and with learning taking place as much outside as inside. Marion Scott describes the Beethoven's Symphony thus:

> … with the fresh-springing tunes of the first movement – the Scene by the Brook – with its murmuring phrases and the bird calls, put in (as he said) as a joke; the *allegro* The Peasants' Festival with its delicious portrait of the country band; the storm which, though not very terrible nowadays as a noise, must always give a strange thrill at the opening where, in the sudden *tremolo* of the basses very swiftly on D flat and the little patter of quavers in the second violins, Beethoven has caught the very feeling of that queer moment before a storm breaks, when the first drops fall and the leaves show their white undersides. And then, when the tempest has past, the final scale upwards of the flute leads into the Shepherd's Hymn of gratitude and thanksgiving which completes the work.
>
> (Scott 1943: 172)

Beethoven we believe was expressing his relationships with nature, a retrospective and thoroughly eighteenth century statement, a naïve notion of a harmonious relationship between man and nature. Sybil Marshall liked this.

Jill's response was fulsome in meeting the music. Her walks with Mrs Marshall in the surrounding fields, where she was encouraged to sense, experience and know as if for the first time, invoked the imagination to be and become the music. Collage and poetry followed. Playing in the Bourne Brook with 'the cuckoo treating us to a lengthy solo', formed a prelude to movement two and the making of a collage with the music playing as they worked and with much to talk and wonder about. 'It was a happy day' (Marshall 1963:189). Movement three saw '… feet tapping and fingers ran up and down the desks. It was as if by common consent that we had decided how to interpret this movement by movement' (ibid: 193). A Dionysian spirit erupts as windows are opened wide with the music as loud as possible and spontaneous dancing on the green across the road: 'No set movements, just interpretations of the music and changes of rhythm when they came' (ibid: 194). And Jill wrote:

> The dancers are spinning round and round,
> Their feet do hardly touch the ground.
> Some shepherds merrily pipe a tune,
> On this summer's day, in June. (ibid: 199)

There was the poetry of Spenser to be read and Hardy's 'Sheep Fair in the Rain' to be introduced as well as the art of smocking … but then the storm and Jill again:

> Everywhere grew dark, but all of a sudden a flash of lightning lit up the room, then the thunder crashed, then it trundled across the sky as though a trolley was being pulled about.
>
> (ibid: 202)

So the question: which instruments were doing what? And this led to the beginning of a discussion and there were now reasons for studying the Instruments of the Orchestra, the life of Beethoven and writing about a symphony. But as providence would have it a storm gathered that Friday afternoon over Kingston and that night unleashed its power in great splendour. Children came to Sybil's gate the following morning to talk about so great a storm and on Monday morning there was much for all to talk about.

The final movement provided a melody to be with the class all day, a tune to be whistled and sung, to be transposed by Sybil's daughter and played on recorders and violins in an impromptu class orchestra. Time was ripe for song writing.

> 'Now, think, put your heads down, cover your eyes up, put your heads down, now, you are just coming out of the church, and you are going, all by yourself, you are yourselves only, and you are going to your own home, what will you be thinking about?' And they all sat and looked at me and I could see their minds, almost the wheels going round. Then I said, 'alright, pick your pens up and I want you to write a poem so that the words would fit to the tune', and one called Jill clapped her hand on her forehead and said, 'Oh! what will she think of next?' And they all burst out laughing but they seized their pens and began.
>
> (BBC *Desert Island Discs*, 11 November 1993)

Sybil is moved by the way Jill captures the spirit of country love while Jill is pleased that her song of 50 years ago still sounds so well as she sings snatches to me before telling me of her mother's interpretation of the penultimate line.

Love Song
My darling, my darling,
Oh will you be my wife?
I'll care for you, I'll share with you,
And love you all my life.
My sweetheart, my sweetheart,

Of course I'll marry you:
I'll cook for you, I'll wash for you,
And I will love you true.
I'm sure we'll be happy,
You need not fear, or sorrow.
So kiss me, don't miss me,
I'll ask your dad tomorrow. (Marshall 1963: 210)

Reflecting on the glory of the term's work, at age 80 Sybil speaks with deep admiration for the way the children had put their trust in her (BBC *Desert Island Discs*, 11 November 1993). The Symphony had provided a grand narrative structure for the term and had enabled Sybil to devise a method, the symphonic method. Perhaps too the term's work had served as a greater narrative for her life's work to date. She was now ready to help others understand what an education through the arts might mean.

Symphony
The music is slowing,
It's drawing to an end,
The rhythm is flowing,
The weaving tunes still blend.
The oboes were singing,
They made a pretty air:
The violins were stringing,
The double bass was there.
The flutes, bassoons, and piccolos
In harmony agree,
And all the swelling music goes
To make a symphony. (Beverley in Marshall 1963: 211)

On Reflection

Writing in the *Times Education Supplement* in 1971, now holding her Cambridge Degree and with experience of training teachers at Sheffield and Sussex Universities, Sybil has a salutary story to relate. Following the closure of Kingston School and at an interview for a local headship she had experienced an immediate and direct challenge from the chairman of the school governors (Marshall 1971: 35). Was it the three 'Ps' in place of the three 'Rs': play, plasticine and puppetry? Sybil is of course affronted by such ignorant provocation and in her article proceeds to make clear the subtle balance needed between the transmission of knowledge and the making and remaking of it. Sybil laments the growing jargon of progressivism and reasserts the nature of what was being misunderstood: 'creative activity'. The creative work that flowed from experiencing Beethoven's Pastoral Symphony had been rooted in long phases of learning about the environment, rural cultures of the past, gratitude and provenance, pastoral poetry, how to interpret biblical text and how to apply skills of reading and writing learnt separately. Sybil had come to see two kinds of knowledge, the pure and the applied. Creativity was a way of applying knowledge, an 'active participation in forms of expression that called for individual creative impulse into play and encouraged an imaginative response to experience' (ibid: 37). Creativity required carefully managed freedom, finely constructed spaces for 'symbolization'.

In this *Times Education Supplement* article Sybil observes a rapid transformation in the character of primary schools. The Plowden Report was being implemented. The report had pointed out that a better balance needed to be found between re-creative and creative approaches to music in the primary school. (There was perhaps knowledge of the way Jill and her class had selected and reworked the songs they knew into fresh contexts.) Again there are questions raised about the reliance upon massed choral activity with a concomitant lack of interest in monitoring progress and providing for individual progression. The importance of music literacy is emphasized as is the place for listening to good music and a challenge that 'not enough is known about how to develop children's creative powers in music. Here, research is needed' (Central Advisory Council for Education 1967: 254). The report as a whole endorses a developmental view of the child and encourages the teacher to experiment and to work out their own philosophy and educational aims. Sybil Marshall had shown the way in this.

Sybil had viewed her experiment as collaborative. It was from the responses of her children that she continually learnt and it is in this respect that she tells of one of her most significant discoveries, the inter-changeability of the arts (Marshall 1968: 59). If it is the case that children cannot be creative at the dictate of the teacher, there needs to be freedom of choice of the medium through which to channel imagination. The case of Jill provided Sybil with evidence. At age six Jill had produced the first of her 'surprising masterpieces', a portrait of Mrs Marshall doing her requisition: 'to see ourselves as others see us! An unsolicited record of what a poor teacher looks and feels like when trying to get a whole year's supplies out of £30' (Marshall 1963: 118). The masterpiece was to be used as the cover for Donald Winnicott's influential approach to creative child rearing *The Child, the Family and the Outside World* (Winnicott 1985). Three years were to elapse before Jill would return to the visual medium, as expression through movement, drama, words and song were Jill's pre-occupation. Impulse directed.

Acts of Symbolization

In Sybil Marshall's book *Adventure in Creative Education* (Marshall 1968), and reporting on her work with primary headteachers on secondment in her role as a lecturer in primary education at Sheffield University, Sybil writes in praise of the project method and of the fruits likely to accrue from a commitment to a sustained concentration on an area of interest decided upon by the teacher.

> Our aim must be to entice the children to learn, but they have to begin somewhere, and part of the teacher's function is to organize the start: it is a bit like an archaeological expedition. Someone who knows chooses the place to dig and leads the diggers to it; but from that point onwards, though he may be in overall control of the operation, the interest lies in what is brought to light. The class has to work individually but in freedom controlled by discipline defined from within the group, not arbitrarily prescribed from above.
>
> (ibid: 57)

Here the teacher's knowledge of what is worthy of being learnt is privileged. It is not the child's impulse that provides the centre of interest and source of knowing but the culture of the teacher. The authority of the teacher is shown in Sybil's meeting with the minds of headteachers. Here she skilfully provides centres of interest that provoke debate and lead to a broadening of perspective. Never prescriptive, orthodoxies always challenged, cultural horizons expanded. There is the claim that knowledge is unitary not a fragmented affair and that while there were of course discrete subjects, their interrelationship was likely to be the source of inspiration and deeper understanding or 'comprehension' as Sybil described it. What it might mean to truly understand served as a challenge to a 'gradgrind' approach to knowledge and its mode of transmission.

If there existed both pure and applied knowledge then of course subjects had integrity but their integrity lay most convincingly in the light of boundary crossing and eminently so through the arts seen as acts of symbolization. It is within the arts, and with it music, that is found the realm of free imaginative play, where impulse is given space to reuse and rework experience and this includes the basics acquired diligently. The discourse was changing. In addition to the 'creative' and 'creativity' there is now 'impulse' and later in an article in the journal *Education 3–13* there is talk of 'aesthetic' qualities in children's art work (Marshall 1976).

Sybil Marshall thus sets out what a richer kind of learning through experience might mean, placing in perspective what is of value both to the here and now and to the future. This is to be and become a person through curiosity, engrossment and a love of learning. Beethoven's Pastoral Symphony is to be known and loved for life, available in the head as an 'old friend' and part of a poetic and pastoral way of understanding. Jill tells of how she was 'happy to learn, secure and confident about a kind of learning that was enjoyable and always a challenge'. Jill's move to secondary school was to be traumatic.

Another Place

Jill's primary school experience had been utterly different to my own. In a large town, in large classes and with strong municipal values infecting every school, I had been largely desk-bound. There was the occasional highly prescribed craft activity, the sitting on benches to sing, bean bags and hoops to structure physical activity, introductions to soccer, cricket and mastery of the forward defensive stroke, and the cane drawing forth shame and guilt. My teachers had followed an orderly, structured and consistent approach to the learning of language and number which eschewed creative process and self-expression. Handwriting practice after Friday dinner time was drudgery before a longed for end of Friday afternoon of football on the playground with its one-in-12 slope and dustbin lid goal posts. My goalkeeping dives involving the noisy sliding of a dustbin lid made an impression I had thought. Diligence in handwriting conditioned participation in football and more than once my taking the field for football was delayed. Central to the final year in primary school was the preparation for the 11+ examination. Hopes were of a place at grammar school while worst fears were of finding oneself in the rough and tumble of the playground of the secondary modern school adjoining our primary school playground. By the end of her time at Kingston Jill had acquired a feeling for art making, an understanding of a making process that included her ideas and feelings. She had a love of language, of writing and speaking. There was a sweet singing voice and a love of dancing too. I was to pass the 11+, but not Jill.

I didn't pass the eleven plus examination. I lived with the guilt of it. No I didn't. In all honesty, it was a case of, well you either pass it or you don't. And I suppose in the back of my mind Comberton was opening. Or in the adult's mind, don't worry if she hasn't passed it, don't make her feel bad about it. But I do know my mother had a long conversation about it with Mrs Marshall and said I should be put forward for the thirteen plus, because she was flummoxed that I hadn't passed the eleven plus. My elder sisters went to Comberton School at the crossroads and when it was my turn to go to secondary school the new Comberton Village College wasn't yet completed so I had a short time at Comberton School. It was unbelievably hard. I can remember feeling stunned. I had written in an italic hand and had to change. I was told that I needed to write faster. We did things as a whole class but we did it to a timetable. We had painting lessons and I had never questioned my artistic ability. I just painted what I saw and when I was satisfied that was it and now I was being judged on what I produced.

When we were at Kingston we wrote what we fancied writing. We put ourselves into it and if there was a space we always drew a nice picture. For this I was now in deep trouble and humiliated in front of the whole class. Here the teacher could instantly order work to be placed in the bin. My confidence was badly knocked. It was the same at the Village College. There were teachers who publicly humiliated their pupils. My life suddenly had totally changed. I was away from an environment where I felt happy, really happy. This alien place with these horrible people that didn't really like you and you didn't want to be there, never sure of myself and always afraid of doing the wrong thing. No wonder I was a difficult teenager.

Jill tells of times when the school bus was deliberately missed so that a walk to school meant missing the first lesson of the day, and the time when a whole day was spent in hiding high up on the gantry of the school's Drama Studio. There was music on the timetable:

… and this teacher was kind and generous, a well-spoken lady. It was a participating lesson, some new songs and some old 'friends' from Kingston days. 'Where the bee sucks', for example, reminding me of our *Midsummer Night's Dream* experience at Kingston. And who should come out of the woodwork but Ludovic Stuart the county music man, who had brought the piano to Kingston and helped us with our recorder playing. Ludovic brought schools together. There were performances in the Guildhall in Cambridge. There was no music club in the school but an English teacher started a dance club, folk dancing with tarantellas and other lovely things. I really enjoyed that. And then came school performances where we danced and chose the bits of music we liked.

I always wanted to become a primary teacher but inconveniently the stepfather of the time died. I needed to work, 'we need your wage'. I had wanted to be a primary school teacher but my mother determined that I should train as a telephonist. I hated it and my job as a telephonist-receptionist was mundane and boring. It wasn't until I became a nanny looking after two young children that I found satisfaction. I knew how to keep them busy, how to make the most of whatever materials were at hand. Sometimes the Pastoral Symphony played while we played together.

Earlier at home in Kingston, Jill had developed the habit of 'lilting': songs learnt in school became jigs and reels. 'There must have been Irish Music in my genes' and there was Jimmy Shand's Band heard on *Family Favourites* on the radio on Sunday lunch times. The desire to own an accordion grew and the gift of a mouth organ came as a bitter disappointment. However, the search for identity was to be boldly confirmed on meeting Johnny in 1967, an Irish boy from County Mayo. Now came integration into the Cambridge Irish Circle with Celidhs and House Dances 'round the kitchen – mind the dresser' and a whole life of Irish traditional music making, the Cambridge Folk Festival, regular visits to Ireland and membership of the All Britain Board of Irish Traditional Music.

As my own children grew up we made music at home together. We played, sang and danced. We especially enjoyed dancing. When the children were independent

I bought myself an accordion and a good friend who had learnt to play at her father's knee in Ireland taught me to play. We are a traditional extended family and now it's the turn of my grandchildren to love folk music. That's what they have been exposed to. When they get in the car it's, 'Oh, put such and such on'. They do like Irish music. Music is about finding your roots, where you belong.

Childhood Freedom

In reviewing the child-centred tradition arising from European Enlightenment thinking of the seventeenth century, Christine Doddington and Mary Hilton argue that at root views of childhood are bound to ideologies of childhood and these have evolved as determining elements of the modern social and political order.

> By the end of the Enlightenment in the early nineteenth century ... two totally different views of the child had emerged in European culture. In Britain, both these views were closely related to the instinctive ideological values of different political parties. On the one hand, conservatives still held to the old view that all children were potentially sinful, and that the poor child was particularly at risk of eternal damnation. The party held that only strict instruction in the scriptures, mechanical discipline and constant surveillance would rescue all children from the influence of the Devil and hence from damnation to hell. On the other hand, liberals and radicals believed almost exactly the opposite: that all children were born innocent, that they had a subjectivity and playfulness naturally given that should be respected by the adults around them, especially those in authority over them. Here history shows us the ways that the values of the adults played out directly on child-rearing and educational practices.
>
> (Doddington and Hilton 2007: xxii)

Arguing in 1911 for release from the oppression of a mechanical system of education that had rested on the notion of 'salvation through obedience', Edmond Holmes produces a foundational text for those in the twentieth century on the side of the liberals who saw in children the possibility of their self-realization. Holmes begins his uncompromising polemic with a proposition that was to provide progressive educators with a powerful manifesto.

> The function of education is to foster growth. The end of which the teacher should set before himself is the development of the latent powers of his pupils, the unfolding of their latent life. If growth is to be fostered, two things must be liberally provided – nourishment and exercise.
>
> (Holmes 1911: 3)

The metaphor of the growing body served to illustrate the naturalness of what is latent within the child. No more would we conceive of binding the body to prohibit growth than we should bind the whole of the child, mind, body and soul. In Holmes's view the West's educational programme was predicated on an ideology of the helpless child with 'mechanical obedience' providing the road to salvation. The instinct to express self was systematically repressed. The instincts to talk and listen; to act (in the dramatic sense of the word); to draw, paint and model; to dance and sing; to know the why of things; to construct things provided the pathway to 'self-realization' (ibid: 165). As Sybil Marshall had realized, for Holmes too, knowledge and understanding required thorough assimilation through self-expression and with 'perception deeply tinged with emotion' (ibid: 85–6).

Central to progressive education's project was the redefining of the role of the teacher, and its anti-authoritarian stance is made clear in the writing here from within a College of Education preparing teachers for the progressive primary school.

> In a progressive primary school the teacher does not play an authoritarian role but is rather a participant in the living and learning situation in the classroom. She has the final responsibility for making the final decisions and setting the boundaries between what is acceptable in the room; but the discipline of the group is based on mutual respect between the teacher and the child, and between child and child, and is gradually assumed as a group responsibility. If the teacher accepts the child and he in return has an affectionate regard for her, he will begin to incorporate the teacher's values and to develop internal personal control.
>
> (Brown and Precious 1968: 26)

This is how Jill had experienced Kingston. There was no 'overt authority' and no 'anonymous authority', but a freedom to be and become in the absence of fear. It was in large part Sybil Marshall's own childhood happiness and intense productiveness that had led her to ask what is it to be a child and what is it to be a teacher. Her work supported a view of education that was for 'growth' and 'self-realization' in the context of what had been given by the past to appreciate and cherish and what sense might be made of it here and now. One major source of Sybil's energy was undoubtedly her depth of knowledge of literature, the arts and the folk culture of her childhood. Her childhood had been fed by rhythm and rhyme, by the cadences provided by both a vernacular and literary heritage. There was a deeply experienced sensibility to her environment, its sounds and images and it was all this that provided Sybil with a remarkable sense of vocation and with a natural authority to teach others.

At the heart of this lay relationships. We recall Sybil Marshall's expression of gratitude for the trust her pupils had placed in her at Kingston as she experimented and made sense of being a teacher. There was no need to make mention of her coming to trust them. Jill's growth from three-year-old interloper to poet, song writer and artist was evidence enough that the arts, singular yet interchangeable, were the place where a sense of completion, of wholeness could be experienced. Jill treasuring the secure and productive relationships of the Kingston schoolroom, learning to feel like an artist, learning how to move from impulse to the realization of artistic form and to appreciate the value of what the anthropologist Ellen Dissanayake understands as the evolutionary drive to 'make special' (Dissanayake 1999), played its part in the formation of her social character, perhaps most clearly expressed in her concern for the well-being and happiness sought through an extended family and bound by a quest for an identity rooted in a particular form of music as a way of life. Speaking of the way her Kingston school days worked, Jill sees music as the thing that brought everything and everybody together. At Kingston art making was a communal matter and the community of the schoolroom mattered.

For Erich Fromm the idea of communal art stands as a potent symbol of a more humane way of life. Here the key tenet of faith is that to be artistic is an activity to be shared with others, allowing one to feel at one with others, and quite unlike the notion of the artist as alone, specialist and detached. Fromm speaks of 'common dances, plays, music, bands, not entirely replacing modern sport, but subordinating it to the role of one of the many non-profit and non-purpose activities' (Fromm 1979: 350). In Sybil Marshall's education through art the community of the schoolroom was a central source of energy and productiveness. The singing, moving and playing of instruments, the making of plays, songs and dances, the making of pictures and the modelling of artifacts as acts of symbolization from which personal and public meaning derived provided for this. For Jill, and unlike her secondary school, the environment of Kingston was flexibile and frequently informal. Jill's earliest memory of music in school was the singing and moving of the song 'Buy a Horse and Hire a Gig'. It is a movement song that has in turn been taught to her children and grandchildren. There are of course many more songs in Jill's head and there is a whole symphony there too.

> If I 'educated' the children in my care at Kingston at all, it was, I hope, to help them to enjoy life. Whatever education they get in the future, no one will ever be able to take that away from the particular little group who lived through the Pastoral term with me in my little school. A true music lover does not always have to have the score before him, nor to keep a record of it continually playing: he can carry the whole symphony in his head.
>
> (Marshall 1963: 213–14)

Chapter 3
Creativity, Culture and the Social Order

No word in English carries a more consistently positive reference than 'Creative'. And obviously we should be glad of this, when we think of the values it seeks to express and the activities it offers to describe.

(Williams 1961: 19)

The difficulty about the idea of culture is that we are continually forced to expand it, until it becomes almost identical with our whole common life.

(Williams 1963: 249)

Clearly, life at school is far more full and creative than it was many years ago.

(Callaghan 1976: 4)

Sybil Marshall's creation of the symphonic method is a story of the 1950s, a time of some dissatisfaction with music in schools, with criticism focused on undifferentiated large group choral singing and percussion band practices. The impersonal recreation of the past was now set against the idea of a more personable creation of the present. A discourse of creativity with talk of impulse, self-expression, feeling and aesthetic qualities was developing and this had a special resonance within the arts. However, in providing a new 'pattern for culture' calling for greater 'self-regulation', 'self-discipline' and 'self-government' on the part of the pupil, there would be inevitable tensions with established and dominant conceptions of the school, the child and how learning would take place and for what purpose. In particular, there would be suspicion, circumspection as well as strong resistance to the liberal cause of promoting subjectivity and the natural playfulness of children.

This episode and the one that follows explore the tensions played out during the years spanning Sybil Marshall's move from Kingston in the early 1960s to Cambridge University where she would fulfil a longstanding dream of completing an academic education, on through Sybil's time as a teacher-educator at Sussex and then Sheffield universities, on to her retirement and to the passing of the Education Reform Act of 1988. This was the period of Jill's making of a family and my becoming a secondary school music teacher. In the previous episode Sybil Marshall provided the case for a culturally rich education respecting and trusting childhood as a form of life in itself. In Edmond Holmes's terms this was a matter of growth and self-realization. If education were to be conceived of in this way, then what kind of social order was in mind? What kind of democratic arrangements were envisioned? What kind of individuals would be created, what kind of institutions, what kind of schools, and who were they to serve? As Carr and Hartnett point out, in Britain, and unlike other European nations, these were the kinds of questions that had never been properly addressed (Carr and Hartnett 1997). There had been no moment in history defining just what education was for and how it should be effected. It had evolved piecemeal with relentless incoherency, contradictions and contestations played out for its soul.

In coming to appreciate the tensions arising between conservative and progressive forces that underlie the crisis experienced within music education during the 1960s and 1970s we will need to understand something of the ways in which music education had been conceived and regulated during the first half of the century and how the question of 'whose music' is considered fit to educate is deeply implicated in matters of social stratification, social control and the social order. From here arises a culture debate. Within all this is placed the influential 'Arts and the Adolescent' Schools Council project recognizing the vibrant cultural and artistic lives of young people and the need for schools and their teachers to respond in imaginative ways. What emerges is a struggle for culture, a struggle for the soul of education. First, however, I call upon Raymond Williams to set out the interplay of three conceptions of education at work in English society. The voice of Williams is particularly appropriate representing as it does a radical perspective advocating moves towards completion of 'the long revolution' and to a more egalitarian and openly democratic order and a common culture.

Civility and Social Stratification

In reviewing culture and society between 1780 and 1950, Raymond Williams suggests three conceptions of education at play and always dynamically interrelated and interdependent. The first, tacit, is the 'training of members of the group to the social character' or 'pattern of culture' which is dominant in the group or by which the group lives' (Williams 1961: 141). This is the natural training or socialization of the individual as they become accommodated to society and through which its ethos and values come to be accepted and sustained. The second, and regulated in terms of the first, is some kind of specialist instruction enabling the individual to contribute to society, an industrial training, while the third is a general education, an 'education for culture'. In this scheme, education has a major role to play in the maintenance of the social and economic order, while at the same time managing to engender those characteristics associated with an educated person. In all this the desire for a common, coherent, integrative culture and cohesive society is strong and remains fundamental to a system of education sponsored by the state and concerned with its preservation. In order to achieve this, education, and with it music education, regulation is required.

The form of regulation I experienced in a boys' grammar school in the late 1950s and early 1960s was representative of a curriculum that had become deeply polarized between the theory and practice of music. There were two weekly lessons, one with pen and paper and mathematical in character and the other singing together and the occasional deployment of the gramophone. The singing class paid attention to different stages of development as a division between A boys, B boys and C boys was made. My membership of a church choir enabled A boy recognition. The singing grew full-blooded and hearty by the second year and before closure of the subject to the majority. Singing was hearty too in the secondary modern school to which I was assigned as a final teaching practice in 1965. There was one lesson weekly and almost always devoted to singing. It was impersonal. A small repertoire of vocal material including the folk song 'My Boy Bonney' satisfied the music teacher, a man with a huge voice and fearsome presence, both developed over a long and dedicated career. The other music teacher, much younger and superficially progressive, but equally authoritarian in style, gave license to my teaching of songs from the musical 'My Fair Lady'. With the classes of both teachers my lessons resembled a choir rehearsal. I was learning to be in control of a class and a director of music. It was impersonal and well regulated and could claim a relationship with at least two of Williams's three purposes. It was orderly, bodies were disciplined and there were songs that might expand the imagination and be of some general value and provide for some lasting personal heritage. However, this was in a secondary modern school predicated on the belief that these children would have a different place in society from those at the grammar school, or technical school where this existed. The platonic doctrine of social stratification for a stable society was strong.

Music, Social Character and Social Control

The most enduring image of the regulation of education comes from fourth century BC Greece and the writing of Plato. Noddings (2003a) points out that Plato works within a framework of clear aims-talk. The aims of education are consistently held in relationship to how music is to be taught and what music is to be taught. There is a sustained integrity and coherence between the why, the how and the what. What kind of society, what kind of young people, what kind of citizens, what kind of schools are the fundamental questions posed and continually deferred to. Plato's purpose is to bring about a static and well-ordered society that knew what was 'good' and what was 'true'. Plato's society was envisaged as small, closed and working from absolute moral standards. Within the programme, unsurprisingly, music has clear ethical purpose. Music educates the soul, affects human character and the whole personality: '… rhythm and harmony find their way to the innermost soul and take strongest hold on it …' (Plato 1988: 88). Music can be of good and bad character. Music's modes and rhythms are to be selected with care. Some are vulgar, some sentimental, not all are equally civilizing. After all, the modes are named after tribes of people, some to be admired, some not. A mode is constructed out of musical proportions, some able to bring about the harmony of mind, body and soul, some not; some able to bring about perfection, some not. In this way of thinking, music education is in need of regulation (Plato 1982). Thus, the character of boys should be developed through modes that were modest, simple and masculine rather than violent, effeminate or fickle (see also Boethius 2002). Music, like the other arts, touched emotion, affected mood and character, and despite being of value as an early years character training device, Plato's theory of knowledge accorded music with low status. Music is less cognitive than other subjects and potentially dangerous. Indeed, this a good reason for it to be carefully regulated. A music education, then as now, was wholly implicated in the moral and political life of society. Music has a place in building not just character but the social character fully harmonized with the social, moral and economic structure of society. Plato provided a blueprint for a stable society where reason and order ruled and where change would be a threat to stability and order. If the mood of the music changed, the walls of the city would shake.

Cultivating Good Taste

There are clear parallels between Plato's regulation and the regulation of English music education between the First and Second World Wars of the twentieth century. Williams's 'social character' function of education in the case of music is revealed in the persistent reference to the inculcation of good taste and civility, and this is achieved through disciplined methods of transmitting approved material that is in good taste. 'The cultivation of taste', a concern for 'music of high quality' and care to avoid 'debased melodies forming taste', 'deplorable little ditties devoid of melody and meaning' are the kinds of sentiments recurring in official documents, for there is good taste and bad taste, good music and bad music. The child needs protection from bad music. Bad music will corrupt taste and with it impede the formation of right character. An ordered society working with common values is the starting and ending point. In suggestions offered to music teachers by the Board of Education in 1927 the following recommendation is made:

> As a rule the music first learned by children should be drawn from our Folk and Traditional songs. These are the true classics of the people, and form the foundation on which a national love of music can be built up … a pupil whose memory is stored with these songs from his earliest school days has the best protection that education can give against the attractions of vulgar and sentimental music when school days are over; and it is not always realized how strong and vital a tie between the members of a school, a college, or even a nation may be formed by their knowledge of a common body of traditional song.
>
> (Board of Education 1927: 253)

Here is a conviction that, through singing, shared identities would be formed and a national community of common values created. Music education was in this way conceived of as an education in citizenship and in many respects to be regulated in the way that Plato had proposed. Vulgarity and sentiment in music militated against 'good taste' and 'good taste' was related to what was civil and civilizing. In the Cambridgeshire Report of 1933, a forward-thinking agenda embracing music education in school and community is set out. But still there comes a clear line of demarcation between what is good and what is bad and what habits of taste need to be instilled through a music education.

> We have so much useless music in our streets, our churches, our restaurants, and our theatres, to say nothing of the mechanized music which recent years have brought us in ever increasing quantity that we may well be tempted to regard music as a nuisance from which we are only too thankful to escape. It is perhaps fortunate that most people simply do not listen to the music which they are obliged to hear: that is, they do not listen to it in the way that anyone habituated to good music listens to a masterpiece.
>
> (Cambridgeshire Council of Music Education 1933: 10)

Those who had determined music education policy during the first half of the twentieth century had been committed to music that civilized, formed character and educated morally. Some ways of life were preferred to others.

Concession and Change

Singing, the appreciation of music and the acquisition of a clearly defined set of skills, techniques and repertoire of music were the common fare of music classrooms following the Second World War. Jill's encounter with the weekly radio broadcast *Time and Tune* showed this well. However, for most there was no impromptu orchestra or study of a symphony through the other arts, and experience often resembled a narrow course of musical training. This was commonly the case at secondary level. Overemphasis on technical matters could frequently get in the way of aesthetic experience and enjoyment. Whilst the Board of Education of 1927 and the Cambridgeshire Report of 1933 had called for careful management of repertoire, the Scottish Education Department in 1955 called for concession. Writing of the choice of music for instruction in listening, music teachers were given the following advice.

> At first it should not be too unlike that which the pupils are accustomed to hear in the cinema or at home. The lively polkas and graceful waltzes of Strauss, for example, are a means of capturing the interest of the pupils who may not respond so quickly to the music of Bach and Beethoven. The simple classics should remain the foundations of good musical training, but the interest of the pupils

in contemporary popular music should not be ignored. When they leave school – indeed, while they are still at school the pupil's interest is drawn towards this very attractive, although perhaps ephemeral, music, which forms so large part of their musical experience. The school's obligation is not to dissociate itself entirely from this kind of music but to teach some discrimination in sorting out the good from the bad.

(Scottish Education Department 1955: 218)

The statement, written in the year of Bill Haley's 'Rock around the Clock' success and only months before Elvis Presley was to have his first recording session for the RCA record label, came on the cusp of an emergent youth culture. The 1955 statement above marks a change of emphasis in policy, recommending that teachers should recognize the interests of their pupils, acknowledging their experience beyond school. However, the nurture of critical judgement and discrimination in sorting the good from the bad, the education of taste, the learned appreciation of music remained a central obligation of the school.

Learning to Discriminate

As Sybil Marshall completed her English Tripos at Cambridge and prepared to move to Sheffield University as a teacher-educator, Jill was growing in disaffection with her secondary school experience where extrinsic matters pressed on the style of teaching and relationships. Primary school experience had ill-prepared Jill for the overt judgement and sometimes public shaming in her secondary school. From a love of school work, fear and guilt now came to the surface and confidence ebbed.

In England post-war austerity was replaced by affluence and a newly discovered level of urban comfort coincided with the importing of aspects of an American way of life. What was of significance for music education was an acknowledgment that there now existed a youth culture and that former authoritarian structures were withering under pressure from outside. Rainbow notes with measured disdain that:

Across the Atlantic the cult of Youth had long formed the essential of that elusive phenomenon, the American Way of Life. The liberated teenager now steadily fabricated paraphernalia of adolescent taste in dress, conduct, language, and music as a badge of identity. The totem apparatus the sociologist was soon to dignify with the title Youth Culture.

(Rainbow with Cox 2006: 318)

Jill had thought that her lyric poetry set to Beethoven's 'Song of Thanksgiving' may well have been influenced by music heard at home, for elder sister Gay would be listening to Radio Luxemburg and the music of Paul Anka was in fashion. There was 'Diana', 'Crazy Love', 'You Are My Destiny', 'It's Time To Cry', 'Lonely Boy', 'I Miss You So', for example. While Sybil Marshall understood well the place of children's private vernacular culture, their playground chant and rhyme, their healthy enfeebled doggerel, she did begin to question the place of such in the school. She recognized too that the notion of 'good taste' was a matter of the 'prevailing zeitgeist at any given time … good taste follows fashion' (Marshall 1976: 25). Taste was not supra-human. However, it was during the 1960s and 1970s that vernacular culture took new forms and imploded on the mind of the child, and the older child became labelled 'teenager' as a category of consumer. As a new kind of vernacular reached the classroom derived from a commercial popular culture of the 1960s and 70s, Sybil was to expresses concern for the nurture of aesthetic qualities in the use of language and the need to sharpen pupils' own powers of discrimination. She makes clear that it is not the teacher's task to discriminate for children but to support them in exercising their powers of discrimination. And here there is an important qualification, for in order to do this they must have a wealth of material to discriminate between and it was the teacher whose task it was to manage this (ibid).

In the case of Sybil Marshall, working with a clear belief about what it meant to be educated and to lead a productive life, her class became a community in which relationships flourished and in which a love for learning grew. Not only were relationships with each other important but with what was being learnt. There were intimate relationships with each other and with the knowledge being shared. Sybil's view of childhood was a positive and realistic one. Childhood was not to be sentimentalized, it was to be understood as best it could be in the circumstances of not being a child. Sybil's curriculum was regulated in turn by the minds of her pupils and her own passion for learning, the value she accorded to living and what would be worth learning for life's flourishing. This was underpinned by the breadth and depth of her own education, by the richness of her culture. Inheriting tradition was pivotal to Sybil's work and this was a responsibility of the school. Oakshott (1972) is clear too that the school is a place where what has been inherited from the past is passed to a new generation. Education is a transaction between the past and the future, a poetic conversation and a personal transaction between the teacher and learner. The teacher is:

> The custodian of that 'practice' in which an inheritance of human understanding survives and is perpetually renewed in being imparted to newcomers. To teach is to bring it about so that, somehow, something of worth intended by a teacher is learned, understood and remembered by that learner.
>
> (Oakshott 1972: 23)

Oakshott is writing about a form of cultural transmission, a relationship between the past, present and future, an 'endless indeterminable conversation' as he described it. What was important was the idea of 'conversation', implying openness, the avoidance of closure or the proposal for any final solution.

Culture is never an easy word and as I review the challenges faced by music educators and the children they sought to educate during the 1960s and 1970s, I will need to create a culture debate and one which has flowed on to the present time. At the heart of such a discussion in the case of music lay the question, whose music should children and young people encounter in the first and formative stages of their lives? At Kingston during the 1950s Jill had met with a vast repertoire of folk and national songs and revelled in music heard on the gramophone unlikely to be heard at home. As well as a whole symphony in her head there remain songs recalled in their totality, songs legitimated by years of benign regulation by those who had acted as the guardians of music education. Arnold Bentley, Kenneth Simpson and Bernarr Rainbow were three such guardians.

Reason and Order Destabilized

Arnold Bentley, music educator and pioneering researcher into poor pitch singing, Kenneth Simpson, music educator and author of the text *Some Great Music Educators*, and Bernarr Rainbow, music educator and leading authority on the history of music education had devoted their professional lives both pre and post Second World War to gaining a better understanding of the place of music in education. Now writing towards the end of their careers they were witnessing a fast emerging culture drawing confidently from progressive and child-centred educational ideas that challenged the authority of the past. From a dominant culture of traditional practices there had emerged a desire to reformulate the basis of music education and to create educational experiences that, in the discourse of the time, would in various combinations satisfy the search for greater relevance, coherence and that which would be thought of as more worthwhile. There was a mood for change. The Schools Council was established sponsoring curriculum development and recognizing the autonomy of the teacher. It was a time of 'breaking out' (Simon 1991), a reaching out for a more egalitarian and open society in which children and young people would be seen differently. Two official reports made the point.

In 1963, the year of Sybil's Marshall's *An Experiment in Education*, came the report 'Half Our Futures' concerned with the education of pupils aged 13 to 16 of average and less than average ability. The report called for a change of attitude towards what was half of the secondary school population and this involved recognizing a need to raise the school leaving age to 16. These pupils needed a fresh approach with attention paid to their interests. Some of their time might be spent beyond the confines of school, and much would depend upon 'the attitude of the teacher to the pupil when the pupil is, in effect, a young adult' (Central Advisory Council for Education 1963: xiii). Among the principal recommendations of the report we find that '… attention should be paid both to the imaginative experience through the arts, and to the personal and social development of the pupils' (ibid: xvi). This as we will see would require an imaginative response of some magnitude on the part of secondary school music teachers. Meanwhile, in the same year the Central Advisory Council (England) was commissioned by government to report on the state of Primary Education and in 1967 the Plowden Report was published endorsing children at the centre of their education (Central Advisory Council for Education 1967). The report recommended movement towards the integration of music with centres of interest and the introduction of small group and individual music making now apparent in some secondary schools.

A significant example of individual and small group instrumental playing in secondary schools was certainly evident amongst a teacher instigated development in the North West of England. By 1966 a consortium of Local Education Authorities in the North West was responding and giving support to curriculum development actively targeted on the needs of the secondary school pupil of average ability. New approaches arising from the project were to become the blueprint for all children. The curriculum framework became 'creating, recreating and listening' (North West Regional Curriculum Development Project 1974). The traditional framework of singing, playing and listening saw the singing imperative slackened and the creating imperative heightened. Those of the tradition of training the voice, ear and eye as the precursor of articulate musicianship felt a sense of rejection. Bentley, who had been engaged in pioneering research into children's poor pitch singing, was unwilling to see traditionally valued activities lost under the 'creative' umbrella. Bentley demurred at what he saw as loss of continuity with the past and the enduring principles of music learning. For Bentley singing was the bedrock of a traditional approach and singing was losing its hold as a central activity in the music room. Bentley questioned the values underpinning the myriad innovations of the time; the idea of creative music making is questioned in particular.

> While children should be encouraged to create their own original music, and be given the means to do this … remembering that they already have a voice as a creative instrument … genuine creative originality is likely to be as rare in school as in the world of music at large. Spending an inordinate amount of time trying to develop original creativity must result in an unbalanced curriculum and the neglect of what for most children and adults would be musically worthwhile.
>
> (Bentley 1975: 44)

Bentley's concern was that appropriate time should be apportioned to an agreed range of activities. In particular there was a crucial balance to strike between learning through the voice and through an instrument. Taylor (1979) echoed Bentley's concern about the neglect of vocal skills, sight reading and aural training. Those seeking to sustain traditional approaches saw music education, like schooling in general, in turmoil. Simpson writes:

> Former certainties of aim are gone; changes in society, and in music itself, have led some to reject traditional curriculum content and methods out-of-hand. Competing voices cry their own particular and often incompatible prescriptions, and the teacher–in-the-middle is faced with a bewildering number of choices about his general class lessons.
>
> (Simpson 1975: frontpiece)

Simpson, writing in the third of a series of *Black Papers* seeking a return to traditional forms of schooling, laments the flood of new ideas that on investigation are in fact old ones 'made over' into novelties and innovations and very often poor imitations of the methods devised by Curwen and Kodaly, for example. These methods are proven through their systematic application from early years, building up:

> ... a store of tonal and kinaesthetic memories, and associations with relevant symbols, and have developed habits of attention, powers of perception, and attitudes towards music which make further progress almost inevitable.
>
> (Simpson 1970: 82)

Simpson concedes that principles underlying these traditional methods have rarely been grasped by teachers. Standards have declined and by this is meant the fundamental ability to sing well and to be able to read music at sight with the voice. In secondary schools there is the problem of poor pupil behaviour, a lack of effort and increasing disrespect for authority. It is in these circumstances that there is a 'fevered search for novelty'. Simpson writes:

> Schooling, as it has evolved, stands for reason, order, objective thought, precision and sustained application – in other words, for the denial and rechannelling of our raw reactions to our experiences. In essence it derives from a small and mostly leisured proportion of the population in the Age of Reason, and some who have submitted to its disciplines have learnt that it opens the way to intellectual delights, ends-in-themselves, which are inaccessible by any other path.
>
> (ibid: 85)

In the name of order and reason Simpson goes on to cite the negative tendencies in artistic movements, those reactions against reason, the early Romantics' interest in legend and the supernatural, Surrealism's rejection of all-explaining reason and the nineteenth-century's Impressionism destroying pure lines of craftsmanship. In place of reason comes shock and destruction. Of course there is a place for educating the emotions but at the present time there is no sensible balance between reason and emotion in evidence. Instead unreason and disorder in the name of freedom predominate. Simpson concludes that in the face of the hostile forces of popular culture, aggressive youth and the demise of authority, music should be cherished for those in secondary school choosing to pursue it. The age of 12 may be the point at which such choice should be available. Rainbow, sharing Simpson's concern for the rejection of tried and tested methods, focuses on the loss of heritage:

> Another casualty of current iconoclasm was class singing itself ... at a stroke the entire repertoire of treble songs drawn from the past, from centuries, was consigned to the dustbin.
>
> (Rainbow with Cox 2006: 354)

Nurture of the voice was proving problematic and the Inner London Education Authority (ILEA 1973), addressing the needs of school leavers, dealt a potential death blow:

> The most obvious and least-skill-necessary activity is singing, and singing is much more profitable when those who do not want to sing are removed from those who do. Therefore singing belongs more closely to the extra-curricular than the curricular.
>
> (ILEA 1973: 8)

When teaching a traditional curriculum in a Worcestershire secondary school during the 1960s and 1970s I had unquestioningly made singing a central activity. Classes had sung from the Oxford Song Book the folk song 'Early One Morning' as well as the art song 'Where the Bee Sucks'. My pupils had listened to a standardized repertoire of music that had come to form the school music canon and there had been a smattering of theory too. I recall a challenge from the school's art teacher as he prepared the set for the school's production of the play *Burke and Hare*. Could we not together compose the play's incidental music? By this he meant improvise music together that would be worthy of recording and become integral to the production. I was coaxed into a way of making music utterly foreign to me. Yet it was this way that was being explored in some other schools by classes as they stopped singing, ceased notating and imbibing information about music. The improvisation of music was something experienced by the art teacher in his art college of the 1960s as part of a broad liberal education. It had never been a part of my own music curriculum.

Music in secondary schools became for the adolescent a place to exhibit apathy, hostility, rejection and for music teachers to respond with a kind of historical inertia. At worst, acknowledging the pupils' musical interests produced condescension and further pupil resentment. A pupil of the time relates:

> It was 1965 and our music teacher tried some experimental lessons when we got to Year 9. We were invited to bring our favorite records to the lesson. I brought Bob Dylan's 'She belongs to me'. I remember thinking this was a really worthy piece of work because both the words and music had been created by Dylan. This encapsulated my ideal of individual expression and what I considered to be authenticity. The piece connected with my interest in surrealism too. The teacher noted the harmonica playing with some disdain: 'it's just suck-blow, suck-blow'. We seemed to be in parallel universes. The teacher always kept a tight lid on discussion to avoid tribal warfare.
>
> (In conversation 2004)

The Arts of the Adolescent

In 1968 the Schools Council's *Enquiry I: Young School Leavers* had shown music in secondary schools to be of little significance for the majority of pupils. The enquiry particularly focused on those pupils close to leaving school, and in Working Paper 35 (Schools Council 1971) the Council looked at the problems in some detail. Why was music among the arts more vulnerable as a secondary school subject than the other arts? Reasoning centred on the cultural dissonance felt by pupils between the formality of school music and the informality of out of school music, by the sharp dissonances in teacher and pupil values. The report noted music in school flourishing where there was 'high intensity involvement' (ibid: 15) and this was clear to see in those activities opted for beyond the weekly classroom lesson that remained obligatory in the first three years of secondary school. The view was that too much might be expected from the class music lesson. If class music were to take on greater meaning and purpose it would need to be linked with a variety of purpose-designed groupings. This implied an element of choice for pupils and opportunities for greater self-determination. The place of literacy in the scheme of things needed to be reconsidered as did the centrality of choral singing.

> However important it may be to make as many pupils as possible musically *literate*, it is still more important to make them musically *articulate* through engagement in playing, singing, and perhaps movement; only through the growth of such active participation can the value of notation be realized. Nor need the form of notation be limited to the five-line stave and its associated symbols ...
>
> (ibid: 20)

A series of recommendations was made. The particularity of the adolescent state of mental and social development would need to be recognized; the gap between teenage sub-culture and what schools offered needed to be bridged; the cohort approach to class music lessons was ill-advised; vibrant out of class activity should be encouraged by an extension to the school day; repertoire needed to be continually reviewed; there was a need for wider ranging instrumental resources; contemporary compositional techniques along with extending the definition of notation were legitimate; interdisciplinary work was to be considered; the recognition of less academic courses was needed as were more generous and relevant staffing arrangements along with improved accommodation. There was an endorsement too of the progress made in primary schools towards a creative revolution.

By Working Paper 54, 'Arts and the Adolescent', written by Malcolm Ross (1975), the plight of music was being evaluated in the context of Robert Witkin's theory of subjective-reflexive action. Ross had grown up singing in church choirs and as an undergraduate in Cambridge reading English he had enjoyed the fine grained singing in his College Chapel Choir and where he had learnt to listen and find musical attunement with those around him. As a secondary school teacher of English during the 1960s he had been inspired by the radio broadcasts given by the poet Ted Hughes and by a course taken at the City Literary Institute in Holborn, and recalls extended drama improvisation in response to Stravinsky's *Rite of Spring*. David Holbrook's *English for Maturity* and the freedom to make the classroom a place of high stimulus and intense expression drawing in the other arts and facilitating extended pieces of highly personal creative writing made good sense and inspired vocation as an arts educator.

Now collaborating with Ross, Robert Witkin, writing from the sociology department of Exeter University, laments his 5 per cent in a school art examination and addresses the complex issue of self-expression, the *bête noire* of anti-progressivism. This was now grappled with considerable intensity through the presentation of a complex theoretical model. Witkin's *The Intelligence of Feeling* (1974) is concerned with defining the nature of 'expressive activity' and establishes a way of 'being' and 'knowing' that involves a reciprocal relationship between the knower and her medium of expression. There are two ways of being and knowing, one through subjective-reflexive action and the other through object-reflexive action. The first way, and the way of the creative artist, involves a yielding relationship between the knower and her medium. The second is characterized by a distancing and objectification unlike the playful engagement the artist enjoys with their medium of expression. In this way it was argued that the artist comes to know the self in coming to know the world of objects. This provides the arts with a clearly defined role in education. It addresses self-actualization, the realization of one's own being and place in the world, realizing oneself through the objects of artistic expression, through the way an instrument is played, the way a composition is created, the way I sing in a choir and always in relationship to that which is not me. The arts in school must, so the argument went, engage with the felt experience of adolescents, their life of feeling, that if recognized would lead to the making sense of self and others through the creative act. In the case of music, Ross, Witkin's co-researcher, called not for 'more performers but more composers, more creators' (Ross 1975: 69). And Witkin observed that of all teachers across the arts, music teachers have most dependency upon what were termed realized forms, existing works, material to be performed, listened to and studied. He noted that in presenting these to the adolescent there was rarely any relationship made with creative activity. Here then was a place of confinement from which music education could escape – the weight of tradition, the burden of repertoire, the overwhelming authority given to tutored skills and particular kinds of musical performance. Witkin and Ross found in their visits to schools that the most common form of classroom encounter in music lessons was a 'combination of the conducted choir practice and formal academic class teaching' and this is precisely what they would have found in my own classroom of the time (Witkin 1974: 137). This was in stark contrast to the greater informality of lessons in the other arts.

The Intelligence of Feeling

The challenge posed by Witkin and Ross implicated teachers in a responsive relationship with their pupils, not a reactive one. Teachers would need to have the intelligence of feeling and understand something of their own 'subject-reflexivity'. Teachers would, as we imagine Sybil Marshall did, need to view children in their wholeness. It was proper for the teacher to get to know the mind of their pupils, to be sensitively interested in what they were thinking and feeling, what might their impulse be to create and express. If the child in an art lesson used colour in a lurid and unconventional way, for example, then this would be something to be understood, not to be rebuked.

The Intelligence of Feeling called for learners to find the freedom to be and to find meaning for themselves. Witkin makes the point powerfully.

> Learning is a process of discovery. When a man is taken by the arm here and there at the behest of an insistent guide, and is told what to look at and what its bearings are in relation to other things he has been shown, he does not feel very much like an explorer making a discovery. He probably feels safe but bored. If he should then meet another man who says, 'Make discoveries, explore the possibilities, find your own way', he will in all probability feel excited but too scared to embark, precisely because he has too little experience of thinking for himself. One solution that might immediately commend itself is to become a sly man, one of life's own tourists. Then he will move where he wants to move but only if the guide book says it is in order to do so. A tourist is sly because he cheats. He pretends to make discoveries while he is busily copying the answers out of the guide book. He is stupid too. Who can be more stupid than a man who cheats by robbing himself of his own possibilities for experience?
>
> (Witkin 1974: 167)

Witkin was thus setting out an uncompromising model of authentic self-expression where there is no fear of freedom and where minds can freely speak, existential anxiety is worked with and self-realization found. In observing music lessons that pupils valued, he notes that there was a warm and relaxed atmosphere 'and a fairly free flow of information between teacher and pupils and, when required, amongst pupils themselves' (ibid: 138). There was a recognition that each child brings a culture to the classroom, a way of seeing the world, with questions to ask, expressive problems to be solved. This is how they are in the world. The challenge for the teacher is to create a space in which the pupil's state of knowing and being can be accommodated. Ross was to find a way of thinking about this problem in the work of child psychoanalyst Donald Winnicott and the notion of 'good enough' mothering.

Winnicott (1985, 1987) assumed that creativity was a normal cultural accomplishment and that it would flourish unless it were in some way impeded by environmental circumstances. Creativity originated and grew in the context of play and playfulness. Motherhood was the model. The teacher could create in the classroom a climate of playfulness where there would be give and take and this would be sufficient to make what in the relationship between mother and child Winnicott defined as the 'potential space', 'an overlap between the subjectivity of the mother and the subjectivity of the child within which gratuitously pleasurable activities can take place' (Ross 1984: 9). Through such playful experiences objects came to be invested with feeling and meaning, objects that in Witkin's theory were engaged with self reflexively and not reactively. In this way of thinking the arts provided a unique way of knowing. The teacher would work towards:

1. establishing the sanctity of mutual truthfulness;
2. developing trust [trustworthiness and truthfulness];
3. being free enough to free students to act playfully, to explore and invent in an atmosphere that is non-judgemental, where error is essential to trial;
4. providing conditions of psychic safety; and
5. being devoted to the child's learning and growth. (Ross 1980: 110).

Ross (1978) provides an example of a teaching sequence undertaken with what is referred to as a 'non-musical group' (1978: 248–52). It is enactive and relies on whole-class work, some smaller group work feeding from and back to the whole and at the same time focusing on individual expressive responses. The work included drumming along to a recording of African drumming sustained for 15 minutes. There was reading of text together, as a whole class finding deep waves of pulse and counter pulse from which a whole class composition was made, recorded, played back and together analysed. A relationship was made with Stockhausen's 'Kontakte' and later there was a reason to listen to Stravinsky's 'Oedipus Rex'; there was score making and an ever onward moving process.

In this example, Ross was setting out a way of teaching music that insisted upon acts of expression, allowing form to be given to feeling and a creative process understood. While Witkin had produced a densely argued theoretical basis to practical teaching, his concept of the creative process was simple enough. This required the finding of a holding form, something that was satisfying and that could be held onto, driving the creative process forward. Once the holding form had been found there could be the working through successive approximations until completion. And here was learning that a feelingful intuition of what was right provided for a deep and authentic form of learning. In the Ross example there is use of stimuli, the recording of drumming, literary text, Stockhausen and Stravinsky, something that the teacher places in the way of the learner, and in Witkin's model something that enables a sensate problem to be felt. This highlights the need for the creative process to engage with something that takes on personal significance. Here there was a critical role for the teacher, playfully energizing the thoughts and feelings of their pupils, helping them to find something of personal and public value. Something resembling an organic process opened up for the class. The outcomes would always be expressive.

The 'Arts and the Adolescent' project had set out to provide a basis for teaching the arts in school by drawing upon what was in the minds of arts teachers and their students. In all this there was a concern for four matters: self-expression and individuality; control of the medium; use of realized form; personal development. Thus, there was an education to be had 'through the arts'. The arts could claim a distinctive place in the school and the education of young people. What was being proposed stood aloof from an education that was instrumental and respectful of the economic well-being of the nation.

The question of the nation's economic well-being now came to the fore. In the wake of problems related to public disorder, unemployment, inflation and the spectre of economic decline, the Keynsian model of social democracy was being questioned, neo-liberalism was finding a form. Minds on the political 'right' were being moved by neo-liberal doctrine and education was being brought to order.

Standards, Culture and Productivity

This first intimation of what was to become defined as a neo-liberal tendency within liberal democracies was to be identified in challenges to the function of education within British society and most pointedly in the culture of education, in its deeply embedded attitudes and values, in its disconnectedness, self-satisfaction and disdain for industry, manufacturing and the world of work. Beck (1998), in examining the blame placed on the teaching profession for the nation's ills, points to an article in the *Times Education Supplement* in 1976 written by Sir Arnold Weinstock (the then chief executive of the General Electricity Council) drawing attention to the failure of the nation's schools and their teachers to promote respect for manufacturing industry (Weinstock 1976). In the emergent neo-liberal discourse there was reference to industrial decline and a nation in decline. Education wasn't performing. In the same year Prime Minister James Callaghan made a speech at Ruskin College, Oxford and reported:

> I am concerned on my journeys to find complaints from industry that new recruits from schools sometimes do not have the basic tools to do the job that is required.
>
> (Callaghan 1976: 4)

Callaghan argued that education was rightly a matter of public interest. The audience was reminded of two fundamental goals:

> ... to equip children to the best of their ability for a lively, constructive place in society, and also to fit them to do a job of work. Not one or the other but both.
>
> (ibid: 6)

While sustaining a dual focus, concern was expressed about two matters in particular: the validity of informal methods of teaching, that is progressive tendencies, and what Williams (1961) referred to as the industrial training function of education. There was a call for a core curriculum, greater application to the needs of industry and greater accountability.

> There is now widespread recognition of the need to cater for a child's personality in its fullest possible way ... There is no virtue in producing socially well-adjusted members of society who are unemployed because they do not have the skills.
>
> (Callaghan 1976: 6)

This was a direct challenge to the progressive view of the child, to a focus on their path to self-realization. Could the arts be thought of as being useful? Could a music education manage to be of intrinsic worth, vital to the child's life here and now, and at the same time serve the demands of the nation's economic prosperity?

Callaghan and those that took an instrumental view of education were rather less concerned about another perceived reason for education, the ideal of the group Williams called 'the old humanists' and expressed most cogently in the words of Matthew Arnold, that each new generation should be inducted into 'the best that has been thought and said in the world' (Arnold 1869: viii). Arnold's words had become emblematic for those arguing for the restoration of standards rooted in a set of traditional values thought of as being embedded in Culture with a big C. Here was a perspective promoting culture as excellence and thought of as a beacon of virtue, a moral force historically engendered by religious impulse. It was this that was being renounced and in its place a cultural relativism was taking hold where no source of cultural understanding or intellectual authority could be privileged over any other.

Here was a purported decline in intellectual and moral standards paralleling the decline in religious faith. But this wasn't the only way of thinking about culture. Raymond Williams and Edward Thompson were amongst those viewing culture as always something in the making and made by real people in real contexts. Culture in this view, as a way of life, was a realm of contestation and struggle but nevertheless one where a shared egalitarian culture might be forged, not sameness but a recognition of equality through diversity and individuality.

In somewhat crude bipolar terms, on the one side stood tradition, civility, a high-cultural aesthetic, a claim to intellectual integrity, rigour, the weight of civilization and the unifying and cohesive force of a mono-culturalism around which a common cultural heritage would be acknowledged, social cohesion ensured and the nationhood verified. On the other side stood the belief in a different kind of common culture. This recognized and celebrated diversity and difference, concerned as much with vernacular expression as with finer artistic expression. At the heart of such dissension lay alternative views of power, authority and democracy, and attitudes towards the legitimacy of a dominant cultural tradition and its call upon timeless and transcendent values. Was music then divinely ordered or inherently multi-cultural?

By appropriating and placing high cultural objects in a dominating and superior position, there ensues the seeking of the components of a product rather than the conditions of a practice (Williams 1963: 48). And a 'selective tradition' creates a rejection of vast areas of what was once lived culture, creating the myth of 'time' as the great valuer (see Williams 1961). The 'rough music making' of the eighteenth century, the 'tin horn' playing of Penzance youth on May Day in 1933, for example, are easily discarded. In focusing on the components of a product the art work becomes context independent; timeless, and placeless aesthetic values are drawn forth transcendent of material culture.

This 'anthropological' way of defining and understanding culture was taken by up Paul Willis (1978) and powerfully expressed through the ethnographic study of West Midland biker and hippie sub-cultures, showing how music formed the symbolic heart of what were very distinctive ways of life. In these cases music confirmed, celebrated and strengthened social identity, the very thing that music in school was, in the view of Willis and others, so clearly failing to achieve for the majority. Willis's way of understanding how the arts could work for young people in their everyday lives in due course came to be defined as 'grounded aesthetics', an idea rejecting institutionalized notions of the arts and in particular the arts in school and their deference to an 'ideology of the aesthetic' (Willis et al. 1990, see also Eagleton 1990).

From the anthropological perspective the way in which music was integral to the human condition, to material existence, was the field of ethnomusicology, and it was ethnomusicologist John Blacking who maintained that music needed to be understood in all its diversity and as human capability, that it was humanly organized sound, a cultural expression of human relationships, existing as a value in human being (Blacking 1973). It was therefore important to speak of 'musics' rather than 'music' and as Blacking was later to write, to see music's purpose as to

> ... enhance in some way the quality of individual experience and human relationships; its structures are reflections of patterns of human relations, and the value of a piece of music as music is inseparable from its value as an expression of human experience.
>
> (Blacking 1995: 31)

And:

> Music should consist of the processes by which people make sense of certain kinds of activity and experience, and that musical value resides not in any piece or style of music, but in the way people address themselves to listening and performance.
>
> (Blacking 1985: 12)

Blacking immediately exposes the cultural blindness of those working inside the Western European tradition. Thus, the way other people in other places make sense of being musically human can inform ideas about what it is to be musically educated. Likewise the consideration of other world views was central to the thesis of Christopher Small who provided a socio-musical critique of music, society and education setting out the ways in which the West had arrived at 'our present uncomfortable, if not downright dangerous condition in our relations to one another and with nature' (Small 1977: 3). Small exposes the relentless triumph of abstract knowledge, arising from a deeply fixed state of mind separating knowledge from the knower leading to a Western European aesthetic of music that proscribes working with images and metaphors presented by the way different musics in different places function socially. Opening the mind to this way of seeing and listening was a source of social transformation where social relationships might be constructed differently. Music could and frequently did offer a form of social critique that enabled a preview of a potential society and at the same time an alternative model of education. Small notes how

> ... we become afraid of the encounter with new musical experience, where knowledge and expertise is no guide and only the subjective experience honestly felt can serve, and retreat into the safe past, where we know what to expect and connoisseurship is paramount.
>
> (ibid: 5)

And how

> ... artistic activity, properly understood, can provide not only a way out of this *impasse* in musical appreciation, in itself an important matter, but also an approach to the restructuring of education and even perhaps our society.
>
> (ibid.)

Rather than existing as an oasis beyond society artificially reconstructed, music can be a part of every-day experience.

For Small it is the artist working in freedom and love who is able to provide the model of what work and what relationships might be like free from a technico-scientific rationality. Here schools might become different and where children would be artists released from the dual role of consumer-producer. Small's account is a serious indictment of Western European musical culture, society and education with the latter reduced to a commodity. Like Williams, Willis and Blacking, Small viewed culture as something to be lived and music as something to be experienced in social relationship. Music in school could be freed from its historical roots and, in the case of Small, become experimental, explorative and a model of ways of relating through music.

If culture was something lived, communally shared and socially transformative then established notions of reason and order resting on a conception of culture as a civilizing continuity of ideas, feelings and sensibilities embodied in great minds of the past and evidenced in great works of art were anathema. Oakshott's 'conversation' and Arnold's 'best' were hegemonies calling for resistance. Reason and order were indeed being destabilized drawing forth reaction in talk of decline in standards and a need to restore Culture with a big C. In this view education was not primarily for the benefit of its recipient. It was not child-centred but subject-centred, Euro-centred and above all, nation-centred. To address the imminent needs of the child, to view them as artists, to consider their ways of seeing reality, their way of making sense, would be a serious dereliction of duty to the future and sustaining the right social order. As we will see, the debate between those intent on cultural restoration and those seeing culture as everyday and ubiquitous came to a head in the making of a National Curriculum for music vividly exposing the contested nature of culture and a chasm of some considerable breadth and depth. The debate further exposed contested notions of a social order and democratic arrangements. The platonic tendency to have faith in ordained ideals and fixed notions of what is good and true was becoming severely strained. Culture then exists to be contested, struggled over, and creativity to be thought of as common to all, or indeed, unusually rare.

Conclusion

Sybil Marshall's enterprising approach in her village primary school during the 1950s revealed progressive trends as she made space for children's impulses to create through the arts. She had come to understand the role of this creative activity as a time of symbolization and part of a creative process, drawing together and making complete wider experience and knowledge. At the same time the growing call for the recognition of children's individual differences ran in tandem with the idea of creativity. In the case of music education, the culture of class singing represented traditional values rooted in a form of regulation through repertoire and a quiet but persistent deference to the promotion of good taste, civility and the maintenance of the social order. Whereas Sybil Marshall represented a teacher experimenting and working out her beliefs and values and shaping these into a belief system that generated free-spiritedness and professional freedom, there remained, in opposition, the conviction that coherence and order required the articulation of aims and the clarification and definition of principles better determining and containing practice. In this clash between subject-centredness with its preservation of tradition and child-centredness with the potential loss or at least dilution of tradition, there lay politically opposed ways of thinking about whose music should educate and to what extent some rather than other ways of life should be deferred to. More fundamentally there were opposing views about the nature of childhood and the extent to which the child's life of feeling should be acknowledged and whether the boundary separating school and not school should be relaxed. In Ross's view music amongst the arts was lagging behind the other arts. Despite recognizing the innovative work of musician-teachers such as Brian Dennis, Murray Shafer and John Paynter, it had 'remained largely aloof from the whole child-centred movement in education with all its ramifications' (Ross 1975: 53). In recognizing that music's task is greatest amongst all the traditional arts subjects Ross offers some explanations. There is

> ... the alleged remoteness of the traditional music curriculum from the lives of young people, the cultural gaps between teachers and taught, the inappropriateness of teachers' training, the demands on mind and skill that the reading of music and the mastery of a musical instrument present for many pupils. Perhaps, too, there is something inherent in the very immediacy of music itself, in its direct and explicit emotionalism that proves to be an obstacle for self-conscious adolescents in the formal school setting ... Perhaps music is, as many musicians have insisted to us, rather a special case after all.
>
> (ibid: 53–4)

Those final (and perhaps ironically penned) words of Ross were to linger and return with force as we shall see later. That aside, the reality exposed by the Schools Council reports between 1968 and 1972 demanded a response from music education and in the case of the 'Arts and the Adolescent' project called for teachers to become co-creators with their pupils, to work in the space in-between school and out of school cultures and in-between the teacher and the pupil and in-between pupil and pupil.

The 'intelligence of feeling' as proposed by Witkin and extended by Ross positioned the arts as having a common purpose. While music need not be taught by drama teachers, music teachers would need to find greater sympathy with the way the other arts engaged the feeling lives of pupils. The young person was alive with musical impulses and these needed to be acknowledged and given form. At the same time this would require music teachers to re-evaluate whose music was fit to educate. The school music canon would need to be reviewed if not abandoned as the use of realized forms (all those songs sung and music played for appreciation), were placed in a relationship to the pupil's own expressive work. If the arts were about self-realization and the making of people able to live well and beyond culture then this would place the arts, in their refusal to concede to the instrumental demands of society, beyond many of the legitimate functions of education. With Witkin and Ross came something resembling a progressive peroration claiming the arts to be a way of being and knowing essentially subjective in nature and for personal development and self-realization. Into this *milieu* the notion of creativity happily nestled. It now required thinking from within the music education community to grasp the progressive nettle and bring about change and to consider what kind of *rapprochement*, if any, could be made with the social order.

Chapter 4
Coming to Know Music

Understandably, the tendency has always been for us to skip the philosophy and
go straight to the 'meat'; the 'things to do'.

(Paynter 1982: 14)

James Callaghan's 1976 intervention was a politically shrewd move, not wishing
to be seen in thrall to the conservationists or the progressives or any other faction.
It was, however, a powerful political signal that it was time to tame the progressive
impulse. The Plowden Report's claim that a school 'is a community in which
children learn to live first and foremost as children and not as future adults ...'
(Central Advisory Council for Education 1967) would be difficult to sustain in
the face of political moves to make education more accountable to society. The
Plowden Report had become the easily identifiable source of progressive ideas
and general concern about the decline in order and respect for authority. Two
particular critiques published in *Perspectives on Plowden* (Peters 1969) help in
understanding some of the tensions underpinning professional and policy debate
during the 1970s and 1980s.

The Plowden Report had widely been seen as an endorsement of child-centred
approaches, a recognition that authoritarian principles of education were now a
thing of the past. While this was to set the pattern for the primary school and the
training of its teachers, criticisms were presented from two differing perspectives.
The first came from the 'new philosophy of education' and the second for the
'new sociology of education'. The first concentrated its efforts on the clarity of
conceptual thinking and challenged partly through ideas incorporating doctrines
of various kinds parading as philosophy. The second saw in child-centred education
a disregard for social factors effecting children's responses to school and an over-
reliance on the child considered as biologically determined to grow and flourish
irrespective of social conditions. In the first case, the weakly articulated claims of
the progressive came under scrutiny.

Knowledge and Mind

Just what was meant by 'to be yourself', 'growth', 'the needs of the child',
'independent learning', 'creativity', 'discovery' and so on? By asking questions like
this the analytic philosopher claimed that it was possible to expose contradictions
and confusions and reveal the paucity of rational and empirical evidence in

support of such proposals. What was missing, so it was thought, was the testing of assumptions, the questioning of beliefs and doctrines, and rational discussion of what were fundamental concepts such as 'education' and what it meant 'to be educated'. The making of educational aims, for example, required a painstaking process of rational enquiry detached from the imminence of classroom practice. Because this approach placed reason and rational thinking at the heart of enquiry the new philosophy was able to articulate the basis of a liberal education, an idea evolving from ancient Greece and ongoing essentialist discussion about the nature of knowledge and the development of mind.

Two years prior to Plowden, Paul Hirst published what was to be a highly influential paper, 'Liberal Education and the Nature of Knowledge', re-published in *Education and the Development of Reason* (Dearden, Hirst and Peters 1972). Hirst writes: 'Whatever else a liberal education is, it is *not* a vocational education, *not* an exclusively scientific education, or a specialist education in any sense' (Hirst 1972: 391).

In avoiding what liberal education is not, Hirst moves to considering the nature of knowledge and the forms it could take, each practical and theoretical and with its own criteria and set of principles. The argument went that it was this breadth of human understanding that was the entitlement of all children. They were to be inducted into what was intrinsically worthwhile. In this way narrow causes and political expediencies were transcended. Education could be distinguished from training and ensure that all children would be acquainted with what constituted unique and significant ways of understanding human experience. There was much here for arts educators to relate to, for they were learning how to speak of the arts as a distinctive way of knowing, the arts as a form of knowledge, as a realm of meaning and as making an essential contribution to the whole curriculum. In the seminal text *Sound and Silence* (1970) Paynter and Aston set out a manifesto justifying the place of music within a liberal education and to establish its fundamental educative character.

A Liberal Education for Musical Understanding

Paynter and Aston's approach readily embraced the idea of music as being of society and culture: it was about a broadening of the mind and much more than a musical training, and focused on the belief that all children possessed the capacity to be as artists able to respond to the world around them and make art in response.

> Like the other arts, music springs from a profound response to life itself and the artist projects feelings into his materials – paint, wood, stone, words, movement, sound or whatever – until the materials become like the reality of his imagination.
>
> (Paynter and Aston 1970: 3)

John Paynter and Peter Aston having experimented separately in classrooms during the 1960s, Aston with the medium of the voice and Paynter through instrumental means, had produced their invocation to creative music making at the same time as Witkin and Ross were conducting the 'Arts and the Adolescent' project. Like Witkin and Ross they readily embraced the idea of an education through the arts starting with the individual, and for a music education to be centred on the child's perceptions and insights. This would expect children to create music in response to things about which they felt deeply, about matters that engaged their imaginations and connected with their inner worlds. Examples from the other arts served to challenge music's backward-looking stance in the curriculum. In response to the question 'what is creative music?' Paynter and Aston write:

> First of all, it is a way of saying things which are personal and individual. It also implies the freedom to explore chosen materials. As far as possible this work should not be controlled by a teacher. His role is to set off trains of thought and help the pupil develop his own critical powers and perceptions. The process of composition in any art is selection and rejection, evaluating and confirming the material at each stage. It is essentially an experimental situation.
>
> (ibid: 7)

Old concerns about the managing of taste in the name of civility were replaced by the education of discernment and discrimination achieved through a freedom to learn and to know the intelligence of feeling. However, as in Witkin's conception, the intelligence of feeling was by no means simply a reaching inward, an expression and knowing of self. *Sound and Silence* expected there to be an easy relationship between the child's expressions and the expressions of other artists. This was Witkin's engagement with 'realized forms' that music teachers had found so difficult to think of in relationship to children's creative work.

In *Sound and Silence* the work undertaken had its genesis in the practices of composers whose works pupils would come to see as related to their own work. The dead hand of tradition had been removed. However, in its place had come a qualified reference to the past. It was the near past and indeed the present that could be most instructive. It was the notion of the contemporary work of the artist that dominated. Modernism's critical ways of thinking, the work of T.S. Eliot, James Joyce and Samuel Beckett in Literature, and Picasso and Mondrian in art had given impetus to the progressive movement in English and art. Now it could be recognized in the case of music. There was a desire 'to give children and young people a genuine experience of what music is really about; to help them feel the expressive power and enable them to use it to say something' (ibid: 23).

Music teachers were encouraged to experiment and *Sound and Silence* provided support with ways offered through which pupils could find a reason for making music. There was always an expressive problem to be found and solved and this required investigation and experiment building up a repertoire of ideas and musical material with which to work and, through an ongoing process of trial and error, arrive at completed work that might well trigger further expressive problems and so on. Thus, the creative process was carefully structured in which the teacher was an explorer alongside the student. This was a major obligation of the teacher as was first hand knowledge of the techniques worked with, and this implied a lively and inquisitive attitude as artist/composer herself. Only then would the teacher be in a position to help students evaluate their work and engage in 'plenty of adventuresome conversation between teacher and class ...' (ibid: 13). In the same way that Ross and Witkin would be thinking about all this, the teacher would be implicated in her pupil's creative action.

Changing the Social Character of the Music Room

In January 1980, I took up post in a Basingstoke comprehensive school and while I believed that I could inspire classes through a natural dynamism, charisma and enthusiasm for my subject, I was to find unexpected challenges from sullen Year 9 students, many recently uprooted from their London birth place. Soon after joining the staff of the school I attended a day of in-service training at Reading University planned as part of the dissemination of the Secondary Schools Council Music Project. The project's director, John Paynter, led the day. Here, we were told, was a new way of thinking about music education, a new philosophy of music education. The idea of a philosophy of music education was new to me. The idea that it was possible to justify action by questioning assumptions and clarifying thinking had not been part of my education. Previous in-sevice training days had been different to this. 'Understandably, the tendency has always been for us to skip the philosophy and go straight to the "meat"; the "things to do"' (Paynter 1982: 14).

Now many of the arguments set out two years later in *Music in the Secondary School Curriculum* were being rehearsed. This was music for the 'majority' and whereas Bentley had left the field suggesting that music in schools should be compulsory only to age 12, Paynter saw no such bounds or reasons not to engage all pupils for the whole of their schooling. And this was possible by freeing the teacher and pupil from knowledge thought of as tradition and convention. The past, the known and that which had been codified were now resources to be called upon as and when needed. We were exhorted to give up the idea of the music teacher as guardian of the sacred flame of tradition in the form of inert knowledge separated from practical application and as essential to be passed on to each new generation. It was time to give up this particular source of teacher authority and duty. These exhortations challenged and ran deep through the veins of those present and into the heart of beliefs and values and to long-held conceptions of a music education. Not all those present were as receptive as I was. We watched video material of children working independently in small groups and later, now led by Piers Spencer, an innovating music teacher of the 1970s, we saw a whole class working in a jazz style noisily independent of the teacher, only for the teacher to call the class to order with a blast of a whistle. These kinds of images were likely to raise profound questions about authority in the minds of those present. Whose music and whose music education was this?

If the social character was formed through family, schooling and work representing the influence of social and economic structures then the freedom for children 'to be' and to 'be trusted' in the way being proposed provided a challenge. No part of my own education and training had imagined the music classroom to be like this. It seemed that this new philosophy of music education might be calling for giving up the authoritarian component of the personality socially formed. I was ready to do this. However, there was scepticism and defence expressed by some present who were not convinced by Paynter's parallel with Monteverdi's epoch changing declaration of a major shift in practice, a move from *prima* to *secunda prattica*, or his assurance that what was being proposed was not iconoclasm, as he left to travel back to York and to conduct Rossini's 'Stabat Mater'.

Within a few days I too declared my *secunda prattica*. What was most obvious about making the change was the discovery that work with classes could move forward organically, that one idea led to another, that pupils arrived at lessons knowing what they needed to do, that there was no end to the idea of experiment and exploration. This was radically different from the idea of sequences of musical skills taught and progression from simple songs to more complex songs with repertoire running dry before the end of term. The most remarkable component of this epiphany was the discovery that I no longer needed to express overt authority. I could be different. Within a few weeks I was writing to my headteacher wanting to share with him the journey I was taking as I departed from long established practice. I was now conducting my own experiment in education knowing nothing of Sybil Marshall, Robert Witkin or Malcolm Ross.

> My mind was fired and I was restless to seek out this thing called creativity, for it was argued that only by placing children in a situation where they had to select, reject, appraise and make positive decisions about sound that the art of music could be experienced and understood. So, into action, cautiously to begin with and with limited resources. The children reacted like caged animals released. Bit by bit they were tamed by their successes, which in most cases were extremely modest. But it was their music. I had no structure for my experiments and mistakes were gratefully learnt from. Music was now pouring from the children and not into them and I learnt how to accept and value their music. The Great Masters gave a wry grin as they came down from the walls thrilled at the music of these young people. The children were at last sharing in the creative process that had given birth to the music of their fore-bearers. At last the beloved art of the masters might be understood by the children. My greatest job satisfaction came from work with lower forms and examination work took on a dreary face. Every new project undertaken with the children opened new doors and a journey of discovery lay before us. I began to understand the meaning of education. All around me I saw doors being closed to children and method being directed by discipline.
>
> (Finney 1980)

Now I accepted a noisy classroom that was busy with activity and I wanted to know more about all this. The questions 'why', 'what if' and 'how' were now at the front of my mind. The Secondary Schools Council Music Project was making a decisive impact on my practice and the status of music in my school. The lunchtime performance of pupils from the Year 8 'remedial' class presenting their compositions accompanying the reading of Tennyson's 'Charge of the Light Brigade' to a mass audience of other pupils and a few inquisitive staff was one of a number of bold statements to be made. The experiment was bearing fruit.

Sources of Creative Music Making

Paynter had composed music from age ten, read Rousseau's *Émile* at age 17, and composed as a student and a professional before coming to teaching, an opportunity to work out ideas about composition's place within a music education. Paynter's ideas crystallized during the 1960s, first as a teacher-educator at a College of Education in the south of England, and then in the music department of York University. It was here that the department's first professor, Wilfred Mellers, had established a teaching model of simultaneously exploring music practically and academically. Teaching invertible counterpoint could hardly be achieved meaningfully without students playing from Bach's 'Art of Fugue', for example. There were other progressive features to imbibe relating to notions of progression and community. Students were able to select courses irrespective of their year group status, and each year began with a whole department project while assessment rejected the sterile formality of the silent big bang examination.

Collaborating with Peter Aston in *Sound and Silence* of 1970, exemplars from the work of child-centred educators within the other arts are freely invoked as sources of justification. Sybil Marshall is mentioned and Marion Richardson's alternatives to copying and drawing technique in art are cited along with David Holbrook's emancipative approach to children's writing. In particular there was inspiration to be found in the ideas of the art critic and educator Herbert Read. For Herbert Read (1943/1958) an education that emphasized feeling and expression constituted an aesthetic education and this was fundamental to general education in fostering growth of what is individual in each human being. It is through acts of expression that we can see what children are thinking and feeling and whereby we can educate.

Central to Read's thesis was a questioning of the prevalent authoritarian concept of morality and discipline that was so easily observable within education and society producing constraint and conformity negating freedom and the growth of autonomy. Thus attention is paid to the relationship between the pupil and the teacher. In writing about the role of the teacher, Read, pre-echoing Witkin and Ross, noted that disinterested observations of classrooms tell him that the most artistically productive situations are where there is reciprocity between teacher and pupil, the quality of relationship is critical. And here there is a 'conducive atmosphere'.

> The atmosphere is the creation of the teacher, and to create an atmosphere of spontaneity, of happy childish industry, is the main and perhaps the only secret of successful teaching.
>
> (ibid: 295)

While this is not the authoritarian principle at work, Read acknowledges that this places great responsibility on the teacher. Read writes hopefully: 'All educators recognize the necessity of not repressing spontaneity, but they leave the child beating his wings in the void' (ibid: 287). The freedom given to the pupil demands of the teacher both criticism and instruction, albeit subtle. And it is through this gentle yet firm dialogue that aesthetic judgement is educated.

Read maintained that before people could co-operate effectively with other people they must understand themselves. Involvement in the arts, as Paynter and Aston, and Witkin and Ross argued, involved exploration of personal ideas and feelings. However, the most important consideration was not the child, not what was being taught or the teacher but the relationship between teacher and child and what was being learnt.

Read's seminal text, despite its over ambitious assemblage of psychological and social theories, established the idea of an education 'through' and for Read it was 'through art' that an individual and society gained a sense of well-being and democracy flourished. Read viewed this as a process of reforming the social order, of invigorating it in much the way that John Dewey had thought of an active citizenry continually creating new forms of knowledge. What I was seeing before me as a music teacher was that this approach, as well as enabling pupils to understand the way music worked, developed qualities of wider value believed to be valuable in other aspects of their lives. In the politics of my school's curriculum making I could now act with political adroitness. There was something happening 'through music'. In being able to articulate more clearly a purpose it was possible to believe that music and the arts justifiably deserved a central place in the curriculum. Yes, all children should pursue an 'aesthetic' subject beyond age 14 and they should do this because such work was worthwhile and satisfying in itself, an education as self-realization. The personal satisfaction gained from work in the arts overrode the demand for more tangible outcomes. This could become a *cri de coeur*.

Music as a Creative Art

Paynter's chief enemy was music education reduced to a narrow course of musical training where tutored skills and proficiencies dominated to the exclusion of imagination and creativity. This was 'Music for the Minority'. Paynter set about emphasizing music as a central element in a general education and this had the potential immediately to raise the status of music within the secondary school. This brought musical improvisation and composition to the fore as well as the art of interpretation in the performance of music. Why, for example, should these arts depend upon the acquisition of conventional skills in notation reading and writing? Tutored skill in music reading might or might not assist in this. Paynter was proposing dissolving the theoretical-practical divide and the integration of technical and expressive matters.

> Children need the creative stimulus of 'using' the skills they have acquired *as* they acquire them. We must try, therefore, to provide opportunities for interpretive decision making even at the most elementary levels.
>
> (Paynter 1982: 123)

Echoing the thoughts of Herbert Read, emphasis was placed on the development of the child's ability to grow in discernment and capacity to make informed judgements of her own. In particular, giving the learner freedom to make decisions about 'how music should go' in the context of composing music provided the learner with the opportunity to know music from the inside. In this view, releasing creativity and imagination was essential to the notion of being musically educated.

In *Sound and Silence*, Paynter and Aston conclude their introduction with the modest proposal that 'creative experiment is only one small part of music in education: but we believe it is a very important part and one that should not be neglected' (Paynter and Aston 1970: 23). The next decade was to see the creative idea taken up with great vigour through a major Schools Council Project. In *Music in the Secondary School Curriculum* (1982) Paynter drew from his own pre-1970s experiments as well as all that had been learnt through the project, and set out the guiding principles that had evolved through the ten-year conversation with teachers, music advisors and others about the role of music in education. Music is justified because, like the other arts, 'it offers unparalleled opportunities for the development of imagination, sensitivity, inventiveness and delight – essential elements in a balanced curriculum' (ibid: xiii). Without music viewed as a creative art, it loses legitimacy as a curriculum subject and its contribution to the curriculum as a whole. Like Witkin and Ross, Paynter is alert to this need to find a place for music and the arts in school and, whether there is utility to be measured or not, they are a distinctive part of the whole. The teacher has a responsibility to

> ... stimulate imagination; there should be continued exploration and discovery in a variety of musical styles, both old and new ... Musical knowledge (notation, history, etc.) is 'not necessary for everyone'; it should be taught when/where it is appropriate.
>
> (ibid: 229)

This version of a liberal education didn't fit well with Hirst's scheme, for the case of music within what Hirst referred to as the Fine Arts was unwilling to grasp the idea of the arts as creating statements of truth in themselves, and was unable to see that the body was in any way mindful and that music's meaning resided inside the musical act itself. Statements about it were something quite different. As we shall see, establishing just what kind of knowledge and knowing music should subscribe to would be a critical matter of distinction. In Paynter's challenge to the authority of the past, with its power to canonize practices into inert procedures and to make debilitating theory, what it was to know music became significant. So, was this new philosophy of music education in fact philosophically grounded any more than was Plowden or the work of Sybil Marshall, Witkin and Ross? In so far as it gave attention to '*a priori* considerations', a phrase used by Herbert Read in criticizing progressives, the answer is, yes. However, the response of the analytic philosophers was at best reserved and this reservation was Swanwick's starting point in his influential work of 1979.

Moderation

In the foreword to *A Basis for Music Education* (Swanwick 1979), Louis Arnaud Reid takes an analytic stance pointing out the difficulty with, and therefore the dearth of, reasoned justifications in respect to the educational significance of a subject like music.

> So it is little wonder that the voluminous talk and writing about art education has consisted largely of the repetition of high-sounding words and phrases – 'self-expression', 'self-revelation', 'expression of the emotions', 'the education of the whole person', 'education for creativity'… and so on.
>
> (Reid in Foreword to Swanwick 1979: 1)

These words and phrases can quickly 'lack disciplined clarity' and this has adversely affected the teaching of the arts. It is in *A Basis for Music Education*, and perhaps for the first time within the history of music education in England, that such an undertaking is accomplished. Swanwick's fine-grained discussion of 'music and emotion', of music's 'meaningfulness and feelingfulness', leads to the establishment of the parameters of music education. A coherent model for action and for the analysis of action is presented. The power of philosophy in making defensible statements carefully worked out is thus demonstrated. By taking such care Swanwick was able to create the basis for his ongoing theorizing of music education over the next 30 years. Swanwick takes delight in phrases such as 'mapping out', 'conceptual framework' and 'conceptual clarity'. And this requires standing at some distance from the action. The practice of teaching is not to be entangled with aims, assessment with learning, the pupil-teacher relationship with subject matter and so on. Each needs to be carefully delineated. The view was that we need fewer experiments in education that lead to pseudo-philosophy and more thinking about 'how are things the way they are?', 'why?', 'what for?' and 'what do we mean by?' Thus, claims made by progressive educators can be questioned, greater clarity asked for. Paynter's philosophy of music education is likely to fail the analytic philosopher's test. Are too many assumptions made about 'creativity', for example? In fact the whole progressive movement falls as being insufficiently grounded. It was Swanwick's model presented as a catchy mnemonic ClAsP (where C is Composition: formulating a musical idea, making a musical object; l is Literature studies: the literature of and the literature about music; A is Audition: responsive listening … as in an audience; s is Skill acquisition: aural, instrumental, notational; and P is communicating music as a 'presence'), with its upper and lower cases, that provided music teachers with an easily comprehensible scheme, rather than a philosophical argument, and that was to satisfy a much needed basis for the thinking about music in the curriculum.

The gap between Paynter and Swanwick was in one respect enormous, yet in another relatively insignificant. The potential for music to be educative through composing, performing and listening supported by the acquisition of skills and understanding of repertoire could be grasped in common sense terms by teachers as simply teaching music practically and in an integrated and coherent manner. Swanwick had established music education as 'aesthetic education' and this recognized that to think music would require that it be felt at the same time. In Ross's *The Aesthetic Impulse* (1984), thinking and feeling together make for 'sensibility' and the 'intelligence of feeling'. If school was to be concerned with knowledge then music and the arts had a distinctive way of knowing. But this didn't answer the question as to whose music was worth knowing or address power relationships, cultural hierarchies and lurking ideologies. Thus, the second criticism levelled at Plowden's door coming from the sociology of education presents itself.

The Anonymous Authority of Creative Music Making

Bernstein and Davies (1969) point out that too little consideration is given to the ways in which children come to school socially and culturally differentiated. Differences in class background, the patterns of family life, for example, are not taken sufficiently into account. The kinds of formalities and informalities met with in the school present barriers to engagement and comprehension for many children. The sociology of education took this kind of argument further in what was described as 'the new sociology of education' and as presented in *Knowledge and Control* (Young 1971). Knowledge was socially constructed, relative and not pre-ordained, and this gave encouragement to the growth of interest in the sociology of music education. The argument went something like this. Schools and school music promote high status knowledge and this comes most obviously through an adherence to a notated tradition, a canon of works and a set of associated performance practices. As such it is unable to value diverse musical traditions, and in particular the practices of popular musicians, and this leads to a culture clash with the pupils' way of perceiving music and valuing musical experience (Vulliamy 1975, 1977, 1978).

The ways in which prevailing ideologies were able to legitimize some music and not others had been exposed. This was not a call for a liberal education but rather a critique of its impotence in the face of social forces and the stratification of society. Thus it was maintained that 'creative music making', along with other child-centred approaches, served merely:

> ... to disguise power relations and social control through new forms of almost invisible coercion ... a deliberate move away from explicit disciplinary practices which could be understood and eventually resisted by working-class children – such as shouting, beating, grading and examining – to implicit, difficult to grasp, covert forms of surveillance and direction – a sort of 'soft control' that continues to promote the class interests of the middle and upper classes within the very process of classroom discipline.
>
> (Doddington and Hilton 2007: 45)

In other words, some children grasped the rules of the game better than others and it was working-class children who were least equipped to succeed.

Certainly, I noted the appalling failure of pupils across the curriculum. These were almost all boys, in the bottom streams, unable to make sense of what the curriculum offered. In Bernstein's terms there was an abundance of 'privileging practices' to uncover (Bernstein 1971). However, in the lower years the creative music making and freedom given to find meaning was working well. Numbers wanting to continue with music as a curriculum subject beyond the age of 14 vastly increased as a result of creating a music department that was open and more amenable to pupils' interests. Nevertheless, there was a salutary lesson to learn about perceptions of older pupils and my own limitations as a music teacher and to acknowledge that Willis and Vulliamy had a point.

'School Music Style, Sir'

On a bright winter's morning in 1984 I started vamping on the weather-worn grand piano in the music room. The music room was in Bolton Block, a mostly single storey building of the 1970s, one of a number of additions to the school's main building needed as the school had grown from its foundation in the 1960s in tandem with the town's growth as an overspill from London. The rooms of Bolton Block had been made for practical activity and for the raising of the school leaving age to 16 in 1972. The hammering of metal, the bubbling of expression and cries of aguish in drama classes, instrumental teaching lessons, the silent movement of girls on domestic tasks and the stillness and contemplation of the drawing class characterized the inner realms of the building feeding a corridor that was noisy and rarely without incident. In Bolton Block the doors, it seemed, could never be closed quietly.

The small group of Year 9 students before me were regarded as needing to spend much of their week with just one teacher who would be helping them to gain functional skills in English and mathematics, and there would be a smattering of humanities to go with it. This special teacher viewed these students as his own, his kingdom of likeable rogues and *maladroits* who would be released for some of the week to the periphery of the curriculum. Music was one such subject. These pupils seemed to enjoy coming to music lessons. It was thought better to receive these classes at the beginning of the day and before relationships within the class had broken down. They arrived with cheery faces, open-hearted gestures of recognition, kleptomaniac tendencies and expecting these lessons to be different.

Knowing the routine well the students joined me in creating music through their playing of xylophones and assorted percussion. I recall feeling good that they were playing the music, that they were having a musical voice as we say now, that they were making the music, that they were being creative, as we said then and as my convictions of the time dictated. As I infected the music with a little syncopation and what I believed to be a Bluesy character, I felt confident that together we were making something worthwhile and stylistically significant. At the end of what became an extended improvisation I asked Martin, a quiet boy, what style he thought our music to be. The reply was short, polite and not without deference, 'school music style, sir'. Martin had exposed the alarming gap between his perception of musical meaning and mine. This was 'alienation'. Martin, along with other members of his class, in due course chose to do music as part of his final two years of compulsory schooling. He achieved a low GCSE grade in music, the only tangible reward for his 11 years of compulsory education. Martin took up employment as a Basingstoke roofer. I am left to wonder what part music now plays in his life and what significance 'school music' holds for him. What the sociological question had raised was a matter of ideology and this penetrated and disturbed the claims of the progressive child-centred educator.

The Problem of Knowledge

Witkin's theory of self-reflexivity had focused fully on the knower and the process of knowing. Ross too was interested in the act of knowing and Paynter in knowing and 'coming to know'. In these cases knowing and knowledge were something to be made in and through action. Knowledge was a process. Knowledge, knowing and the knower, were now a focus for clarification of purpose and another perspective through which to view what was to be taught and the place of the child in this. Those on the side of the child might speak of knowing, those on the side of the subject might speak of knowledge. Knowledge, skills and understanding were taking central place in the onward movement towards a National Curriculum. These were to become foundational concepts within discussion of curriculum structure and goals.

In the wake of James Callaghan's Ruskin College speech had come a Framework for the School Curriculum (DES 1980) in which the aims of school education were set out alongside the structure of the curriculum. There is the identification of the need for a core to the curriculum which all pupils should be entitled to and which would ensure 'sufficient grounding in the knowledge and skills which by common consent should form part of the equipment of the educated adult' (ibid: 5). Thus the start of a debate about the curriculum was signalled and which was to culminate in the making of a National Curriculum. There followed intensive activity by Local Authorities and schools. The six stated aims were generous in their scope. But into the discourse now had come what was to become a foundational pillar in all that ensued: the acquisition of knowledge, skills and understanding.

In response to the Framework, Ross saw the place of the arts in the curriculum marginalized, and proposed five fields of knowledge as a way of integrating subjects: language; maths and science; creative arts; humanities and religion, and technology. In Ross's view together these formed the core and provided a holistic view of human experience. To privilege any was educationally and epistemologically irresponsible. Ross was fearful of the rise of instrumental thinking, thinking without feeling, without sensibility; thinking led by economic ambition, thinking for profit and by 'the apparent drift towards materialistic self-interest' (Ross 1981: 6). It is the arts that can provide an aesthetic dimension to lives, and this is concerned with quality not utility. Why would this dimension of human existence not be 'core'? A liberal education would expect no less.

Ross was chiming to some extent with Her Majesty's Inspectorate who were encouraging an approach to curriculum planning that recognized a number of essential areas of learning and experience as a way of bringing coherence to the curriculum. The debate became relevant to my own work as my school's curriculum committee set about reviewing the school's curriculum and working broadly within the areas of learning and experience as set out in the document *Curriculum Matters 2* (DES 1985a).

These areas were designated as aesthetic and creative; human and social; linguistic and literary; mathematical; moral; physical; scientific; spiritual and technological. However, the committee decided on some amalgamation and conflation of areas, and the spiritual was omitted altogether. Those of us teaching the arts were seen as spearheading thinking about the aesthetic and creative area. The teachers of music, drama, art, film, physical education and English were called upon to work out the distinctive contribution of the aesthetic dimension within the curriculum. We were to set about defining the nature of aesthetic knowledge and understanding, the kind of progression this would call forth and the kind of objectives desirable in our subjects as pupils progressed through the school. While other groups found it agreeable to work with the general curriculum model being developed, where behavioural objectives, linear progression and the accumulation of easily assessable knowledge was the way, we were playing a different music. We had discovered the value of 'expressive objectives' as proposed by Eisner (1979), working on the basis that the outcomes of aesthetic engagement could not be easily prescribed and in the belief that assessment through appraisal involving the pupil would be the preferred way.

Some subjects found themselves in more than one group. English teachers, for example, were split between the aesthetic-creative group and the linguistic group. The aspiration that each area of experience would reach across all subjects only partially succeeded as the need to create a school timetable and secure staffing limited any serious or sustained philosophical inquiry. The final report from the school's curriculum committee revealed the victory of instrumental rationality as it used the economic well-being of pupils and society as the central rationale in making a curriculum. There was to be a particular emphasis on science. In this view the arts were to serve as recreation, leisure, pleasure and entertainment. The arts and sciences as cultures apart had been reinforced. The possibility that music and the other arts be viewed as key contributors to aesthetic education, with a particular way of seeing reality and able to support and assist in the prospering of all other ways, had not been grasped.

What Kind of Knowledge Do We Want in Music?

The voices of science and technology had been loud in the process of curriculum development in this Basingstoke school. The dissemination of value free knowledge to its pupils was thought to be crucial. Education here was to be functional and instrumental. There were credentials to bank. Colleagues sometimes spoke to me of 'value judgements' in pejorative tones and I wondered what other kinds of judgement there were. The idea of teaching children to make value judgements and how to interpret the world appeared to be viewed with suspicion and thought to be inferior to the acquisition of value-free knowledge as objective, firm, hard and of the real world. The idea of the 'real world' was often cited in discussion with the implication that the arts were of another world. And the headteacher spoke of our need to keep our feet on the ground.

Music, as with all subjects making a claim for a place in the school curriculum, had validity to the extent that it was able to establish objectives that would be amenable to 'objective' assessment. Thus, at examination level a certain kind of knowledge qualified as being assessable. Well codified harmonic progressions and melodic patternings, musical historical truths and established interpretations of music fitted well. This kind of musical knowledge had been socially constructed and rested upon a canon of works and procedures that endorsed high status knowledge long codified, reduced and abstracted from musical experiences and from personal and social meanings. The objective model that could reliably measure held strong sway. The polarization of subjective and objective reality was firmly in place. The Certificate of Secondary Education (CSE) examination in music introduced in 1965 and designed for the average and below average secondary school pupil breathed its final notes in 1985, asking of its candidates: 'For what activity was Cavallie-Coll renowned?' The divorce of fact and feeling was ready for a reconciliation. School music and its assessment as loss of happiness, as Ross put it, had a case.

The publication *Assessment and Progression in Music Education* (Preston 1986) marked a sea change in approaches to music in the school curriculum. Recognizing music as an aesthetic discipline, the report pointed out that aesthetic judgements are personal and that precise criteria for making these can not be laid down in advance of a musical encounter. To attempt to do so would be to deny the personal nature of the individual's judgement. However, this was not to suggest that judgements in music were simply subjective, a matter of personal taste and preference. Aesthetic judgements were 'in one sense personal but in another, communicable, open to inspection and capable of negotiation' (ibid: 10). Inter-subjectivity could lead to meaningful disagreement and consensus. The issue was whether reasonable grounds could be found to support judgements. The process of negotiating value created its own kind of truth and objectivity.

> It is not possible, in the arts, to make *right* or *wrong* judgements; the only thing that is possible is to be prepared to 'take one's coat off', so to speak, and get down to an argument.
>
> (Aspin 1982: 48)

The choice, it was thought, was not between relativism, where there was no basis for determining value, and absolute truth, where given truths waited to be applied. In a subject where it was crucial for pupils to learn how to make judgements, to become discriminating and to decide for themselves what felt right, the knower was at least as important as the known. Musical appraisal, musical criticism and the discourse of music were at the heart of assessment, and the pupils themselves needed to be inducted into making decisions about the value of their work and the work of others. Assessment was therefore about teaching self-assessment and self-assessment was learning. The report noted too, and chiming with earlier public statements, that music was more rewarding for both teachers and pupils in those areas of the curriculum not formally assessed and that the problem lay not with assessment as such but with the ways in which it was frequently conceived of and carried out.

The report coincided with government moves to revise approaches to assessment. The limitations of norm-referencing were recognized by the Minister of State Sir Keith Joseph. Criterion-referencing was to be adopted in an attempt to broaden access and to allow all children to show what it was they knew, understood and could do. This was a key feature of the General Certificate of Secondary Education (GCSE) examination instituted in 1986 and deliberately setting out to be more inclusive than previous examinations and to function both formatively and summatively. The argument for fresh approaches to assessment in music rested upon music as a key element within the aesthetic realm, as a bearer of aesthetic knowledge or aesthetic knowing as it now became more frequently referred to. The shift from 'knowledge' to 'knowing' was significant and one that Dewey had recommended earlier in the century. Use of the word 'knowing' was a means of giving status to awareness and perception and the recognition of the involvement of states of mind, all in contrast to another kind of knowledge, where description, words, statements and propositions held status.

Along with the other arts, music was able to establish an identity where the hard dualisms of fact and feeling, cognition and affect, objectivity and subjectivity were, if not completely lost, at least suspended. At the heart of aesthetic knowing was feeling, and feeling was knowable. Reid (1980) pointed out that feeling, thought of as immediate experience, is present throughout our waking consciousness and is engaged with more or less depending on our concerns and dispositions. Feeling bears most significantly on our knowing when we are orientated towards beliefs and values, when we care about what we are doing. Feeling, unlike emotion, was therefore an aspect of cognition and Reid (1983) proposed the term 'cognitive-feeling' to help in this way of thinking. This was in contrast to the approach where music is linked to emotion. In this view, and still the most common within the cognitive psychology of music, there was an assumption that the subject listened to music with a contingent emotional response, a stirring up, a reaction of some kind. Perception is arrested by the musical stimulus. This discounted the possibility of the subject both moving the music and being moved by it, of investing feeling and meaning in it, of being in a dialogue with it (Witkin 1974). It posited a view of the human subject as passive and without agency. Yet we know musical perception to be active, interpretive and knowing, and while the seat of feeling is unknowable and not 'intelligent', non-cognitive in fact, it is through the processes of aesthetic experience that unknowable responses become knowable and intelligent. It is this that distinguishes the aesthetic curriculum. The term cognitive-feeling was helpful.

Fact and Feeling

The CSE examination asking for knowledge about the French organ builder Cavallie-Coll was symptomatic of the hegemony of privileging knowledge. This was knowledge that was thought to approximate to fact.

> Cavallie-Coll, Astride (b Montpellier, 4 Feb 1811; d Paris, 13 Oct 1899). French organ builder. Of an established family of organ builders, he studied in Paris ...'
>
> (Sadie (ed.) 1994: 148)

Reid argued for the inadequacy of thinking of music and the arts as statements of truth, as subjects with a knowledge structure existing independent of the knower, waiting to be unwrapped and for each new generation to be inducted into. This was the rationalist view of knowledge where knowledge transcended human experience and sense perception, and consisted of frameworks of concepts, procedures and rules. Music and the arts could be considered in this way. But for Reid, to engage with the arts at once dealt with a different kind of knowledge. This he referred to as direct knowledge through acquaintance and experience. 'All propositional knowledge of music is empty if not based on direct, intuitive, first hand cognitive experience. Experiential intuition is essential' (Reid 1986: 14). For Reid the musician engaged in her art is 'coming to know', for in the creative act, whether as a performer, composer or respondent, the knowledge which is discovered is not fully known until the making has been completed. The artist is working in dialogue with his medium and the meaning is in the making. In this way experience-knowledge becomes the *raison d'être* of the arts and is concerned with a form of knowledge that stresses that which is tacit, personal, revelatory and insightful.

As Reid implied, this is not to say that 'knowing that something is the case' in music is not without value. To know 'that Cavallie-Coll ...' is valuable knowledge providing we have listened to organs and organ music or even played them. Indeed, we find learners searching after this kind of knowledge once they have gained and valued experience-knowledge. Ah, I hear a Cavallie-Coll organ, like meeting an old friend, an irreducible experience, an event with meaning and realization (see Dewey 1925/1958: 330). The musician feeling and shaping a phrase in performance or a listener experiencing this are in a state of coming to know and revealing musical understanding of a unique kind. Reid cites Yehudi Menuhin as he talks to a pupil in a masterclass.

> Until the current flows from the toes to the fingers ... and you feel the weight and movement of the body ... you won't quite 'get' the music.
>
> (Reid 1986: 42)

Paynter began his ground-breaking report of the Schools Council Secondary Curriculum Music Project (1973–82) with a historical overview and this showed how, since the institution of music education in England in the nineteenth century, the intuitive had been continually threatened by the formal, the practical by the theoretical. The learner's search for personal meaning and relevance had been overhauled by the external world of non-negotiable concepts, structures and formalities, by the inertia of fact and theory. Significantly, the GCSE examination introduced in 1986 declared a concern 'to encourage imaginative teaching in schools and foster a greater understanding of music through more *direct experiences* of the creative processes involved' (DES 1985b: 1 (my italics)). On the most common sense and practical level aesthetic experience was equated with the direct experience of music.

The Proof of the Pudding

Stuart opted as one of the first to be prepared for the new GCSE examination in music. The Department of Education and Science produced National Criteria for each subject and in the case of music these were 'intended to encourage imaginative teaching in schools and foster a greater understanding of music through more direct experience of the creative processes involved' (DES 1985c). The guidance recognized the need to build from existing experiences in school and to acknowledge areas that pupils are most interested in. The idea of criteria referencing was clearly exemplified. Music teachers were left with great freedom about planning the two-year course of study. The range of music produced by pupils was potentially vast and the teacher would be hard pressed if large numbers were in the class to manage individual approaches to composing and performing, affording different levels of freedom and varying degrees of constraint.

Stuart had learnt the piano at an earlier stage, given up formal lessons and had become more recently committed to working with his Korg synthesizer. Stuart was not short of inspiration and in the three compositions submitted for examination he demonstrated the capacity to synthesize his life's musical experience and at the same time his wider life of felt experience. The balance between his formal and informal knowledge including his life of feeling enabled him to work intuitively, with aesthetic sensitivity and with what appeared to be a dream-like understanding. His most striking composition had the title 'Forty Years of Peace'. Just how much did he know about the music he had created? Was he aware that he had worked within an arch-like structure, that he had used a *passacaglia*, and that the octave piping effect featuring in his introduction and coda was a telling symbol of the awesome dread of war that he clearly wanted to express? There seemed to be a great deal of implicit knowledge here that was in need of valuing and that might or might not need exploring further. Stuart had exercised imagination to the full.

Such work was possible for Stuart through the development of that particular form of knowing and understanding that Reid had set out. This was the embodiment of knowledge, skills and understanding. I had not taught Stuart *passacaglia*; I had not taught him how to manipulate the soundscape of his synthesizer. I had not provided him with exploratory tasks that would build up a vocabulary of musical gestures, ideas and feelings that would lead to the identification of a sensate problem and enable the making of a holding form from which he would move to completion. Stuart had found his own sensate problem and evolved a creative process of his own that approximated to Witkin's and now, in Paynter's fashion, I could put Stuart in touch with further realized forms that might help him make sense of his 'coming to know' and feed his ongoing work as an artist. Stuart represented the triumph of the child as artist, and now publicly endorsed. The work produced by the class I believed to have an imaginative sparkle. Each student's work was distinctive. There was Claire's short two part xylophone dialogue, with every phrase carefully shaped and duly silenced in expectation of the next, Danny's jangling rock guitar pieces and Lisa's suite for oboe not without an idiosyncratic turn of phrase. Together the work of the class was a vindication of the creative imperative. I believed that what the class had experienced was not so much useful but memorable, personally significant and a contribution to their on-going process of self-realization. In the case of Stuart and many others in the class an education in and through the arts appeared to have established some level of critical awareness. They had been given space to be, to think and feel together, to ask questions of each other, their teacher and themselves and this was quite unlike much of their school experience. Martin, so insightful about school music in Year 9, was happy to continue with school music and be a part of the GCSE class, for this was one of the few places in his school where some personal meaning might be found.

All in the Garden is not Roses

In embarking on the 'Arts and the Adolescent' project, Witkin and Ross had believed that teachers would benefit from developing theory-informed practice. The theory that was created grew out of sustained and wide-ranging discussion with teachers. Where classrooms were most productive, arts teachers were speaking of the need to find creative stimulus, a need to learn to control the medium of expression, where there could be a profitable connection made with realized forms and where personal meaning and personal development were in evidence. From here a theory was created and this in turn would enable teachers to reflect further on practice, refine theory and practice and so on. However, as Ross writing in 1989 ruefully reflected in his overview of the last 25 years in arts education, the theory had at best been partially grasped and in such a way that practice was rarely informed by it (Ross 1989). And in the same volume Witkin reflects on 'the implications of teaching of a rigorous expressivism'. Five points are made. Teachers must be able to elicit knowledge from the felt life of their pupils and this requires the removal of the divide between school and non-school. They need too to seriously attend to the acquisition of skill, control of the medium, for without this self-expression is badly served. And realized forms are critical both in engaging children with heritage and with the contemporary imagery with which they daily surround themselves. Finally the matter of evaluation is addressed and here teachers are exhorted to avoid succumbing to typical academic models that the school readily provides. Instead the process of evaluation should be no different to the process of the evaluation of art in general (Ross 1989: 34–6).

By now Witkin and Ross are writing in the shadow of the 1988 Education Reform Act (DES 1988) and finding themselves swimming against the tide. The idea of the arts working together rested on the questionable assumption that arts teachers would want to work as a community and put aside narrower interests. While music teachers were no more or less inclined than teachers of the other arts to find common purpose as an arts community, music had been transformed by a model provided by the GCSE examination in which the status of propositional knowledge had been severely downgraded. There was a strong sense in which music was being thought of as an arts subject and providing for a creative-aesthetic education. The fruits of progressive thinking within music education of the 1970s and 1980s were most clearly seen in the flowering of pupils' imaginative compositions submitted for examination at age 16. The country's music advisors, still of considerable influence within their counties, had for the most part willingly moved towards the idea of music as a creative-aesthetic subject. The Schools Council Secondary School Music Project had encouraged music teachers to experiment. It had provided an open invitation to meet with the interests of their pupils chiefly by offering space in which to work with their own ideas and feelings. However, Paynter's model of the music teacher as co-composer, co-adventurer, able to create workshop-like, open-ended, conversational environments of mutual respect was by no means common, remaining something of an ideal requiring a range of skills that few teachers possessed or were motivated to acquire. For example, there was an expectation that pupils would develop the role of critic amongst their fellow creative artists. And we recall the observation made by Rainbow (1989) in his disdainful review of experimental music in schools gathering strength in the 1960s and 1970s.

> The new technique, so adventurous in concept compared with traditional methods, attracted many young teachers who started creative work with their classes. But an element essential to success in this activity was an ability on the teacher's part to guide and sustain positive criticism of children's efforts in performance.
>
> (Rainbow 1989: 351)

Rainbow's point penetrates. And Read had warned about the dangers of leaving the pupil to 'flap like a butterfly' just at the point where teacher support and intervention was crucial. In other words, the knowledge and imaginative insights, the well practiced personal pedagogies and clarity of purpose of progressive music educators who themselves were able to work in highly sophisticated ways, could not be easily translated into a pedagogy for others of reliably satisfying progressive principles. Great subtleties of relationships required by the teacher which rested on a certain kind of commitment to the nature of music as a creative art and above all a commitment to developing an identity as teacher-composer, were needed. Quite unlike the culture of Visual Arts education where a common appreciation of the centrality of the making process unencumbered by performance traditions, and with a mildly anarchic persona in the school, was well established, music maintained an ambivalence towards the pre-eminence of a making curriculum centred on composing. For music teachers working within benignly authoritarian institutions increasingly expected to serve instrumental ends and whose identity remained within the environment of performer-analyst, a 'fear of freedom' was to be expected. Schooling remained a fundamental pillar of social character formation for a society that required economic dividends from its investment in education.

Within the child-centred progressive arts movement there was an assumption at work and set out in David Holbrook's reflections on the development of a creative approach to English teaching in the 1960s. The child had an inner life and this was a precious and vital part of the whole child. This inner life implied an unconscious self which it was thought played a part in the process of coming to know and understand. Of course, not all teachers were disposed to recognizing this and even if it were acknowledged, there would be a question raised. Wasn't this a private matter for the child and one not to be impinged upon? And here the problem moves back to Herbert Read. It was Read, in the thrall of the claims of both Freud and Jung, and Jung in particular, who developed the idea of psychic integration through the arts, an unconscious process that needs to be recognized, quietly and knowingly understood by the teacher. This interest in the artistic personality placed the existential first or at least in co-existence with the more rational. Personal individuation is not left to chance and is as significant as received knowledge and culture. Artistic endeavour, the process of making, was an act of integration. Paynter (1982) in addressing the question 'Why teach music in school anyway?' concludes by arguing that music's ultimate educative value lies in processes that allow for 'a symbolic seeking after order and integration' (Paynter 1982: 92).

> ... the process of inward symbolization is educative in a special way; whoever strives for the 'wholeness' of coherent expression in sounds, words, paint or clay or bodily movement, seeks to 'make sense' not only of materials but also his own experience. From this point of view, the arts occupy a unique position in the school curriculum, and we certainly should take them much more seriously than we do.
>
> (ibid: 134)

The making process, coming to know and understand music in this view is deeply humanizing. In Paynter's (1995) tribute to the work of David Holbrook, a chapter titled 'Working on One's Inner World', there comes a moving description of a creative process involving the work of a class of primary school children in the Yorkshire Dales in the 1960s. There is some resemblance to the bright summer's day when Jill and her class had been taken into the Cambridgeshire countryside by Sybil Marshall as they began their experience of coming to know Beethoven's Pastoral Symphony. In this case it is the character of the flying birds observed that leads the class into their creative writing.

> We talked about making some music. Someone suggested that we would have tambourines to be the beating of the rook's wings. We agreed. We thought what we would have for gliding. Someone tried top C and G (on recorders). It goes C then the tambourines, then G and so on. The leaves were falling all the time.
>
> (Paynter 1995: 130–31)

Paynter proceeds to describe the process of making in which the children's ideas are continually evaluated in practice, empirically tested, and in which artistically intuitive judgements work towards what is felt and known to be right. In this case a piece in ternary form had been created and like Stuart's GCSE composition contained far more than could be known by the makers in the process of making. Skills and techniques had been mastered and musical conventions revealed. The model of learning was inductive and in this way there could be a coming to know and understand, a process of making and revealing. There was something akin to Reid's engagement of cognitive-feeling and for Paynter a 'working on one's inner world' towards cultural expression, and meeting with what until now has been unknown. The teacher was now to help pupils speak their minds, to move towards a different kind of knowledge, a knowing that this is ternary form.

Ross (1978) had been greatly impressed by the significance placed by Winnicott on the taken for granted processes that bring about psychic integration as a part of the 'maturational process'. For the creative process to be life enhancing, authentic, culturally productive and at the same time self-realizing, the inner world would need to be included and it was play that formed the bridge from unconscious phantasy to reality. In this way the conflicts and contradictions of life find a place in artistic form. This making sense is the making of meaning.

In this process Holbrook is clear about the kind of teacher needed.

> The least piece of writing, if the teacher has established the context for proper 'giving', will be a meant gift. Of course, it depends on what the teacher's attitude is to human beings. If he can not believe that every human being has an inward need to find himself, in a struggle with love and hate, and between the subjective and objective worlds, then he probably won't get given poetry.
>
> (Paynter 1995)

Here we return to the reflexivity of the teacher-pupil relationship. Was it an unreasonable demand for such relationships to be forged in the classrooms of the 1980s, for the music teacher to find a playful disposition of generosity, yielding to the ideas of young people that allowed for the teaching of music to resemble a co-exploration? For the child-centred progressive educator the demand was no less than an ethical one.

Conclusion

The 'Arts and the Adolescent' project had exposed the moribund antiquity of music in the secondary school at a time when teachers in the other arts were receptive to and modelled the idea that central to an education in and through the arts was personal development, self-realization: self-expression could be harnessed in the name of cultural growth and knowledge of realized forms. Key here was acknowledgement of a creative process to be entered into, a bold collusion between teacher and pupil, pupil and pupil. While a range of experiments in music education characterize resistances to the *status quo* during the 1960s and 1970s, it was the work of teacher-composer John Paynter who, through working in classrooms and studios with children, their teachers, with those learning to be teachers, those studying music in the university as well as those wanting to make music in the community, forged a way of working that drew from learners imaginative and creative responses. There was something of Sybil Marshall's working from felt experience, from personal insights unselfconsciously stirred into a process of making involving the exploration of musical techniques waiting to be placed in the context of personal imagery and motive. It was the mind of the composer-teacher that observed closely the unfolding process of thinking and making and it was this that became the secret garden of music education reform that no amount of sharing, discussion and collaboration between teachers could adequately shape into a commonly grasped pedagogy. The subtlety of the knowing-not-knowing teacher who would need to intervene sometimes boldly, sometimes imperceptively in the creative process proved a challenge. Nevertheless, as evidenced in the GCSE examination the music educational map had been re-written. By maintaining that reform starts in the classroom rather than the academy, Paynter had disregarded the 'new philosophy of education' concerned to define aims as a necessary academic precursor to action, and by advocating 'all kinds of music' as the entitlement of all children had disregarded the 'new sociology of education'.

A guiding principle of the Schools Council Music Project reads:

> MUSIC MAKING is more important than musical information – which is only a support for music activity. 'Theory' cannot by itself, lead to musical understanding; it exists principally to explain what has already been experienced. Our first task is to involve young people with music itself. 'Knowing about music' can never be a satisfactory substitute for the living reality of musical experience.
>
> (Paynter 1982: viii)

Knowing about music, knowledge of a subject, delineable into a framework of concepts was in the minds of the rational philosophy of Hirst and Peters, was some distance from Louis Arnaud Reid's clarification of aesthetic knowing and its potential to be of 'personal significance' and intimately related to a concern for existence here and now, with relationships and the making of meaning. While this distinctive way of knowing was assumed to be common to all cultural manifestations of music making, the adolescent was quick to observe cultural deficits in the practice of teachers unable to broaden the cultural base through which knowing like this could be accessed. There were those who saw pop, rock and ethnic music well placed to challenge the hegemony of what was ordered by a dominant ideology. Developments within the sociology of knowledge had fuelled the belief that young people's alienation from schooling could be related to the de-legitimation of the knowledge that they came to school with. This was a matter of class and power relationships and in this view much more than Witkin and Ross's 'finding of the space in-between' or Paynter's 'working on the inner world'. In fact the liberal progressive educators in this view under-estimated the way societal structures and social class impacted on achievement and the relative success of music education. The culture debate was being sustained.

Paynter, for his part, made clear the significance of popular musical idioms and acknowledged the role of imitation 'as a point from which creative ideas can flow' (Paynter 1982: 117). And his sponsorship of a remarkably eclectic *Resources of Music* series, books for the classroom and books for teachers, revealed a generous acknowledgement of music as having great social significance. Although I saw no priority in giving Martin access to his vernacular through school guitar or drum lessons underlining my ideological positioning as a music teacher, I was able to encourage and celebrate the pop and rock musicians, all boys, in their GCSE submissions who had developed in school, out of school musicianship, alone and in community. And these boys were awarded grade A's for their work alongside those who had been nurtured through school and private individual instrumental lessons over a sustained period. However, this world of the 'other' was in need of understanding. Had the aesthetic, the creative, the existential come to be privileged over the cultural and social? How would this be if reversed? I would need to venture into a de-schooled environment to find out.

Chapter 5
Music Embodied, Music Regulated

From within the child-centred progressive perspective espousing the goals of freedom, self-expression and self-realization, particular kinds of relationships between teacher and pupil and between pupil and pupil were strongly implicated. The pupil's nascent insights, ideas, feelings and working hypotheses expressive of their personhood were to be looked for and cherished. While the discourse created recognized the school as a regulatory force and an agent of state authority, it also saw in the school the place of possible deregulation where life could be lived in its fullness and where particular requirements of the social order would be unself-consciously accommodated, disregarded or explicitly rejected.

Child-centred progressive educators frequently had drawn from the idea of the natural playfulness of children, of their inquisitiveness and desire to make sense, to discover and create. In the arts the progressive tendency translated this belief into making the school a place where, as Herbert Read put it, there would be 'a conducive atmosphere for expression' (Read 1958: 295), where teachers would listen to and support the ideas of their pupils and nurture their artistic minds, where in Paynter's terms there would be lively conversations between the child as composer and teacher as composer and where in Sybil Marhall's terms a great deal of cultural heritage would be shared. There would be no anonymous authority and the teacher would work without deception. Sybil Marshall, Malcolm Ross and John Paynter were three such gifted teachers.

But what if we were to take a step beyond the school to a self-made informal learning situation where young people of their own volition were learning how to be and become musical? Would not this inform the debate and at the same time evaluate and perhaps make legitimate the claims of child-centred education? What could be more child-centred than children at play regulating their learning for themselves? In 1987 an opportunity to explore this idea arose through the study of a group of four 15-year-old boys becoming rock musicians. This was also the moment when a National Curriculum was being schemed. An official curriculum was in formation and to be implemented for the benefit for all children and young people in all state supported schools. This chapter is thus able to juxtapose the informal with the formal, four boys' search for musical meaning and a self education alongside a curriculum prescribed to ensure the sustaining and making of a particular social order.

In personal terms I had developed a commitment to a music education that sought self-realization through music working in tandem with what I believed was worthy to place before my classes. This was conducted within the institutional framework of an urban comprehensive school. Moving beyond the constraints of the school and my own ideological position I would have much to learn from examining an informal learning environment. In attempting to understand what it meant to learn for these boys, I had in mind a view of culture as 'lived experience', this being a form of making new by listening to culture and appropriating it to current needs and future aspirations. Culture would be ordinary.

I saw the work of Jon, Chris, Neil and John as strongly countering my work in the classroom, as taking a form that my work could never take and a form that could never be replicated within the institutional framework of the school. Music in school, even in its most progressive form, was regulated. I was pleased that my students offered individual rock compositions for the new GCSE examination and awarded high grades. I was happy to loan equipment to burgeoning rock musicians and for them to rehearse in the school's music room. But there was no place in my imagination for how the practices of a non-school rock band might be part of the school curriculum. These ways of working were private and with all the characteristics of informality. These young people would be involved in their own process of socialization and free to create a value system of their own.

There was no shortage of literature telling about spontaneous music learning in many different cultures and about the looking, listening and copying that formed the stock in trade for these ways of learning. Music learning in traditional societies (Cooke 1978), the learning of music without a teacher (Rice 1985) and other sources within the anthropological and ethnomusicological literature provided models very different from music learning in the school. But perhaps most arresting was the vivid account of 'profane culture' told by Willis (1978). The book's sleeve note reads: 'The sheer surprise of a living culture is a slap to reverie. Real, bustling, startling cultures move. They exist.' And Willis goes on to tell of two sub-cultural groups, bikers and hippies, and the dynamics of their constructed cultures. All this offered ways of learning and making culture beyond the bounds of the hyper-institution, typically the school (see Willis 1990).

I was interested in the values inherent in these ways of being musical and becoming more in human terms. In these cases the well-being of both the individual and the collective was what music was for. Music education in these places had a humanistic goal. In the case of Willis this was oppositional to the social order. This humanistic way of seeing a music education was very different to the way it was viewed as functioning in the school, for although there was concern for students' personal well-being and social development, there remained in place music thought of as an object, a form of knowledge with a conceptual framework determining and legitimizing its existence. It wasn't what people did to make sense of their lives amongst others doing the same. I was embarking on a profound learning experience. My learning was likely to be slow and enduring.

The Researcher and the Researched

The group of four boys, *Cell 1* by name, began rehearsing under my roof, my teaching room, and thereby established a dependence on me. My role at this stage was 'caretaker', the person who showed a little interest in them, the person who loaned equipment and locked up after their meeting. However, within weeks of taking on this role, another group that I had started to study collapsed, necessitating the development of a new kind of relationship with *Cell 1*, now rehearsing in the school's drama studio. It was from this point that the investigation proceeded to cover a period of six months. My role changed little by little from outsider to outsider-insider as trust was built. At times, my 'realness' was challenged and found wanting. Why did I leave the Caribbean Club early after their gig? What were my deeper motivations for carrying out my investigation? Was the group being taken seriously? Were they to be wrongly classified by an 'ignorant outsider'? The teacher was performing a role they had not commonly encountered and certainly one that wasn't expected of the music teacher. As an ethnographer I was learning by 'hanging around' as both participant and non-participant observer and, albeit slowly, finding patterns to the culture as it became less hot and more comprehensible.

The relationship was able to grow as I took on the role of recording engineer. I became an appendage to the group and this helped to work through any kind of judgemental role in what transpired. After a period of two months, a verbal contract was negotiated whereby I would be free to describe and interpret events as I saw them but that my findings would be shared with the group. This feedback and subsequent dialogue proved to be a vital technique in yielding ever richer data. Study of the group was confined almost entirely to 'musical activities'. There was no attempt to encroach upon their 'out-of-music activity'.

The Actors

The group shared a great deal. Unlike their parents, all were born in Basingstoke. They lived at the southern end of the town and attended the same 11–16 comprehensive school. Jon (bass guitar), John (lead guitar) and Chris (drums) had known each other from same primary school while Neil (vocal) attended a neighbouring primary school and first made contact with the others at secondary school. Here Jon, John and Neil shared the same timetable for the most part during the first three years of school life.

The group's lives had counter-pointed the second phase of Basingstoke's development from a market town of 25,000 to a population of 100,000 that depended upon hi-tech and service industries. Basingstoke was becoming a popular location for company headquarters. There was a high level of employment and the town was deemed to be economically successful.

The town's rapid expansion began in the mid-1960s with migration from the London conurbation. More recent settlers represent a wider north-south migration. Many of the town's pre-expansion institutions had benefited enormously from the growth of population, and newer ones were flourishing. Basingstoke's culture was expressed in a wide range of activity. Majorettes and marching bands, a symphony orchestra, choral society, community church, sports centre, country music club, male voice choir, American football, Welsh society, Caribbean club, folk club, jazz club, aikido and karate clubs, subway culture and vandalism characterized the cultural diversity of the town. An estimated 30 rock bands were in operation.

Formal educational provision after the age of 11 was supplied by eight 11–16 comprehensive schools, a Sixth Form College and a Technical College. The school attended by the group had recently incorporated the word 'community' into its title. In addition to traditional evening classes catering for vocational and leisure needs, twilight short courses were offered for the ten to 14 age range. This was in part a response to the loss of 'after school' activities caused by the long-running teachers' dispute and a general concern in the town about an increase in vandalism. The school also provided a base for community-initiated needs. Six rock bands made use of the site.

Jon's parents settled in Basingstoke in 1967. They describe their own formal music education as 'very basic typical school lessons'. Jon's mother had piano lessons for one year. Their listening now centred on 'classical pop'. They disliked modern jazz, opera and punk. Jon had one elder brother, Simon, aged 18, who listened to punk, psychedelic, ska, folk and heavy metal. Jon's pattern of listening was very similar. Simon played in the band *Antithesis* (formerly called *Strontium Dog*). Jon is a 'junior' member of this group.

Primary school music is described by Jon as 'a useless singalong with tambourines'. Two years of violin lessons at primary school are described as 'a useful musical experience' but little was understood.

> It was a 'play this, play that' style of teaching producing what the teacher wanted. There was no flexibility.

At the age of 11, conscious listening began. This demanded two to three hours daily. Once an instrument was acquired, listening sessions were integrated into private practice, a process of imitation and the generation of new ideas. Jon has consciously modelled his style of playing on groups such as the *Apostles*, *New Model Army* and *Metallica*, although he claims that any experience is grist to his mill. He was not aware of any single outstanding influence. Jon brought to *Cell 1* important stylistic values learnt from the parent group *Antithesis*. This experience equipped him to act as discrete leader and facilitator of *Cell 1*, the ethos of which he insists is developed jointly and freshly. For Jon, music is seen as:

> … a wide form of communication. It is used to express feelings and anything else the composer wishes. In my scene, it is used as a form of communication between like-opinionated people.

Although Jon insists that music cannot be summed up in a couple of paragraphs, nevertheless central to the concept for him is 'communication'.

John's parents settled in Basingstoke in 1970. His mother recalled a 'sketchy' formal music education with assemblies regularly featuring the recorded voice of Kathleen Ferrier. Their listening now centres on classical and folk although mother enjoys pop and especially Michael Jackson. Like Jon, John is the youngest member of his family. He has two sisters, Debbie, aged 23, and Janine, aged 21, and a brother, Bryan, aged 22. Debbie played the flute, piano and classical guitar and listened to *Pink Floyd* and 'piano music'. Janine played the recorder and French horn 'with more enthusiasm than success', as John puts it, and listened to Barbara Streisand and 'slow love songs'. Bryan played the E flat tenor horn. He too listened to *Pink Floyd* amongst other groups.

For John, primary school music provided opportunity to learn a variety of instruments but these were not taken up.

> I remember singing along to tapes and television programmes with the little notes that light up and the big kids getting the best instruments off the music trolley.

However, he did receive piano lessons privately but failed to practice and stopped going. After teaching himself a few chords on the guitar, he took private guitar lessons. Here he received a good grounding in rhythm playing but came to resist the teacher's funky style. He became bored, practised the wrong things, wanting to go in a different direction. John describes the lessons as useful but wanted to develop his 'lead' playing. The teacher's agenda insisted upon achieving 'rhythmic competence' before allowing for this. John's conscious listening began at the age of 12 and he recognizes the influence of *Deep Purple* and other heavy rock bands. He finds the style of some heavy metal bands like *Iron Maiden* 'dynamic, powerful, interesting and very musical'. He was taught by his brother to search out unusual music in second hand shops. Like Jon, John spends time listening, imitating and generating.

Neil was born in Basingstoke on the Buckskin Estate, an area of public sector housing sometimes stigmatized in Basingstoke. His parents settled there in 1964. Both parents see themselves as 'having no musical talent whatsoever'. 'Chiming along to a teacher on a piano and singing around the piano with teacher playing all the music' is what is recalled. Mother did attempt to learn to read music and to play an instrument in secondary school but failed. Father's secondary teachers are described as 'elitist and as having no time for talentless pupils'. Neil's own primary school experience is summed up as 'the dreaded chime bar!'. 'You haven't heard of a professional chime bar player, have you?' he asks.

Neil has an elder brother, Darren, aged 17, and a younger brother, Richard, aged ten. In the home, Neil has experienced a variety of music handed down from parents and elder brother. Father presented light rock, Blues, rock 'n' roll, heavy rock and military band music. Mother enjoys the music of the *Beach Boys*. Elder brother went through a classical phase then on to *Dire Straits* and rock 'n' roll. Neil concedes that his love of rock 'n' roll may have grown out of home experience.

Neil started listening to his own music at the age of 12. Jon introduced him to the *Sex Pistols* when he visited his house but Neil didn't listen intently at first. He soon 'grew into' real punk, recording over the *Sex Pistols* and acquired *Crass*, *Conflict* and other premier punk tapes. Recently he has been listening to rock 'n' roll. He admits to being heavily influenced and admits that his beliefs have been moulded.

> *Crass* and *Conflict* have given me a lot of thinking to do because their lyrics make so much sense. They really have brought me out and ironed out feelings I never knew I had.

Neil cannot easily say how much time he gives to music. 'I almost *always* have a tune in my head, and hum, sing and whistle a lot.'

Chris's parents settled in Basingstoke in 1966. They describe their school music lessons as 'average'. Father's listening centres on rock-classical music like *Sky* and James Last while mother focuses on popular vocal music exemplified by Barry Manilow and Jack Jones. Chris has an elder brother, Jonathan, aged 17, who plays contemporary music such as the *Cue*, *Angelic Upstarts* and *Political Asylum*.

At primary school, Chris played in the school orchestra on drums and was given 'rudimentary instruction'. He also benefited from a year's drum lessons at a Local Education Authority Music Centre where he learnt the techniques of 'breaks', 'fills' and 'beats' etc. and 'was shown how to read music'. These lessons were seen as being useful but were limited by 'lack of space to expand your own ideas'.

Chris has consciously listened to music from the age of eight and has focused attention increasingly on drummers such as Nicko McBrann (*Iron Maiden*), Clive Burr (*Iron Maiden*'s first drummer), Neil Peart (*Rush*) and Tristram Fry (*Sky*). These he is convinced have greatly influenced him. He has enjoyed contrasting the styles of *Iron Maiden* and *Sky*. Chris has attended five *Sky* concerts. This devotion to the group *Sky* is a source of teasing from the other members of the group. He listens to an hour's music daily and, for family-social reasons, limits drum practice at home to two sessions weekly. He used to drum along (with hands, sticks or voice) in his private listening but just listens now.

Getting It Together

The group came to birth during the first term of their second year of secondary schooling.

> There's a lot of dispute over whose idea it was between me and John ... we were
> just mucking around then. We didn't realize it was going to be serious.
>
> (Jon)

John, Jon, Neil and Dave (no longer in the group) began by drumming with biros
on pencil cases and photograph albums. This was a stage marked by fantasy and
'dream planning', all without any musical equipment.

> We all had little dreams ... we were like building the band and saying who was
> playing what before we had any instruments.
>
> (Jon)

This burgeoning of musical ambition was part of wider peer group phenomenon
in which a number of boys initiated their own musical educational programme.
For members of *Cell 1* it was a time of promiscuous social activity centring on
'getting it together'. Equipment was being acquired and the group spluttered and
started to progress during this 'out of tune guitar stage'. Membership of the group
and commitment to relationships was uncertain. Individual skill mastery was being
worked out in a group situation. Practices would last for 30 minutes and then
disintegrate into a 'muck around'. But there was a dramatic awakening to the part
music offered to how they were living their lives and making sense. The 'out of
tune guitar stage' was a dramatic contrast to the 'biro-dreaming stage', a coming
down to earth.

> It told us what we previously thought was that we were just going to pick up
> guitars and we were going to be excellent like that it showed us.
>
> (Jon)

> Hendrix! I thought as soon as I picked up a guitar I would be dishing out burning
> solos. It wasn't quite like that.
>
> (Neil)

> It was fun.
>
> (Jon)

The group came to see that they had to do more than play 'fast solos' and 'twiddly
bits'. They had to 'get it together'. The arrival of Chris on drums provided the
stimulus for this 'getting it together'.

> A drummer makes all the difference, I think. We didn't sound too good without
> a drummer, but as soon as he came there was more like a professional air. It
> seemed as though we knew what we were doing.
>
> (Jon)

He also kept us in time.

(Neil)

Rehearsal patterns continued to be erratic. Shortage of amplification, difficulty in negotiating practice venues and general organizational failure were persistent sources of frustration. Exceptionally, intensive practice took place during school holidays. On one occasion, this represented three consecutive days' work of three hours each day.

The group had grown in understanding and defining what they believed to be their unique ethos represented by their independent spirit. This, they believed, was made possible by the fusing of their different cultural backgrounds which became harnessed into a dynamic unit by a common 'political commitment'. They had become sensitive to the patronizing attitude of those who see them as 'up and coming kids'.

We're just stupid little kids, we'll grow out of it, we'll become normal again …
maybe we will.

(Jon)

The trouble with being still at school is that no-one listens to us or takes us seriously, although we are possibly more politically aware than they are.

(Neil)

The chorus of their song 'Armchair Anarchy' expressed this feeling of impotence in a world beyond their control:

But it ain't so easy to shout how we feel,
When we live at home, we got no money,
Nothing's real.
Dependent on others for our food and clothes,
Living off the things we need from the ones we loathe.

Jon's association with *Antithesis* was the first strand of a wider network. Jon's brother, Simon, is an important source of approval. Tapes of *Cell 1*'s work have been sent to Ramsy, the singer of the group *Political Asylum*, and in turn Ramsy has communicated with Jon and encouraged their work. *Political Asylum* are based in Stirling, Scotland and were first heard by Jon at a London gig. Jon identified with Ramsy and entered into correspondence. This has also occurred with the bass players of the Scarborough group, *Indian Dream* and the Bristol group, *Disorder*. Addresses of the musicians are gleaned from record sleeves of compilation LPs. Jon and his brother have produced a magazine called *Black Dove*, which circulates to the network of like-minded 'musicians' and to a local audience amongst their peer group and any thought to be sympathetic. During the first term of their fourth year of secondary school, the group had performed to an invited audience in the school's drama studio, and the second term of their fourth year saw them on stage at the Caribbean Club and giving a second performance in school. The third term of their fourth year afforded the group a street performance as part of Basingstoke Arts Day. This series of performances is acceptable by their school as a community service component of the 'Trident Scheme', centred upon a period of three weeks' work experience at the end of their fourth year. The actors have made their stage, an emergent culture, an amoeba swimming free. So what were the defining characteristics of their culture, their system of beliefs felt and known inside their creative process?

Value Formation and Personal Growth

Over the six-month period the group worked out a creative process that began with foreplay and experimentation. The act of tuning up became an art in enabling whole sequences of interplay. The sounding of the open strings was the cue to initiate the musically expressive gestures as a way of expressing what was known, what was available for use, and what could be playfully integrated into short musical conversational pieces. All this served as re-affirmation of memory, the self and each other. The group's musical building blocks were assembled, extended and reviewed. From here, and with the nuancing of musical gestures, individual skill mastery was worked at. A search for the right sound and its right feeling was what really counted. As a 'non-instrumentalist', Neil took upon himself the role of controlling this situation. For example, he commonly seeks to gently manage Chris's virtuosic drumming outbursts. Neil in due course calls the meeting to order with Chris making a final flurry confirming Neil's decision. The foreplay is complete.

Patterns of music making for the group develop into an upward or downward spiral of activity. Once the right feeling is generated, all that is good can be released. But all this involves risk. Learning to trust in one's own feelings and the body from which they flow is the challenge. Fear of failure will secure failure. To defend will deny the full exercise of powers. There can be failure or there can be exhilarating success. If failure is met, it must be learnt from, not denied. Success cannot be planned for.

The group makes a point of ending the rehearsal early if the spiral is ascending and satisfaction achieved while alternatively the descending spiral is lived with, analysed and learnt from. The source of the fall is examined and usually explained by bad feelings, feelings that have not been 'ironed out', dealt with and clarified. For example, the experience of a school day has not been dealt with adequately during foreplay. There is usually a mutual forgiving and the fall forgotten and hopes for a better tomorrow. If the forgiving is not accomplished then a period of unsettled behaviour ensues. 'Jon may throw a wobbly and leave the band', says John. These rare occurrences have to be dealt with. They become a source of group history, experience to draw upon. When satisfaction is found, it is known and celebrated. There is a regular hint of this as the ending of a song is realized, where there is an unwillingness to let go, a refusal to give up what feels good and right. This could mark embarkation onto the 'jam', the endless exploration of pleasure, but *Cell 1* rarely takes the trip. It is thought to be wasteful and there is the danger of over-indulging individual virtuosity.

In the song 'Something in the Air', there is opportunity for John to deliver intensive musical gestures. When the 'vibes' are right, his movement art is developed as a sure way of affecting full meaning. This takes Jon into a supine pose and his reverie authenticated. Jon often finds himself foot-tapping but as bass this is something to reflect upon, for it is his responsibility to ensure stability and structure. As bass he must be the rock. To dance the music would be too great a risk and could throw everything into turmoil. There is a discipline to master. Chris's commitment to meaning is demonstrated in a curling of the lip and this comes to be a sign that the group understand and look for. Neil is anxious to demonstrate commitment and believes that he should try to be relaxed so that he can be sincere and truthful.

When the good has been felt, quiescence descends upon the group. This is marked by a refusal to discuss the experience. Words are redundant. There is a taboo on breaking the magic. This may last for half a minute or more until Jon breaks the spell, 'Shall we do it again? Let's prove it weren't a fluke'. The quiescence may naturally signal the ending of the rehearsal. An alternative manifestation of satisfaction is a refusal to quiesce. Instead a musical celebration is 'enjoyed'. This takes the form of playing an arrangement of 'Old McDonald had a Farm', 'Wandering Star' or the 'Hovis Theme'; in fact, any commonly rejected piece that can through mocking become accepted.

The group comes to know that the more pre-planned a performance, the more dangers lurk. Everything depends upon the spontaneous. Another form of active celebration sees the group changing roles in playful fashion. When I play back recordings of their work, the group re-enact each other's playing in silent imitation by taking up their instruments. Here too is a gentle mocking and a sealing of group identity. If Neil's American football is with him then something other than musical playfulness may grow at the end of a rehearsal.

We have seen the contribution of the playful body to the learning process and musical and physical gesture used as the building block of experience, as the way of translating what is felt into more articulate form. The group are *being* musical and gaining in personal knowledge.

Private and Public Realms of Knowing

Knowing music without words is enjoyed by the group. On the other hand, what they know with music cascades into a verbal realm of great intensity. Beyond the group's collective songwriting there is the poetry notated in Jon's magazine, their school English Department's 'personal diary', writing that I as researcher encourage.

We recall that the group is looking for 'the right sound' and 'the right sound' means 'the right feeling' and this validates the creative process. If 'the right feeling' is achieved then only 'the right words' will do and they cannot easily be given. The group uses no language in relating to pitch other than 'high – low' and 'up – down'. There is no naming of pitch levels or chords. This area of expertise is understood by 'looking and listening'. In this sense, the group admits to 'reading music', the reading of hand shapes, the learning of motor structures. This exercise ranges from the casual glance from ten metres to the intense close up 'mirror work' where guitarists are brought within bodily contact range. The transmission of material in this way is endorsed in concerted playing. This mode of behaviour has been rehearsed extensively in private listening where play-along techniques have been used. The group increasingly relies on listening alone and the 'look' becomes cursory. But the guitarists look continually at their own motor structures, a source of self-conscious behaviour.

The group learns that the achievement of musical fluency goes with 'feeling good' and this leads to quiescent states. These states are key indicators of success and movement towards the attainment of goals. The pleasure of being musical includes the opportunity to create values and to continually re-evaluate them. They are able to become aware of changes in attitude and personality. The group enjoys exercising what they call 'mental skills'. By this they mean staying in touch with a critical perspective on the world as well as going beyond an unaccountable subjective dream world. They 'face the music' in public performance.

If teachers of music and the arts were unable to grasp the implications of the work of Witkin and Ross, and this is Ross's judgement in hindsight (1989), ignoring the child's expressive act by working outside of it, then in *Cell 1*'s creative process without the presence of a teacher and the constraints of a regulated classroom, there is freedom found to work expressively, to learn to trust what is subject-reflexive action, to know in action and to understand subjective states. The creation of the right environment in which self-expression is possible depends on sufficient playfulness. This facilitating environment is by no means given but emerges as part of their setting-up/tuning-up process, working through the day's experiences where they have not always been in control of their expressive lives. In coming together they look for freedom to be. *Cell 1* learn how to learn, a process whereby they come to understand their changes in attitude and personality, their making of identity and a personal system of values, their ability to exercise mental skills, to dream *and* to be wide-awake. They know much of being musical and this is firmly rooted in trust in the body as the mediator of experience and generator of spontaneity. This means an openness to feelings, the necessary precursor of good musical behaviour. Foreplay becomes a critical element in this creative act. Their body consciousness forms the essence of transactional behaviour. There is a continuum of gestural expression emanating from the unarticulated world of inner feeling through the manipulation and nuancing of what becomes known to the finely articulated musical utterance. That what is known of music resists translation directly into discursive symbols is signficant. However, the richness of what is known with music cascades into a highly articulate world of critical consciousness in which language plays an important part.

Cell 1's musical world, in its imaginal roots and value orientation, attempts to embrace the whole of life and thus, being musical, is thought of as embracing the whole of life. To isolate music from their being and becoming would be to give it up to the world too easily. That music education failed in this respect for the group is shown by their withdrawal from the arenas that claimed to be the purveyors of music learning. In those places there was simply not enough realization of self. *Cell 1*'s every word, gesture, response and interaction is thought of as heavy with value and significance. Their whole educational programme and its music is only to be communicated as a belief system.

Silencing the Past

Arts educators have repeatedly argued for the intrinsically worthwhileness of artistic endeavour. The distinction between extrinsic and intrinsic learning is helpful. Maslow views the former as dealing in content and skills. 'It is controlled from the outside, a learning of impersonal associations, and it is extrinsic to the personality of the learner' (Maslow 1973: 159). In this view intrinsic learning is about becoming a particular human being; it is learning that accompanies the profoundest experiences in our lives. Extrinsic learning sees the teacher shape the learner. Intrinsic learning sees the learner shape themselves. A great deal of debate surrounds this interplay between the locus of control in learning and neatly encapsulates argument about child-centred and subject-centred arrangements. The move from external control to internal control is what is meant when learner autonomy is spoken about. John, Jon, Chris and Neil as *Cell 1* demonstrated well a model of intrinsic learning where they were able to know about the particularity of their 'human being' accompanied by profoundly committed experiences. In the same way Stuart in Chapter 4 following his GCSE music course had found the freedom to learn and in his compositions expressed personality shaped from the inside.

Intrinsic learning relates to the idea of self-realization. But in the discourse of the Education Reform Act 1988 that was being schemed while *Cell 1* was rehearsing there was no talk of intrinsic learning or learner autonomy. Beyond common sense arguments for a manageable and coherent system of schooling based on traditional subjects and with continuity and progression in learning assured, there were powerful driving forces for reform. The *Black Papers* of the 1960s and 1970s had made a contribution to a form of neo-conservatism concerned about a threat to social cohesion and national identity. Thus, the notion of cultural restoration figured large in attempts to make a National Curriculum deferring to a more stable past. Coupled with this was a political imperative that had grown in strength from James Callaghan's acknowledgement of education for industry, concerned with entrepreneurship and training for the real world. Together, in the name of the moral and economic order, the state claimed to be fully justified in re-establishing its authority through the control of state education, wresting it away from professional interests, from the producers of education and passing it to the consumers. The child-centred progressive tendencies of the previous 30 years would be erased.

Music teachers had been moving towards assimilating 'all kinds of music' to their cause and this freedom to select from past and present, recognizing cultural diversity, had become a valued part of their credentials and an aspect of their growing confidence and attention to diversity. The formation of a radically different examination at age 16 recognizing the interests of pupils and encompassing 'all kinds of music' provided a model for music teachers to work with and for the community of music education to celebrate. While unresolved debates surrounding culture, traditional values and contested forms of knowledge once again came to the surface, music teachers attended meetings organized to canvass their views on what form a National Curriculum for music should take. They did this with enthusiasm and with conceptions of music education to defend and promote. There was now a common conviction about the role of composition as a creative and essential activity and a growing consensus about learning music by doing. Above all else was the belief that pupils themselves had musical ideas and feelings that could be expressed in ways personal to each. Music could be promoted as a practical activity and this needed, if necessary, to be defended.

However, there had been talk of classroom practices taking on the form of a dull orthodoxy. There were many cases of predictable patterns of small group work in which the acquisition of skills, as part of the process of composing, was limited and whereby Year 9 pupils had learnt how to stagnate and regress rather than progress. And singing, the substance of a traditional music education, was now uncommonly heard in the secondary school. Although a broad range of stakeholders, including representatives from the music industries, formed the Working Group set up by the Secretary of State to propose a curriculum for music, they were strongly advised by HMI, who were well qualified to hold the best overview of the situation through their large number of visits to music classrooms. It was HMI who had addressed the idea of continuity and progression in their publications of 1984 and this was now central to the making of a National Curriculum for music. What was now increasingly becoming clear, as my headteacher of the time announced, was that the past was largely to be forgotten and a new culture forged.

New Order Thinking

The making of a National Curriculum based on a set of subjects, one of which would be music, did little to promote the arts as having a common purpose. The quest of Witkin and Ross to understand 'how it is that we can value the creative arts in a way that acknowledges them as central to the educational process'

(Witkin 1989: 24) had been overrun by official moves made since 1980. Even the enlightened thinking of HMI in attempting to frame the curriculum through 'areas of experience', one of which was the aesthetic-creative, was now of no consequence. However, in a National Curriculum consultation document of 1987 making clear the distinction between Core (English, maths and science) and Foundation (history, geography, PE, art and music) subjects, it was proposed that all pupils should continue with some study of all the Foundation subjects and that 'in the fourth and fifth years they should be able ... to pursue a combined course covering art, music, drama and design' (DES 1987: 6–7). In due course the Music Working Group set up to advise on the new curriculum was lukewarm about this, seeing a potential threat to GCSE music. Each arts subject was now defending its corner. There was a great deal at stake.

Music, as a Foundation subject and of lower order than the Core subjects, was late to be considered in all this. The Music Working Group (DES 1991a) produced a clear rationale for music that was in line with the developing principles of creative-aesthetic education, and there was a sustained commitment to holding together the activities of composing, performing and listening and in promoting music as a practical subject through which knowledge, skills and understanding would develop. The group's sensitivity to and defence of recent curriculum developments was considerable alongside a call for singing to be restored to a position of equality with instrumental playing. However, by Chapter 3 of their report, where the group set about creating a rationale for the structure of attainment targets and programmes of study, their obligation to the requirement of the Education Reform Act (ERA) (1988) to specify 'knowledge, skills and understanding' led to proposals that were to prove problematic (see Swanwick 1992a, 1992b; Pitts 2000). The report argued for the centrality of listening, composing and performing activities and that it would be appropriate to think of these as 'skills'. Doing became thought of as skill, as practice, not as knowing, knowledge and understanding. In this way the doing, the making, the experience of being musical as a way of knowing in and for itself was given up to knowledge about music. The report proceeded to argue that the 'skills' of performing and composing could not be acquired and developed without an attendant degree of knowledge and understanding of concepts related to music:

> ... of the ways in which music is notated, recorded and shared, and of the contexts – historical and geographical and social background of a piece if they are to talk about and critically appraise it.
>
> (DES 1991a: 13)

This of course was right. But the group had, despite a hint of recognizing that knowledge might involve a subtle form of cognition and be more than conceptual, aligned musical knowledge and understanding with the propositional, with knowledge of this and knowledge of that, with words and with concepts. In due course, the National Curriculum Working Group's *Teaching Music in the*

National Curriculum (Pratt and Stephens 1995), aware of the curriculum's recent revision (Dearing 1994), pointed to five fields of knowledge: knowledge of musical elements; knowledge of musical resources; knowledge of how music is communicated; knowledge of how music reflects its historical and social contexts, and knowledge of musical character, styles and traditions. Thus they write:

> Above all it is essential that knowledge is developed through experience rather than by didactic instruction, and that it is largely derived from, and applied to, pupils' own work within the music curriculum.
>
> (Pratt and Stephens 1995: 33)

But now that music ceases to be a statement in itself, experience-knowledge as aesthetic knowledge with its highly prized tacit components is lost to a form of knowledge beyond the music.

The achievement of the Working Group had been not inconsiderable in the light of strong pressures coming largely from beyond the music education community. The aesthetic dimension of education, recognized from the time of Plato and Aristotle, and reaffirmed again and again and consistently so during the twentieth century, had been expunged from the nation's consciousness by the Education Reform Act of 1988. Now, there was not only an absence of an aesthetic dimension to the language of official discussion but of any recognition of its existence. The philosopher Marcuse, a constant and insightful critic of instrumental rationality, may provide a clue to this way of thinking. Marcuse argued that the aesthetic dimension had come to be seen as a place where freedom from the demands of necessity could be found; it was not the real world, and with this a considerable cost had been exacted (Marcuse 1955/1987).

The life work of educators such as Dewey, Read and Reid in raising the status of the aesthetic dimension of human experience, in distinguishing it from the study of aesthetics as a branch of philosophy, as a philosophy of art and as contemplation of formal elements within works of art and giving it an everyday significance as a mode of awareness, had been disregarded. Did the curriculum high priests see in the aesthetic realm the dangerous potential for 'freedom from necessity' and a serious incongruence *vis-à-vis* the new curriculum, or were they distracted by the attraction of a particular form of cultural education, and with it a set of particular moral assumptions? Was the aesthetic identified with the soft and subjective, with the sentimental and progressive? Was the word aesthetic simply too difficult?

The kinds of attainments proposed by the Working Group in their *Music 5–14* document (DES 1991b) unsurprisingly took the form of statements, easily calibrated. The process of making the National Curriculum had yielded to old dualities: now experience was opposed to knowledge, practice to theory and the intuitive to the formal, and these kinds of awkward dichotomies surged forth in plenty as the process of making the curriculum proceeded. Despite a conviction about the holistic nature of musical experience, the Working Group had developed a way that made this difficult. Despite the intervention of Swanwick and the establishment of a meaningful attainment target 2 as Listening and Appraising, the draft programmes of study showed little understanding of what this might mean in practice or how it might relate to attainment target 1, Performing and Composing. The subtle relationship between experience-knowledge, of the immediacy of knowing, and mediated knowledge, was barely to be found. The result was the inclusion of dead matter, matter pre-determined and insisted on in the programmes of study that had the potential to demoralize the pupil and the teacher. Before long pupils in the early years of secondary school were gaining knowledge of ternary form and musical epochs from the outside, a distant cry from the emergence of a ternary form in the Yorkshire Dales as the children's 'Flying Birds' came to rest. The philosopher Susanne Langer understands all this well.

> People suppose that to understand music one must not simply know much music, but much *about* music. Concert-goers try earnestly to recognize chords, and judge key changes, and hear the separate instruments in an ensemble – all technical insights that come themselves with long familiarity, like the recognition of glazes of pottery or of structural devices in a building – instead of distinguishing *musical elements*, which may be made out of harmonic or melodic material, shifts of range or tone colour, rhythms or dynamic accents or simply changes in volume, and yet be in themselves as audible to a child as to a veteran musician.
>
> (Langer 1953/1979: 106)

The Working Group had found itself needing to accommodate an unrelenting demand for a particular kind of knowledge and understanding. The Group's final report was in any case to be overrun by government dictat. In making a National Curriculum there was a key reform at work insisting that knowledge be independent of the knower. Education was about equipping children with knowledge and there was to be one size of knowledge to fit all.

Diverging Pathways

As the coming of a National Curriculum approached Swanwick had produced in *Music, Mind and Education* (1988) 'a cogent and workable theory of music education' (Swanwick 1988: 6), building on his philosophical enquiry of 1979 in a quest to understand the nature of musical experience and music as mindful activity. In doing this Swanwick is himself mindful of ensuring that music has a credible cognitive position retrieved from the dangers of emphasizing the arts as serving subjectivities and self-expression, the danger of 'separating the arts from the main business of life and education' (ibid: 37). The business of life is not thought here as what *Cell 1* above had considered the business of life and education, their making sense of and understanding the world into which they were growing, their growing in critical awareness of their place in the order of things and how they might be able to shape this. Rather, Swanwick's business of life and education required a world independent of the knower and it is this that the philosopher of science Karl Popper provides (Popper 1972). This is a world of ideas, theories and propositions that is continually inherited, revised and added to, a 'third world' beyond the physical world (world 1) and the world of mental states (world 2). Thus the potter reciprocating with the clay or the musician vocally shaping a musical phrase, their media of reflexive self-expression, are at the same time engaging with a world 3 of ideas about what they are doing. Their world 2 state of mind is acting as an intermediary between this world and the physical world of the clay or vocal tracts shaping the phrase. In this way there is an objective element to consider. The two-dimensional model of subject-object, the maker-the medium, the me-the not me, is exposed as a limiting discourse and in Popper's view as a source of subjectivities, infinite regress and dogmatism. In his book *Objective Knowledge* (1972) Popper criticizes the expressivist theory of art, the idea that the creator gives form to feeling. For Popper, expression is a low order matter, meaning is of little significance and dwarfed by the evolutionary power of knowledge. All this had become important to Swanwick's theory that set out to establish higher status and credibility for music and the arts. And in the light of discoveries concerning children's development of musical understanding through composition, a way of thinking about the multi-layered nature of musical knowledge and its unfolding was proposed (Swanwick and Tillman 1986, Swanwick 1994). By doing this, the key official demands for continuity and progression in the curriculum could be addressed. Swanwick was swimming with the tide and critically engaging with the problems presented by the issue of progression in learning. In seeking to accommodate to official requirements a clear space is created between the child-centred progressive focus on the significance of subjectivities, the child's being and becoming and a necessary objectivity and order in things. Ross and Swanwick were in different places, moving in different directions. The work and creative process of *Cell 1* made little sense to 'new order thinking' while for Ross the group might well offer much that could usefully inform the practice of music in school. But even for Ross there needed to be reappraisal, while at the same time remaining in a place from which to challenge the distasteful reality of the now official fundamental interest in a particular form of progression, assessment and accountability.

In Ross et al. (1993) Harre's attention to 'individual identity' and human engagement is drawn upon (Harre 1983). This is in the cause of assessing 'aesthetic understanding' which is elaborated into four aspects: its conventionalization; its appropriation; its transformation and its publication. In recognizing the child as growing inevitably into cultural conventions, these become both the starting and staging points for the development of aesthetic understanding. Conventions available to us within our culture are appropriated for the making of personal meaning followed by a search for uniqueness and personal distinction before 'social ratification'.

> Contrary to the stereotype, the expressive impulse is in fact unsatisfied in us until the work is placed in the public domain, albeit anxiously and with some trepidation, as an effort of communication with and an invitation to validation by others.
>
> (Ross et al. 1993: 56)

Ross et al. set out an argument for the assessment of aesthetic understanding, not unlike that proposed by the *Assessment and Progression in Music Education* (Preston 1986) as a sensitive conversation between teacher and pupil, pupil and pupil and ultimately as a personal conversation that the pupil has with themselves. In a climate of new order thinking this becomes a radically alternative conception of assessment, one that is neither normative nor referenced to an agreed set of criteria and clearly at odds with the dominant thrust of public policy and ways of guaranteeing accountability.

> Traditional assessment practices would conform to the reductive tendency of non-aesthetic engagement, by predetermining the knowledge that the pupil shall show evidence of. The pupil selects from her experience in order to fit the function of the question she is asked. Where questions function to make rigorous selection and particular ordering of experience a necessity for the one who answers, it is perhaps little wonder that the more open and active form of aesthetic knowing should have evaded traditional assessment criteria and even been judged unassessable.
>
> (Ross et al. 1993: 58)

Here is the sustained defence of the child as a particular individual whose creative work is *sui generis* and which rather than adhering to some arbitrary pre-determined artistic standard contributes to an ongoing debate about values. Assessment is self-assessment and becomes peer assessment moving out towards the validation by a wider community. Assessment is coming to know.

However, the defining of pre-determined knowledge was to be expected if the process of learning was to be politically accounted for. Public policy was firmly dedicated to the specification of outcomes and for Ross this is an unacceptable intrusion upon both the pupil and teacher's creativity and the preservation of aesthetic learning and the nurture of aesthetic understanding. This ethical demand for a process which would yield the unexpected, which would be open enough for the learner to make sense and, in Maslow's terms for the learning to be personally significant, is sustained by Paynter as he reviews progress within music education over the past 30 years in the 1992 publication *Sound and Structure* (Paynter 1992).

While noting the reform of the examination system and the creation of GCSE as a significant step forward, Paynter recognizes too that the idea of creativity as being concerned with imagination, invention and innovation may not be recognized by all. There is still more work to be undertaken in making this clear. As in *Sound and Silence*, *Sound and Structure* provides detailed support for the teacher and a section 'The Workshop in Action' maintains the idea of the classroom as a place where ideas are generated inside a creative process made by the teacher and with their students.

> The teacher's role is vital to the success of a composition workshop. Nothing can be left to chance, and there is no substitute for good planning. It is crucial to anticipate the kind of guidance most likely to be needed (or the reasonable expectation of what will be produced in response to given starting-points). At the same time we must allow for the unexpected and be ready to encourage it when it appears. It is important to know – from personal experience – what *may* happen. This means being active ourselves in creating and performing, and being inventive and innovative in our teaching.
>
> (Paynter 1992: 27)

As with Ross there is a fundamental distaste for the pre-specification of outcomes. The teacher plans for an open-ended inquiry while being sufficiently aware of possible lines of development and expressive outcomes. *Sound and Structure* reaffirms the role of the teacher as a subtle enabler who has considerable knowledge of repertoire and compositional techniques and who is able to continually affirm the potential of the child's ideas. The music room as workshop is a place where relationships are developed both musically and humanely. The process, like that enjoyed by *Cell 1* is thought to be humanizing. But this is not how Ross (1995) is seeing the state of music in schools.

Ross now makes a devastating critique of music education, pointing out its inability to genuinely reform and pursue aesthetic and artistic goals. The problems identified at the time of the 'Arts and the Adolescent' project had not gone away. Refusing to see music as a special case within the arts, Ross characterizes music teachers as being disinclined to actualize the musical minds of their pupils or to create a climate of mutuality in which these might grow. Composition, the activity thought to draw music closer to the other arts in their aesthetic aims, had failed in this. At best music teachers have gone only half way towards embracing an appropriate model of the arts in education. They have been ultimately restricted by a teaching persona built on their own musical authority rooted in skills, techniques and knowledge about music. Ross maintains that music teachers conceive of music in pre-modernist terms. Too often children have been taught in such a way as to render their ideas, thoughts and feelings impotent. Unlike the other arts music has failed to develop a pedagogy that ensured the meaningful engagement of young people.

Whereas Paynter had come to see the one-dimensional approach to knowledge and understanding adopted by the National Curriculum as problematic and diminishing the possibility of composition achieving its potential, '… should we not be asking what kind of knowledge is appropriate to the subject' (Paynter 2000: 26), Ross observes teachers in the other arts as being more resilient to official demands and able to sustain their long commitment to the arts as being concerned with individual acts of expression. Before too long Ross's insights were supported by research into the teaching of the arts (Harland et al. 2000). Where the arts were well taught pupils acquired increased art form knowledge and skills, personal and social development, and the enrichment of communication, expressive skills and creativity. In music, unlike art and drama, pupils registered a more limited range of achievement of these desirable outcomes. Unsurprisingly, pupils in the case of music noted a missing space in which to draw on their own meanings and find relevance.

Conclusion

Government reforms seemed to be achieving very little in music. While teachers appreciated the confirmation of a common curriculum structure, many nevertheless, and based on my own many visits to schools, appeared disorientated and frequently somnambulant in respect of the kind of curriculum development being imposed upon them. When close surveillance threatened in the form of inspection they awoke, coped and performed. Most were unwilling or unable to colour the curriculum with insight or interpret it with generosity. It was something to fit in with demanding adaptation and compliance (Plummeridge 1996; Finney 2000, 2002). As a high-stake assessment regime emerged along with the idea of continual school improvement and ever more efficient outcomes from the investment in education, so teachers were beholden to micro management within their schools. The regime had created curriculum stagnation marked by a dearth of classroom innovation. An official model of music education had been created and there was mounting evidence to suggest that it was deficient.

The text *Music Teaching in the Secondary School*, written by an Ofsted Inspector, set out a view of effective music teaching for the twenty-first century. The work shows teachers how to manage and control learning outcomes that are largely non-aesthetic. The knowledge and understanding gained is far removed from the conception set out by Reid in earlier times. The case given of the Blues is exemplary in this respect.

> By the end of the project pupils will be able to: use a standard 12-bar Blues sequence, play chords in C major, have listened to and recognized the use of ninths in three pieces of music, know the names of notes in chords I, IV and V.
>
> (Bray 2000: 22)

There is no mention of musical qualities, of human interest or of felt experience. The core of aesthetic endeavour seems to have been lost. The Blues doesn't seem to be about the way people feel or how these feelings become musical. It is barely worth becoming acquainted with. This is some considerable distance from the work of *Cell 1*, where embodiment and intrinsic learning ensured an existential component to their creative process that made for meaning. The official curriculum had lost both the child and the teacher who together could be playful, curious, insightful and with an impulse to create, discover and make something new that was of personal and public significance. Knowledge had become separated from the knower.

Basil Bernstein (1995) had shown how the principle of the market has come to dominate and define the organization of official discourse of schooling. This he argues leads to a new concept of knowledge and of its relation to those who create and use it.

> Knowledge is divorced from persons, their commitments, their personal dedications ... Knowledge, after nearly two thousand years, is divorced from inwardness and literally dehumanized. Once knowledge is divorced from inwardness, from commitments, from personal dedication, from the deep structure of the self, then people may be moved about, substituted for each other and excluded from the market.
>
> (Bernstein 1995: 87)

Bernstein points out that the mediaeval curriculum in its subtle counterbalance between the sacredness of the Trivium and the secularity of the Quadrivium made inwardness a prior condition of knowing and in this way the knower and the known enjoyed a productive and humanizing relationship. Recent educational reforms in Britain enshrined in a National Curriculum eschewed 'inwardness'. Self-knowledge, self-revelation, personal insight, feeling, aesthetic experience and existential concerns are silenced as education is thoroughly reoriented. When this happens pupils are likely to feel a greater disjunction between school and out of school, between school and felt-experience, between their humanizing goals and quite another agenda. Curriculum managers came to present knowledge as a bland conception standing independent of the knower, a profane triumph over the sacredness of human interests. The state educational bureaucracy set up when the Conservative government implemented its educational reforms successfully silenced the child-centred progressive tradition. While at one level, the values of the cultural restorationists had made relatively little impact (see Shepherd and Vulliamy 1994), on another they had been successful, for the curriculum was now to be thought of as a set of discrete subjects. There were knowledge, skills and understanding to be acquired and these arose from a conception of culture depending on repertoire selected from the 'European "classical" tradition, from its earliest roots to the present day; folk and popular music; music from the countries and regions of the British Isles; other musical traditions and cultures' (DES 1992: 12). There remained unresolved tensions between cultural conservatism and multi-culturalism leading in Gammon's view to 'botched categorizations' (Gammon 1999: 1).

However, far more successful than attempts at the restoration of a culture had been the technicist triumph coming from the other thrust of Conservative Party thinking. It was this which had produced a set of what Bonnett (1996) calls 'New' era values.

> ... the concerted attempt to radically change the culture and ethos of the
> school into something akin to a commercial business enterprise has at its
> heart the identification of pre-specifiable outcomes (the product) which meets
> the requirements of those that education is to serve (the customer). This is
> accompanied by an edifice of quality checks and procedures to ensure that
> 'delivery' occurs in the most cost-effective way (euphemistically, 'assessment'
> and 'appraisal').
>
> (Bonnett 1996: 28–9)

Bonnett argues that with these values in the ascendant the teacher-pupil
relationship as a source of authentic understanding is fundamentally fractured. For
the classroom to be a place of authentic transactions the teacher will be listening
to the pupils' responses to what has been put in their way, to the concerns that arise
from stimulation and provocation.

The high degree of reciprocity involved here suggests a triadic relationship
between teacher, learner and what is at issue, which is essentially poetic in character
– poetic in the sense that it celebrates *receptivity* and *participation*: engagement
that is open to the call of what is there to be thought in its summons to individuals,
rather than the preoccupation with imposing a pre-formed structure on otherwise
unintelligible 'data', or with seeking detailed pre-specified outcomes (ibid: 35).

In promoting authentic self-expression Bonnett makes clear that this has nothing
to do with *doing one's own thing, a free for all and anarchy*, and points out:

> Authentic self-expression must involve acknowledging that one is the author
> of one's own actions, and it is this sense of personal responsibility that gives
> them (children) their feeling of meaningfulness, a feeling that is lacking if one
> is simply carrying out someone else's instructions. Or complying with what is
> commonly expected.
>
> (Bonnett 1994: 110)

Cell 1, in wanting to be and become 'more' through music, developed understanding
of authentic engagement, expressed as ironing out feelings, being open and honest,
learning to trust and so on. They were concerned too to be non-compliant, shapers
of their own learning and wanting to move towards publication of their work
and reaching outward to a particular cultural scene. They brought to their work
knowledge of specific cultural conventions and stylistic boundaries, and as in
Harre's model adopted by Ross et al., moved through a process of appropriation,
transformation and on to publication. It was this issue of working from specific
cultural norms and conventions that we recall in Chapter 4 Martin had politely
raised as I drew him into a culturally amorphous school musical event.

In reviewing the 'Arts and the Adolescent' project (1989) Ross, after conceding
its inability to engage teachers at a theoretical level, noted a potentially more serious
failure of the project. This 'lay in its adopting a neutral view of art, unrelated to
the processes of social production and centred solely on the psyche of the artist'

(Ross 1989: 8). The aesthetic-creative model of music education left a thicker, more developed notion of cultural understanding to chance. Ross acknowledges that it might well be Willis's notion of a 'grounded aesthetic' rooted in the appropriation of material culture that will usher in a vibrant concept of cultural education serving to disrupt and invigorate a dying concept of the arts as aesthetic-creative education and as the source of self-realization. In all this there would be a need to consult pupils. Their own voices would need to be heard.

Chapter 6

Pupil Voice

I actually feel that school has grown to be the way it is now because of being threatened with detentions, being rewarded with commendations. Everyone has split themselves by their own frame of mind into those who say, 'I want to be good, I want to get commendations. I want to get rewards. I want to get stuff'. Other people, they know this is hard and it's so much easier to fall below standard. Then you get a bad reputation and there's no chance to redeem yourself. Teachers work on reputations. It splits people, it splits the school.

(Brian, Year 8)

Ross (1995) had questioned whether the period of curriculum development in music education following the reforms of the 1970s and 1980s had brought about any significant change in pupils' attitudes towards the subject. In Ross's view music teachers were yet to find an appropriate pedagogy. 'Music Education has a sad history' (ibid: 185). Music teachers were not able to create a climate of mutual concern or find expressive problems worth solving. There was an absence of lively discussions about how work might progress and there were few music teachers taking on the role of composer working alongside their pupils. They were teaching music at a distance and upside down.

Swanwick (1999) finds a way forward in proposing that music, informal and inspiring for pupils out of school, might need to develop a curriculum model that is more flexible, where 'musical eventfulness' rather than 'sequenced instruction' become the norm and where diverse resources from outside school continually enrich and informalize the nature of pupil engagement. The music teacher would become a community musician, a generalist able to draw upon and harness diverse resources. There are rich veins of talent beyond the school gate and community musicians and arts organizations increasingly impact on student enthusiasms and latent talent. Pupils would be able to engage with music at their own pace and, in their own way, and be released from pre-specified learning outcomes. But this would require looking at the structure and function of secondary schools themselves.

Jean Ruddock's analysis goes a step further in asking: 'what kind of pupils do we want?'; 'what kind of schools do we want?'

Schools, in their deep structures and patterns of relationship, have changed less in the last 15 years or so than young people have changed. Out of school many are involved in complex relationships and situations, both within peer group and the family and they may be carrying tough responsibilities. Schools, in contrast, often offer less challenge, responsibilities and autonomy than students are accustomed to in their lives outside school.

(Rudduck 2002: 1)

Rudduck argues that there needs to be a better fit between schools and young people, a better understanding of their capabilities, their accomplishments and their capacity to analyse social situations and to intelligently inform teaching and learning. There is a need to see the young as 'being' rather than 'becoming', learning to value the here and now rather than travelling on an imagined escalator from childhood to adulthood, a message intensively reinforced within school. The pupil has a voice and listening to this can transform school for pupil and teacher and enable a review of the traditional structures of schooling. We know very little about what pupils think of their music teachers, of the ways in which they are taught, and the ways in which they think music might be taught in school.

Pupil Voice, Participation and Democracy

The Schools Council 'Arts and the Adolescent' project consulted almost 4,000 secondary pupils aged 11 to 16 about their experience of school by inviting them to construct a hypothetical curriculum. Other researchers of the time explored pupil perspectives by talking to pupils and then re-constructing their realities, analysing the social dynamics of the school and publishing in academic journals, but as Rudduck and McIntyre (2007) point out, there was no notion that the school in which the pupils lived and worked, as a community, would be seeking to elicit their voices in the name of whole school curriculum development and whole school improvement. It was during the 1990s that this became a reality. Rudduck puts forward four arguments in support of pupil voice:

Argument 1: We need a better fit between young people's capabilities and their standing and responsibility in school: talking to pupils can help us bridge the gap.

Argument 2: The Children's Rights movement is behind it and 'everybody's doing it!'

Argument 3: School improvement gains from pupil participation.

Argument 4: The qualities that we look for in young people are those that participation and consultation can help develop.

(Rudduck 2004a)

Here there is movement beyond simply eliciting the perspective of the pupil. Now there is an open conversation that would support change, improvement and an ongoing fuller participation in the life of the school. There is the potential to connect with the quality of day-to-day classroom encounters between pupil and teacher, their ways of relating, the manner of their dialogue, creative intimacies and the symmetry-asymmetry of their relationships. It asked questions about the social climate of the school and of each classroom. The movement sought to harness pupil insights into the social reality of school life and classroom experience and to find ways in which the school might be more responsive to pupils' social maturity and capabilities. There was synergy here with thinking about Citizenship Education, and the belief that pupils would develop an 'active disposition towards democracy' (Crick 1999, 2002). The school, and the classroom, could become places of lively conversation, healthy dispute and the creation of new values. If this had been the ambition of arts educators of the 1970s following the trail of Herbert Read's democratic education, now it was the whole school that could model and work out such ideals.

In the Rudduck and Fielding paper 'Student voice and the perils of popularity' (2006), antecedents of the idea of consultation, participation and democracy are highlighted. At Bedales, an independent boarding school, there was a parliament and student involvement in the monitoring of their own progress, as well as a degree of freedom in exercising choice in learning activities. And there is Harold Dent's new secondary school in the late 1920s where pupils could 'exercise choice in a framework of responsibility and trust', along with Bloom's post-war ideal of replacing 'fear of authority ... fear of failure ... and the fear of punishment' (Rudduck and Fielding 2006: 222). The pupil voice movement of the 1990s saw a way of countering the demoralization of a centrally imposed curriculum, which caused a distrustful culture of accountability and uninspired children. If these were 'freedom's children' then they were the most obvious source for creating new values and greater democracy.

What kinds of needs were expressed by those consulted about their experience of school? Key themes to emerge from the Economic and Social Research Council Network Project (ESRC 2003), involving 300 teachers working on a range of pupil-consultation projects, were 'security', 'respect and fairness', 'challenge and support' and most of all, 'responsibility and autonomy'. What emerged from interviews with pupils was a desire to have opportunity to make decisions about their learning and to have the scope for active, problem-solving work on real issues. Beyond this, pupils wanted to be trusted to help others with their learning and to have control over their own progress in learning. It was a call for greater participation.

Autonomy

It is not difficult to link the idea of autonomy to the discourse of child-centred progressive thinking of earlier times and with the Enlightenment ideals of self-government, freedom and self-realization. The pupil voice movement again raised questions concerning the ways in which children and childhood were thought about, and within the sociology of childhood in the 1990s efforts were made to convince policy makers to take childhood seriously. Here childhood was viewed not as a biological reality but as a social construct. While schools were slow to change, children were not. Children need not be thought of as having inferior status to adults, as being restricted to subordinate and restricted roles, dependent or as a minority group (Wyness 2000). They could be always seen differently and recognized as competent actors, willing and reliable contributors within their social contexts of home and school. In the case of music, we saw earlier the capacity of *Cell 1* to act on the world and research was now revealing the extent and levels of musical engagement of pupils out of school (North et al. 2000, Lamont et al. 2003). Witkin's deeply held conviction that in music and the arts the adolescent could enjoy the same state of being in school as out of school, and Willis's reminder that the young are already 'culturally energized' were again matters of great and urgent interest. Schools and their music had changed little in this respect. The crisis of confidence within music education was about inclusion and how it was that so few pupils in the middle and upper years of secondary school were able to create and maintain a positive school music identity.

In order to make sense of issues arising from the quest to make music in school meaningful for all pupils, and to penetrate the mounting rhetoric of despair, I set out to understand the case of one class and their music teacher in one secondary school. I wanted to investigate the pupils' and their teacher's attitudes, motivations, ways of knowing and perceptions of the learning and teaching of music – a search for the significance, for them, of their weekly encounter with music as a way of life. Would the experience cohere with the burgeoning musical identities of the pupils and the more established musical identity of the teacher? Would it be a positive experience? If it was, why was this? To understand the significance of the weekly music lesson, it would be important to understand something of the teacher's and the group's experience of school in general as well as their experience of music out of school. My task would be to construct a version of the social reality of a group of 24 children and their teacher. This would require a sustained enquiry. What did I find?

Perceptions of Schooling

School for this Year 8 class was proving to be an uneven and sometimes stressful experience. Many struggled to make sense of much of their week. Levels of engagement were variable and there was little experienced that was truly memorable. What was it all for? Were they learning to tally because they were going to be bank clerks? Were they trying to get good at science because they were going to be chemists? They were very unclear about the purpose of their education. They were easily frustrated in their quest to learn by the teachers who didn't make connections with them, teachers who as Abi put it, 'don't understand things'.

Their model of a good teacher is demanding. The good teacher not only presents the subject matter well, but also understands what meaning it might have for the pupils. Learning, they maintained, needed to be social, talkative, supported and celebratory. They wanted learning to be active and physical so that they could show who they were, how they felt and what they knew rather than simply a facsimile of their teacher and her curriculum. They wanted to work at a pace they felt comfortable with, becoming engaged in their own way and deciding for themselves that something was worth doing, making decisions, being creative and knowing more about themselves. They wanted to place the imprint of their personality upon the curriculum. They were capable of spending sustained periods of time in the pursuit of learning out of school: their majorettes, their dancing, their singing and listening, their cooking, their rearing of guinea pigs, candle making, drum practice in the garage, football practice, model making, the creation of volcanic timelines and the taking of things to pieces to see how they work. They become engaged in learning in school when experience is heavy with value, and this means when it engages with their life of feeling, when it touches core concerns so that knowing and understanding are personalized: learning empathy for children without homes, the wonder of human reproduction, dancing to their Caribbean music, the creation of mythological creatures in art, the Human Rights poem in humanities and the telling of stories about other people in history. In some subjects and with some teachers these desired ways of being are peripheral, palliatives or absent, while in others they are recurrent and central.

Perceptions of Musical Schooling

On Friday at 11:15 am each week the class's storm-tossed ship finds a safe harbour. They will be learning more about music and more about how to do it. Their teacher is one who 'understands things', 'a Peter Pan with intelligence'. Their one-hour lesson begins and ends with music. They will be calm at the beginning of the lesson and attend to music. They will attend to their music teacher and to each other, showing how music is to be created, and before the end of the lesson they will be performing something they have created themselves that has never before existed and they will be valuing each other's endeavours. They will know what it is to improvise and compose music, to become informed musical critics and to reflect upon their musical tastes and preferences. Their teacher will connect with them and touch their core concerns and convince them that whatever they are asked to do can be done.

> Yes, you can do it, you really can. You will surprise yourself. Go on Michael, you can do it, go on. Just have a go and use your ears.

There will be new and interesting things to learn, stories to enchant as well as much music to order consciousness and relieve the tension between the here and now and the future. They will be given creative spaces, opportunities to negotiate and re-negotiate meanings, so that the intentional and incidental knowledge of schooling may invite in and interact with the intentional and incidental knowledge of non-schooling and there will be surprises, discoveries and disappointments. Girls will work with boys they don't like and cope with the expressions of male dominance, and the boys will be learning something of this exercise of power too. The class will experience a dialogical style of teaching and learning where their world views exert influence on proceedings and they will go to lunch content in the knowledge that learning can have meaning.

The music teacher muses on the possibility of having the class for four lessons a week as they do in humanities: 'Just think what could be done', and he has a wish list of resources that would make such an enterprise meaningful: a library of drums and the potential for DJ-ing come to mind. Many of the class's musical aspirations can't easily be satisfied by the music teacher and the school. The resource implications are formidable and the school is not a 'leading school' within the city. It is a Specialist Sports School and not a Specialist Arts School and this affects funding. However, a goodly proportion of the class will major in music beyond the compulsory music curriculum as part of an expressive arts programme. The music teacher's vision is of his pupils being makers of culture and in this to rub up against and resist his own, to sort and sift values for themselves, to share in the joys and sorrows of his musical life as he presents a range of possible ways in which they can be musical and become musicians. He works hard to acknowledge and celebrate what it is that the pupils bring with them to the classroom, their musical worlds, their functional and dysfunctional school week, their desire to be known and to know music, to know each other better and to make a classroom musical culture that can be adapted and harmonize with their musical learning beyond the school gates. From the class we select four pupils and move into an action research mode. We want to test out the idea of pupil participation.

What Us?

Morgan, Brian, Rachel and Tyson are 12 going on 13, well established in Year 8 and in the same class for most things. Despite the school's boy next to girl seating policy, Morgan and Rachel sometimes manage to sit next to each other, Brian and Tyson never, and as Brian says, 'it doesn't take much to set us off'. For all four, along with the rest of their class, the novelty of the new school in Year 7 has worn off and Year 8 has become the much documented limbo and something of a mystery (see Rudduck 2004b). Like the rest of their class their minds are concentrated on their school's finely tuned system of rewards and punishments and this is at the forefront of their concerns about school and the source of what appear to be daily injustices. They know that they should know that in their school 'it is cool to achieve'. And they know about 'the right to teach – the right to learn', for this moral principle is to be read at the front of every classroom. As I came to share in their understandings I realized that making connections with moral principles was not an easy task. Their moral way was rather an uncomplicated search for goodness and mutuality as found in relationships with each other, and, critically, their teachers.

Their tutor group, which forms the basis for most of their teaching groups, is a lively bunch. The start of each day is tutorial time, a buzz of social clatter making a transitional space between home and school. There are groups of twos and threes as well as larger clusters distinguishable by gender, class and commitment to schooling. There is the cross-chat about last evening's missed call on the mobile phone, the harsh bonding jibes between boys, the comments that hurt made to the outsiders Tania and Shane and the gently exercised pastoral care of their tutor.

Their tutor, a teacher of five years' standing, speaks of the group as having been a handful before Christmas, disorientated and losing the plot, their science teacher of needing to impose a tough regime of drills and a 'persistent and insistent' approach, and their art teacher of seeing the class as 'an interesting bunch. I never know how they are going to be. You have some sessions with them when you think, "shall I give up teaching? Am I professionally incompetent?"'

Making Sense

Art, along with drama, music and PE feature strongly in their preferred list of school subjects. They like doing things. They like the process of making and celebrating what they have made, they like to make connections, see how things fit together. In these respects it is expressive arts subjects that most obviously enable the class to gather meaning and purpose and build confidence. Expressive arts teachers are encouraging, thinks Brian, and furthermore proposes that they have to be, for how else would pupils risk expressing themselves, committing their ideas and feelings to public scrutiny.

Their school teaches students to be aware of and make use of their many intelligences, and most hold on to the discovery that they are 'body smart'. But for Brian this is rather more than the usual cognitive construct. Brian tells of a more complex and richer notion with the body providing a source of agency and identity:

> Your body can show how you are thinking, what you are thinking, the way you are quite basically, the person you are. Your personality, who you are. If you can. Things like music can help express that. It's just a way of getting it out of your body. Most lessons are sit. You're just sitting down answering questions out of a text book. And really kids of our age prefer to be doing something else. Practising something on the keyboard like we do in music or something different like in drama. Acting out. I suppose art's different even though it's still on paper, because it's still another expression. I suppose that's why they are called expressive arts. We had a brilliant lesson on Wednesday in art. We are all doing a God-like creature that you'd find in a jungle. I did a tiger, orange and

black lines. So it looked like a tiger with red eyes and everything. It was really good. I thought so.

Opportunities to be like this are far from the general pattern of experience and in stark contrast to the lessons that are a matter of exposition and practice, where students feel insufficient support and where there is little opportunity to bring something of themselves to the learning. Above all else they want teachers to 'make connections with them', to have 'teachers who understand things', for this is how it was in primary school. Tyson recalls the secure world of the primary school and contrasts it to the impersonal world of secondary school and his search for trusting relationships.

> Primary teachers were interested in you, knew which television programmes you watched, which football team you supported. You could have a joke with them. I liked the chat at the end of the day making everything feel all right. There are too many systems and procedures in secondary school. We've been knuckled down and it still doesn't change a lot of people. Some teachers when we don't understand them blame it on you. We learn when we can talk about it, discuss it. Life skills is good, the teacher talks with you as if you were mature and you feel OK. Everybody loved their primary teacher. Teachers in secondary school need to trust us more.

For Tyson, as for many of his class, secondary school has been difficult to make sense of and the transition from primary to secondary school has proved difficult. In Tyson's year group of 250 pupils the Head of Year identifies 25 per cent who have not settled well and who have become to some extent or other problematic, disaffected or disengaged, 25 per cent who are not working with the school's systems that are intended to promote effective teaching and learning. Tyson receives his fair share of negative points, occasional detention as well as commendations. Tyson's form tutor views him as being always pleasant and polite, very sociable and liked and has been elected as tutor representative on the Year 8 student council. However, his tutor notes that he is slow to take responsibility for his own behaviour. Other teachers tell more:

> ... amiable and good on the surface, but very disruptive ... has difficulty in accepting authority ... others do look up to him, some through fear rather than respect ... loses concentration easily and gives up if he feels the work is difficult ... enjoys being at the centre and the one to whom others defer ... probably the strongest personality in the group, he is an intelligent boy.

The Head of Year has a 'top twenty' list of troublesome students, cases that the system regularly refers to him. Of Tyson, Rachel, Morgan and Brian, it is Brian who has hit the top twenty in Year 8 and his teachers view him as problematic.

... a boy whose tactics are very covert and one who is adept at putting the responsibility on to someone else ... one who can be malicious with words and who enjoys winding people up ... easily distracts others, stirring them to misdeeds and who does not respect the right to teach and learn ... Brian is always not on task.

But, as we saw at the head of the chapter, Brian is thoughtful about how school is working for him and his contemporaries and tells of a school that is two schools, a school heavily dependent upon the use of sticks and carrots, a school where for some you get caught in between, a school that is difficult to access.

Unschooled Music

Morgan, Rachel, Tyson and Brian are stilled by their music lesson, and value being taught by a teacher who doesn't get stressed. They go to lunch at ease with themselves and with their school, or perhaps it is just Friday. None of the four has had formal musical instruction in or out of school but music is playing a significant part in their lives. Their out of school music curriculum involves listen-move-sing, with a good balance between learning that is both planned for and casual. Most obviously this out of school curriculum is called upon immediately after school and at home, as they find another space in which to make the necessary adjustment between school and home life. Rachel, like Morgan, dances for as much as two hours with the help of a karaoke machine, while Brian and Tyson move between their Justin Timberlake body waves, BMX biking and football. Brian has a guitar and is beginning to pick out rhythmic riffs as he listens to his mini-disc, something he has learnt to do in his school music lessons, and Tyson has recently retrieved his keyboard from the loft. For all four, Justin Timberlake is their man and *Justified* their album.

All this is a private engagement with music, providing the necessary antidote to the experience of school with its fraught relationships, unsatisfying promiscuities and the treadmill of anxiety and boredom. Morgan alone of the four is learning music in a public space beyond school. For two and a half hours each Friday evening it is Morgan's time to be a majorette. This involves missing the television soap EastEnders and there is more than a hint that the time is coming to move on from majoretting, notwithstanding all the badges and medals which have been gained, but preparation is in hand for a national competition and that presents a reason for carrying on.

My observation of Tyson's impromptu body waves as he enters his music classroom to the music of Justin Timberlake provided a cue to begin the process of selection and form the group who would be offered the challenge of taking on curriculum leadership through the use of their unschooled musical talents. The music teacher agreed that Tyson would be a good choice and someone in the class who responds to careful nurture. Brian seemed to be a good choice too as someone who had already shown insightfulness into his difficulties with classroom learning and who, like Tyson, is a body waving skateboarder. I further proposed Morgan, knowing of her majoretting skill and detachment from schooling. The music teacher added Rachel as a student with talent in dance and whose verbal incapacity results in limited success in some curriculum areas and who appeared to be low in confidence.

We were now ready to invite Brian, Tyson, Rachel and Morgan to design a teaching episode for another class in their school, making use of their talents developed through their out of school engagement with music. Their desire to be valued for who they are and for what they have to offer, being treated as responsible and with leadership potential, would now be tested. What impact would this have on the students? What impact would it have on the students they were to teach and what might be learnt about the students' own theories of teaching and learning? The students were about to be asked to undertake a challenge that they least expected from their school.

Becoming Teachers

The students were surprised by the invitation to become teachers. There was initial diffidence and while Morgan and Rachel were quick to acknowledge their majoretting and dancing prowess, Tyson and Brian were less sure about their talents as concern about how they wished to present themselves came to the fore. My suggestion that Tyson and Brian were skilled body wavers was deflected into their perceived potential as guitarists, keyboardists and drummers. However, they were now gaining in commitment to the project and agreed to meet weekly to plan what they would teach and how they might teach it to a class in Year 7. Meetings were convened and their music teacher maintained a log.

At the first meeting the leaders reviewed their talents with support from their music teacher and myself. We agreed that:

> Tyson learns things quickly on the keyboard and this week had learnt 'Mission Impossible' managing to teach another member of his class in his music lesson. He likes to play the drums too but above all else is a whiz with the Michael Jackson shuffle. Rachel dances a lot at home, Morgan is brilliant at baton twirling and dancing and Brian is a dab hand at guitar and of course, a good dancer too.

The group became convinced that they could work on a routine that involved twirling, a dance, the guitar and keyboard. The boys' proclivity to body wave and shuffle remained on hold.

An early decision was to use the Justin Timberlake song 'Like I love you'. The music, a fusion of soul and punk, advertised as deferring to the worlds of Stevie Wonder and Michael Jackson and with distinctive riffs and pervasive rhythms, was considered ideal. It was easy to dance and move to with a chorus that proclaimed 'if you let go, the music should groove your bones' and requested the listener to 'sing this song with me'.

The leaders viewed Justin Timberlake as the new Michael Jackson and his music would be familiar to all those taught. Now the four were provided with a space and tape recorder and asked to document progress through an audio diary. If the leaders felt they had come up with something significant they would stop working and make an audio note. Enthusiasm was growing as they pointed out that one lesson would be insufficient. A sequence of three lessons would be needed. An intuitive grasp of structure and wholeness of experience was quick to emerge. Morgan led the case for beginning with demonstration, with a modelling of the skills to be learned, with the presentation of a clear vision of what might be achieved. This proposal met with a counter proposal from Tyson making the case for holding back the picture.

> We will need to show them first and then teach them new skills ... no, we should teach them new skills first and then show them our skills, we should teach them our skills first and then get them to show us ... we can do our routine at the end in the third lesson ... they do that in PE ... but if we show them first they will think wow! and want to do it ... no, they don't do that in PE. We need to think how our favourite teachers teach and maybe copy some ideas ... we can play calming music, something they know and like ... we can give commendations ... Year 7s like commendations ... we can give certificates to everybody just for taking part ... we should not just give them to the best ... we need to ask if they already know what they are learning.

This kind of discussion came to represent a subtle analysis and sometimes explicit enquiry into the methods and strategies adopted by their best teachers that made sense for them as learners and what it was that alienated them as learners. The group decided on an opening performance to inspire, although they realized that this would be a considerable challenge and serious risk. Brian and Tyson had by now resolved to share their body waving talents.

The leaders were engaged in a creative process and wanted to make something special. They had established a 'holding form' and now the messy, hard graft of moving from the vision to actualities had begun.

As planning proceeded so we realized the strong empathetic grasp they had of their Year 7 learners' needs and experience, and their music teacher noted:

> This is very exciting. How are the young culturally energized in ways which we can re-inforce? These young teachers do not seem to have a problem with thinking about the culture of the children that they are going to teach. Many teachers do!

It was time to draw from the student-teachers their purpose. They provided not an instructional objective but a procedural one linked to pedagogy.

> Our objective is to get the whole class to perform in small groups our special out of school skills and abilities and to put these altogether in a final performance. We want them to find new ways of responding to music.

The leaders became ever clearer that their opening performance would need to inspire, that there should be scope for choice of activity and that each of the leaders would work with a group of about eight students before drawing the class together. Uppermost in their minds was the need to engage their charges from the outset, to present a picture that would allow learners to see vividly what it was that was to be emulated and learnt. They were determined that all learners would succeed and that the sequence of lessons would end in celebration. This would take the form of final performances by each group showing what had been learnt in a climate of mutual respect.

A frequent item of discussion centred on ways in which to reward the students' achievements and it was agreed that all would receive a participatory certificate, while there would be a learners' consensus through which the best group would receive particular acclaim. From the leaders' perspective three criteria for success would be addressed. There would be the valuing of positive attitude, commitment and a willingness to help others. There would be the recognition of the most accomplished performance as well as the group who exuded most spirit.

Meetings continued with reasonable regularity but there were to be continuous disruptions to the process and it proved difficult to find times when all four were present. One week Rachel was not available as she had been excluded from lessons for fighting. Rachel's absence promoted Morgan's disengagement and then her majoretting equipment was left at home. Then there was Brian's holiday in Lanzarote, Morgan's absence during the last week of term and Brian excluded from lessons for accumulating ten negative points and taken out of rehearsal by a senior member of staff. On this occasion Brian's behaviour had been consistently bad in every subject except music. And then there was Tyson's internal exclusion when he declared on his mid-year report that 'teachers in this school don't know how to teach'. At times sustaining the project was difficult. The commitment of their music teacher and support from the headteacher played a crucial part.

As the planning progressed, so there were times of serious self-doubt amongst the four, concerns about street-credibility and the obvious fear of failure. Tyson's lapses in confidence were most noticeable and here Brian took on the role of mentor to Tyson and also exercised a subtle leadership role within the group. Brian reassured Tyson that he would support him and make sure he succeeded. Their music teacher noted that:

> Brian is working as a skilful teacher. He is reassuring and initiating a joint professional journey where there is no superior-inferior relationship. He is very encouraging, supportive to his friend. Here is a student who can be a 'tricky customer' in certain lessons working in a very sensitive way with another 'tricky customer'. It is good to have Brian on board. He is particularly perceptive,

artistic. Would Brian's skill come more to the fore if the school's arts culture was a true microcosm of the student's home or street culture?

As time for action approached so the student-teachers suggested that it would be helpful if they could observe the Year 7 class they were going to work with. This was to be a salutary experience as their reflections show.

> They were a naughty class, only a handful looked as if they were listening, might be difficult to teach them … Linda is naughty … what if we played the music when they came into the classroom … what if we rewarded them with commendations … I think they would listen once we started teaching them because it was interesting … I think that I would 'bop' them if they played up.

Now the leaders saw the challenge as one of turning the class around. They knew that they would need to engage the class throughout and develop positive attitudes. The experience had to be a good one. The event had to be memorable. There was no room for failure.

The Teaching and the Learning

The venue chosen was a soft-lighted dance studio, a warm space inviting performance intimacy. The Year 7 class entered expectantly and sat in two pre-prepared rows and without a word the jagged yet softly arresting riff from Justin Timberlake's 'Like I love you' brought forth the dance and majoretting of Rachel and Morgan before Brian and Tyson presented a dialogue of mime and movement. Their audience was intrigued, remained attentive throughout and at the end applauded. A gauche explanation followed from Tyson with questions that were as wonderfully rhetorical as those of any beginning teacher. Each leader then worked with a group of eight students modelling their skills to the track 'Cry me a river'. There followed coaching and a process of continual nurture. Each group showed what they had done, a move that the leaders believed would ensure consolidation of learning, in the salutary and statutory plenary. The class left for their next lesson. The leaders were elated.

> It makes you think on your feet. I like my group. They were really good … They were doing their own thing … Linda was on task! … We played the music and it calmed them down right away … It makes you appreciate what a teacher has to do. Teachers need lesson plans … Everybody seemed to have enjoyed it. It's not a big thing anymore.

The second lesson a week later saw the leaders encouraging students to develop their own ideas, transforming the material offered in the previous session. As before, a plenary to consolidate progress brought the session to an end:

> They needed my input at certain times … They were learning how to respond to the changes in the music … The students followed instructions easily … It was easy to use their ideas.

The final session allowed learners to polish what they had produced in preparation for the final performance. Final performance time arrived and took the form of an act of celebration incorporating the much considered certification of achievement for all students and a special award for the most successful group decided upon by the whole class. Tyson concluded the event with a short thank you speech.

> Thanks very much for taking part in this project and helping us to help you. You've been really good in behaviour and practicals and every one of you were good. I hope you enjoyed it as much as I did.

From the questionnaire given to all members of the class taught, 97 per cent thought the standard of teaching in the three lessons was 'good' or 'very good' and 90 per cent that the teaching had helped them to be 'creative' or 'very creative'. These were some of the Year 7s comments explaining how:

> Morgan was very positive and helpful … she showed me clearly what to do … taught me how to baton twirl … she showed me first and then I go off and do it by myself and if I got it wrong Morgan would help me.

> Rachel helped me by showing me how to do the dance moves easily, she repeated the moves to make it easier … Rachel got to know me and was very pleasant about explaining the task… she showed me clearly what I had to do … she supported us … she encouraged us and joined in with us.

> Tyson showed us what to do and how to do it … he had confidence in us … he said, 'You can do it'.

> Brian was understanding and he helped us all the time even if we couldn't do it and he always said we were the best … he gave us confidence … he asked us what we wanted to do.

In open forum discussion with the whole class there was appreciation of the way their ideas had been used and students repeatedly spoke of how their learning had been supported and how their student-teachers had encouraged them. If they didn't get it right they were helped to get it right. It was fun and interesting and by being 'dancical' they had come to know the music really well. They had learnt to listen carefully. The music had been an inspiring choice.

> Listening to people like Justin Timberlake and Eminem means you can feel like them and feeling like somebody else feels helps a lot, especially if things have

happened in their life that are happening to you. It's good to feel like Justin Timberlake. We need models and heroes.

There was appreciation of the way the student-teachers had communicated – *few words, our words, movements.* All this was contrasted to experience in many of their school lessons. There was a strongly held view that their teachers talk at them too much – *talk to themselves really* and don't provide enough time to do the work. A member of the class spoke of the routine of being asked for ideas only for them to discover that the teacher had the best idea. And here the students returned to the expressive arts curriculum that they experienced in school.

> In expressive arts you can express your personality … you can be really creative without anybody telling you it's wrong … in art they don't tell you how to move your hand … you can tell people a message through your drawing and music … in expressive arts you can show your talent … expressive arts is about working together, it teaches you to work as a team … if there is somebody who can't do it we help them.

For one student the whole experience was like a game of Jenga. Jenga was a game well known to all the students. The game involves either building or dismantling a tower made of wooden blocks. The task is to avoid making the tower fall. The object is to be the last player to stack or dismantle a block without knocking the tower over. Interestingly, the students viewed the game as collaborative. Matt explained:

> They gave us a piece of the puzzle, a starting point and we built on it … in Jenga you have to work together … you don't want to let anybody else down … you have to concentrate to do what you need to do … you have to agree on the moves. If somebody is doing it wrong you have to help them out, not shout at them. You have to support each other – it's no good just having your own idea.

In the Year 7 Focus Group four students talked more about how they had been helped to feel *creative* and to *achieve* and to *feel good*. They liked the way the student-teachers expected them to bring in their own ideas:

> I think that when you are dancing you are not like a robot, you can put your own personality into it. You put your own facial expressions and gestures into it. It's not something you have to do like a robot. If you make something up you can show how you feel. It is not something that you have to do. You like doing it. Being a robot means doing it automatically and you don't enjoy it. In some lessons you just have to copy out of books.
>
> (Matthew)

For Emily, while the experience had been characteristic of Jenga, the making of a jigsaw came to mind. She was especially impressed by the group's presentation at the outset. This had been inspiring and was like seeing the whole jigsaw, the jigsaw that they were going to make together.

> The four leaders became the corners of the puzzle and we all filled it in so that by the third lesson it was ready to be seen. It was a pretty picture.
>
> (Emily)

Doing Something Useful

The project had taken up much of the second half of Year 8 and came to culmination in the final weeks of the summer term. This meant that the school year had ended positively for Morgan, Tyson, Rachel and Brian. As the project had developed so Tyson volunteered to assist with the school production of *Bugsy Malone* and in the event played the part of a boxer. His short, carefully crafted mime in the ring was impressive. In his end of year assembly he gained three awards and was taken out for a meal that evening by his parents. In this event he may have eaten too much for he was not feeling too well for the next morning's performance of *Bugsy Malone* extracts in assembly. Morgan is still talking about giving up majorettes and Rachel has not been in any more fights. Brian's form tutor is speaking positively of Brian's attitude. His head is high and he is giving winks, nods and smiles. It was Brian who had most to say about the experience of curriculum leadership:

> I thought it would be tougher than it was. I thought it would be a bit more of a struggle. I thought that they might not co-operate as much as they did, that they wouldn't be enjoying it so much. I thought that they might not be bothering to do it. 'Let's not do it, let's be stupid.' They helped me in a way as well as me helping them.

> All the times we had off from lessons practising we were doing something useful. If we had been in lessons, we would probably just've been messing around. Just not doing anything at all, not learning anything new, not using ourselves for anything useful, decent. But then we got the time off to practise getting better at something, the opportunity to do something better and we did achieve something. Without the lesson plans we would have been stuck, but then again you can still improvise on bits but you still need a basic structure for the lesson.

> We want to keep involved in all this. We don't want to let it go. We want to see how far it could go. I feel more positive about school in so far as you can understand the teachers. We taught three times in two weeks not five times a day, five days a week. That must be tough, harder than we appreciate. You can understand why they get frustrated so easily, which makes you better towards

them. My attitude in class has definitely improved. We learnt how it feels if nobody is going to co-operate. Managing a class must be a learnt discipline, how to make them quiet without going over the top. I think I am a much better judge of what good teaching is now. Good teachers make sure their students are happy, at ease with what they are doing. They let their students have ideas. They are fair. They don't work on reputations. It's a shame to be back on full timetable.

I definitely feel more confident towards their class, but I am not sure about more generally. I feel more confident about standing up in front of people as a group. You are not going to get up and dance in maths. I really don't think there is any way maths lessons can be made interesting. I feel more adult and would like to have more responsibility.

Intuitive Practitioners

As Morgan, Brian, Tyson and Rachel moved into Year 9 so we presented three further opportunities to sustain and develop their identities as student-teachers and leaders of others. They were challenged to become teachers of teachers as they taught their special skills to a group of 24 trainee music teachers, then to a Year 7 class in another secondary school and finally to a Year 6 and Year 1–2 class in a primary school. Nerves returned about their opening presentation in teaching the teachers; they decided not to risk their opening performance, something they were to regret as they later reflected just how supportive, encouraging and receptive the teacher-trainees had been.

> They weren't over opinionated and that was great. They gave us thoughts and said what they wanted and that was what we needed. We only planned the introduction and took it from there. We just improvised. They asked us if their ideas were OK. They were catching on so quickly. They were going with the flow, merging ideas. Some acted like big kids, some like grown ups – already teachers. Hannah was cool. She loved it. We lost all sense of time, it could have gone on for ever. It was like nothing else mattered. Like when I go out and play football and then I suddenly say, 'Oh, no, what's the time?' and I'm late for tea. In the car on the way back we felt so good, just saying how brilliant it had been.

For their part those taught identified eight significant attributes of Tyson, Morgan, Rachel and Brian's teaching:

1. Confident expression of authority
2. Relating and empathizing
3. Quality of instruction
4. Level of challenge

5. Chunking of material
6. Degree of support and encouragement
7. Creating a teaching and learning dialogue
8. Capacity to share a love of their knowledge

By midway through Year 9 the student-teachers were teaching in a primary school and their ability to think on their feet was seriously tested in taking on the challenge of teaching five- and six-year-olds. The class teacher confirmed the student-teachers' capacity to inform the professional knowledge of teachers and their potential to contribute to the improvement of schooling.

'They Haven't Noticed I'm Different'

But, as Brian foresaw, as they demonstrated their capacity to take on responsibility, grow skilfully as teachers, declare a deepening empathy with their own teachers and with those they taught, reputations were hard to change. Where they were making an effort to engage and learn in subjects and with teachers that had not always made it easy for them to do this, their past reputations held firm among teachers. Mid-year reports were discouraging as the students' eyes ran to effort and behaviour grades as the key indicators of approval, progress and hope. The student-teachers were reminded once more of their deficits. Tyson's targets reiterated the need to display a more positive attitude, to ensure total concentration, to complete homework and to develop a work ethic. Brian was called upon to change his attitude, to concentrate 100 per cent and ignore distractions and to realize that his behaviour was selfish. Morgan needed to find greater focus too and to discover self-motivation so that tasks could be completed. The perennial call for Rachel to become more actively involved and more assertive in lessons featured less than before.

However, their Head of Year was able to report a dramatic change in Brian, now well out of the 'top twenty', and viewed Tyson as being much happier with himself. Rachel's music teacher noted her growth in confidence with her speech and in this respect she was outstripping her twin sister. Morgan seemed much the same and was soldiering on with majorettes despite finding her instructor ever more authoritarian as her troop's competition success faded.

For both Morgan and Rachel options for the next stage of their schooling provided the opportunity to opt for Health and Social Care and they were enthused about this. Morgan's mother had suggested a career as a child psychiatrist or a lawyer specializing in child abuse. Tyson and Brian thought these kinds of ambition unrealistic as their minds became set on emigration to Canada and a world of professional ice hockey. Brian remained philosophical about school and life.

> Year 7 and 8 just fly by. Year 7 feels like another school. I'm starting to understand things much better this year. People, cultures, things that happened

in history and why they happened. Words mean something. In Year 7 you're too concerned to get friends. Now school is a great place to be, like one big social network. I can't wait for lunchtimes. It's bad to grow up with criticism, some do, but some grow up with encouragement. The way it is can affect your whole life. Being criticized all the time makes you look stupid. Being encouraged all the time makes you feel great.

Their music teacher has learnt to give the students responsibilities in class, in nominating them as 'lead learners' and values having come to know them as responsible young adults. In interview he reflects too on the structures of schooling that make change problematic and that prevent the students' voices from being heard.

> I see them as more confident, more strident, they seem to understand a lot more. They seem empowered, almost with another knowledge. I've spoken to them so many times about different things and, these days, it is an interaction rather than an adult speaking to a young person who responds when spoken to. They say that they understand teachers a lot more. And whether they understand me a bit more, I don't know, but this understanding seems to have given them the power to talk to me on an even footing. I have begun to understand what they can and cannot do, well, there is no 'cannot' at the moment. This project has helped me to understand that there is a lot more to these pupils, in fact to all young people. It has affected the way I teach, the way I plan my lessons. I use the idea of 'lead learners' a lot. I have pretty much done that before by strategically choosing more able students, or even less able students to model or scaffold an idea or activity. Now I think more consciously about the disaffected students when choosing models. I ask the students how they want to learn. 'What is the problem with the way we have done that? Shall we try it your way? What is your way?' They will always tell me. This boldly challenges a philosophy that many of my colleagues expound and that is that we have to spoon feed the students. 'We have to lead them by the nose even in Year 10 and 11.' This idea irritates me so much. No wonder they misbehave! Our student researchers challenge this directly. They have their self-respect and knowledge to share with each other and us, with some help of course.

> I tended to think that I am the artist, the resource, I am the live music maker. Now, however, I am seeing the whole class as the resource. Each class is a dynamic resource. I look for this every hour that I teach. I am now thinking about ways forward for schools. I would love to change the culture of teachers. I would love to be part of something that changes teachers' perceptions of how to teach and how to learn, and above all, how they might regard their students. It would be good to see a culture change in the school.

One of my appraisal targets is to disseminate what is being learnt from this project. I have presented our findings to various teams and individuals. While the management are interested, this is where it stops. I don't think my colleagues are willing to go the whole way and make radical changes. They acknowledge there is a problem. The management put new systems in place, they rejuvenate old ones but there is nothing wrong with the systems that we already have. It is our perception of the students, that's the culture we have got to change. It might take a long time to address.

The answer to school improvement is in the students and their perception of what we are trying to do with them and how we give them responsibility. They want responsibility and autonomy. Colleagues acknowledge that they have got all this responsibility in primary school and then they come here and it's just suddenly gone and they're lost in a *melee* of bodies and movement around a massive building. When I made my presentation to the senior management team I know that I provoked a great deal of thought. Whether we ever have change here I do not know.

It is about the way the school views the staff and students. We have a kind of collegiate system here, organizations within organizations. Power is ceded to those like me who lead an organization, the expressive arts faculty. Often I will step to the fore and lead the school in productions and concerts. However, at the end of the day we have an authoritarian and bureaucratic structure in which everybody has their place. The students, I fear, come very low in the line of authority. Is it all about systems that keep people in place? Perhaps 'keep in place' isn't the right term.

Preserving the Expressive

The case of a successful music department as found at Tyson's school, where all pupils followed a course in the arts from 11 to 16 and with a third engaged in music between the ages of 14 and 16, was not typical. Despite 25 years of reforming and adapting the curriculum in order to enable all pupils to show what they know, understand and can do and despite repeated calls to recognize a wider range of pupil achievements, little had changed for a significant number of pupils. What counted as success continued to deny the broad range of personal attributes and capabilities. The expression, for example, of what one teacher of Tyson et al. described as 'pupils' creative side' had little currency on the ladder of success. In the climate of the first years of the new century, where narrowly defined goals drove both teachers and pupils, the challenge was great. Official doctrine set in place with the establishment of a National Curriculum had silenced a basic need for self-expression and creativity. The subjective lives of young people, their search for greater knowledge of themselves, for discovery of who they are, what they could do, who they might become, their search for self-esteem and personal meaning have been overrun by a curriculum focused on a form of knowledge detached from the knower.

The result of a target-orientated model of education leads too often to what Seymore B. Sarson calls 'passionless conformity' (Sarson 1990: 82). The disjunction observed by the music teacher between his school's rhetoric of pupil participation and the reality of the pupils' subjugation in this case is stark. Pupils in the school understood well the ways in which their expressive arts curriculum was different. They saw its potential for drawing in more of themselves than was frequently the case elsewhere.

Ross (1978), in exploring further Witkin's distinction between 'object-knowing' and 'subject-knowing' in championing a creative self-expression position for the arts, writes:

> Action that seeks to put as much distance between the feeler and his feelings as quickly as possible – actions that seek release from feeling through the cancellation of feeling – are to be sharply distinguished from self-expressive responses that are genuinely creative.
>
> (Ross 1978: 42)

And this makes sense too in terms of Bonnet's challenging notion of 'authentic self-expression'. In music lessons and in the other arts the pupils in this school knew well that you could choose to 'hide' or be real, truthful, authentic in expressive arts lessons. This was much less a problem in the rest of the curriculum where frequently there was no expectation that the work would engage subjectivities, personal concerns and interests. It felt good when it did.

Writing in 1997 Paynter affirms a commitment to thinking of music as … 'a manifestation of thought and perceptual judgement' (Paynter 1997: 5). Music remains educative because it invites the mastery of thinking and making. Certainly Tyson, Morgan, Rachel and Brian wanted their Year 7 class to take part in making, making pieces of a puzzle with which to make a picture that felt right, complete. They bypassed the idea of specific learning outcomes by placing emphasis on providing an experience that would be eventful and special, and free to yield expressive and creative outcomes of unspecified kinds. There were to be surprises. Student responses and turns of imagination were to be welcomed and nurtured. There would be appropriation and transformation of what was given. The process of making was not a complicated affair anymore than making a cake might be. It was Dissanayake's notion of 'making special' or as Hickman thought of it, 'making aesthetic significance' (Dissanayake 1999, Hickman 2005). For Dissanayake the act of 'making special' represented an impulse central to human evolutionary adaption celebrating the capacity to make art. Hickman (2005), a visual arts educator concurs, noting that there:

… are many who do not consider themselves to be artists, but exhibit all of the tendencies which artists often display: a passionate desire to create something which looks good and feels right – something which has particular significance, whether it be a birthday cake, a garden, or a hairstyle. In such activities, intuition, expression, skill and a consideration of aesthetic form – all attributes of artistic activity – are considered important. What everyone needs is the opportunity to create and when the occasion calls for it, to create something of aesthetic significance, that is, something which has meaning for the person who created it. The term which I prefer then is 'creating aesthetic significance'. 'Creating' because of that word's association with creativity and inventiveness, concepts which have a particular resonance when talking about human development; 'aesthetic', because we are concerned here with the senses, while 'significance' is associated with meaning and 'signs' which are highly expressive and invite attention. I am not aware of any culture in the history of humankind which does not create aesthetic significance.

(Hickman 2005: 102–3)

Consulting pupils, making schools participatory, more open and where relationships might become more symmetrical and gain greater authenticity, represented an antidote to the demoralizing onward move towards the micro management of schools and of classroom transactions supported as this was by an audit culture of overbearing stature, a triumph of 'top down, paternalistic and managerial thinking' (see Jorgensen 2003). The idea of 'pupil voice' offered a fresh perspective on a child-centred education by recognizing not childhood's naturalness, but its agency, its potency, its way of seeing that was different and that was as much about being as about becoming. However, the neo-liberal superstructure demanded much more than this as school improvement and individual attainment of higher standards ruled the rhetoric and practice of public policy. If music in the secondary school was 'ill at ease' the need to 're-define roles, and to be proactive in finding fresh ways of working', fresh ways of thinking about music in the school were urgently needed. As the National Curriculum of 1999 came to be re-envisioned in preparation for a new curriculum in 2008 two initiatives presented themselves, the one sitting comfortably within official policy and now attuned to the particular characteristics of music, the other drawing upon models of music making beyond the school gates and the informal practices of popular musicians in particular. If the music educational river had become idle it was now energized by these two powerful currents emerging from quite different sources and working in the common cause of better engaging young people in music education.

Chapter 7
Music Education, Music Education, Music Education!

The United Kingdom is at the forefront of measuring and reporting student learning, and implementing strategies to raise levels of attainment.

Years of international research evidence have demonstrated that a new curriculum precisely along the lines of that now being introduced is the key to continued growth in educational performance for the individual, the school and the nation.

The foundation on which it is built can no longer be seriously questioned: the international jury came in years ago, and it is nationally important that we get on with it.

(Boston 2008)

In 1997 the Conservative government of John Major fell and with the slogan 'Education, Education, Education' the education policies of Conservative governments of the past 18 years were taken forward by the new Labour government. The tone and temper was of course different, but much remained unchanged. The marketization and regulation of education as a consumable continued but now there was appeal through notions like the power of transformational leadership, emotional intelligence, emotional management and new forms of teacher professionalism, and in due course the promotion of product customization defined as personalization. The previous sole reliance on re-structuring to bring about desired changes was producing diminishing returns (Hartley 2007).

Alongside this came a fresh drive to define Britishness and bring some resolution to what Beck (1996, 1998) referred to as 'Moral Millenialism', the quest throughout the 1990s for a civic, moral and cultural re-ordering. This now came in the form of Citizenship Education. At the same time, Education Secretary David Blunkett had set up the National Advisory Committee on Creative and Cultural Education (NACCE). The NACCE's terms of reference were:

To make recommendations to Secretaries of State on the creative and cultural development of young people through formal and informal education: to take stock of current provision and to make proposals for principles, policies and practice.

(NACCE 1999)

While greater emphasis was now placed on the raising of standards in numeracy and literacy, there was a recognition that creative and cultural education was needed if every young person's potential was to be reached. The language of a new child-centredness was developing and discernable in the statements from both the Department for Culture, Media and Sport (DCMS) and the Department for Education and Skills (DfES).

> Our cultural heritage, together with creativity through self-expression, offers a way of developing the talent of the individual and their understanding of a diverse and complex world around them.
>
> (Blunkett 1999: Foreword)

> The opportunities to explore the best of contemporary culture and to express individual creativity are two vital components of any education system committed to developing the full potential of all its pupils.
>
> (Smith 1999: Foreword)

While there is reference to expression, self-expression and individuality, the key ideas now moving within the rhetoric of policy making were 'full potential', 'talent', 'social inclusion', 'creativity', 'diversity', 'inclusion', 'standards', 'raising standards', 'continual improvement' and 'global competitiveness'. There was to be a cool, confident and economically energetic Britannia. Blair called for children to be taught how to be competitors. The neo-liberal ethic of individual enterprise and entrepreneurship was fully endorsed.

The NACCE report recognized that education was situated in many places – the home, community and school, and that education was a matter of both formality and informality. This chimed with a growing appreciation that music education too should be thought about as being in many places. There was Swanwick's call for music in school to connect with music 'beyond the school gates' (Swanwick 1999) at a time of growth in agencies providing music for youth in the community and arts organizations offering outreach programmes. By 2001 John Sloboda was asking 'Where is music education?', thus exposing the challenge facing those responsible for providing a music education. With this came a direct challenge to school music teachers.

> Classroom music as currently conceptualized and organized, may be an inappropriate vehicle for mass music education in twenty first century Britain. Hints of effective parameters of a more effective music education environment may well be found in the somewhat anarchic mixed economy of out of school music provision in this country.
>
> (Sloboda 2001: 243)

Swanwick and Lawson's earlier observation that 'music in the English secondary school seems ill at ease' (Swanwick and Lawson 1999: 47) had sounded out amidst wider clamour about the well-being of music education in school. There was a crisis of confidence and Cox (2002) called for the music education community 'to be ready to re-define roles, and to be proactive in suggesting fresh ways of working which enhance the musical experience of young people, and revitalize ourselves as teachers and musicians' (Cox 2002: 131). This challenge was a precursor to the findings of a study of young people's music in and out of school commissioned by the Qualifications and Curriculum Authority (QCA) (Lamont et al. 2003). While there were encouraging signs of positive attitudes to music in school, perhaps unsurprisingly a more robust commitment by young people to music out of school was the case and much of this informal in nature. The researchers conclude:

> The current challenge for school music is to maximize the experience of *all* pupils during the statutory period, and to help those who show additional interest in music beyond the classroom to develop that, recognizing the value of their own contributions, developing their individual skills through valuable social, cultural, and primarily musical experiences and activities, and providing the confidence to partake in musical activities in whatever personal and social context they choose.
>
> (ibid: 240)

Concern for standards in literacy and numeracy had meant that implementation of the NACCE report had been put on hold. However, a strategic way forward was found in 2002 through a flagship government initiative. Creative Partnerships set out to 'develop schoolchildren's potential, ambition, creativity and imagination [by building] sustainable partnerships that impact upon learning between schools, creative and cultural organizations and individuals' (Creative Partnerships national website). The creative citizen in Tony Blair's view would be one who contributes to 'a true enterprise economy for the twenty-first century – where we compete on brains, not brawn' (NACCE 1999: 6). If the music teacher and pupil as artists was now a lost icon, artists thriving independently of the school and its structural constraints were a resource well placed, it was thought, to nurture pupils' and teachers' sleeping creativity. By 2003 minister of education David Miliband had set up a working group to find ways of supporting music education further. From here a Music Manifesto was developed under the banner, 'more music for more young people' with the aim of providing greater opportunity for young people to be involved in musical activity. Music education was thus seen as a special case by government. It was a good thing and made good sense in terms of the government's commitment to social inclusion.

Outcomes and Standards

All this was taking place in the context of a revised National Curriculum of 1999 and unlike previous editions there had been a concerted effort to establish a set of values, aims and purposes underpinning the whole curriculum and to see schools as a part of wider interests. There was a need for schools to collaborate with 'families and the local community, including church and voluntary groups, local agencies and business' (DfEE 1999: 10). In this way the two broad aims of the curriculum could be achieved. The first addressed learning and achievement while the second called for the promotion of pupils' spiritual, moral, social and cultural development, an attempt to make sense of the agitated moral and cultural debates of previous years.

Of considerable significance in the case of music was the creation of nine descriptions of attainment reinforcing earlier demands for, and finally establishing, a fully fledged linear model of progression. In this way the idea of the child as a *sui generis* artist moving towards the conventions of culture and the shifting consensual judgements of musical communities would be difficult to countenance or sustain. There were now more targets to be met and non-negotiable standards defined. Music in the curriculum had for some time been in transit from providing a 'creative and aesthetic' education with a concern for artistic integrity and engagement in a creative process that would yield not always expected outcomes, to being an education for a particular conception of 'musical understanding' and with greater interest in society and culture, social relevance and usefulness. Musical traditions, genres and styles along with their relevant conventions and devices were to become key ideas in bringing about a re-conceptualization of music in the curriculum.

This move to provide nine levels of attainment was of course a key policy imperative to bring the curriculum's Foundation subjects in line with Core subjects, thus making a fully coherent assessment structure that would be more easily accountable and data efficient in serving the school improvement agenda. At the same time there was great conviction and sound reasoning behind the claim that by establishing bench marks of achievement, learning and progress would be better served: teaching would be better focused, learning would be more efficient and pupils more engaged. The reported slackness in the early secondary years might be overcome and progression from primary to secondary school be more assured. Creating nine level statements which moved incrementally onward was a not inconsiderable achievement and one which generously recognized music as a making and thinking art form. The statements of attainment tell what it is that pupils will be able to do. They will be able to discriminate, express, perform, create, evaluate and so on. However, this had created a quality gap. The 'how well' any of this would be done, the fluency and expressive qualities to be revealed and the quality of thinking and feeling engaged with were missing. This would have required recognition of a less cognitive core traditionally linked to the development of sensibility, the intelligence of feeling and the more general idea of aesthetic understanding.

The statements were attuned to the general conception of progression in knowledge, skills and understanding. Progression in music was to be marked by a particular form of cognitive shift and the verbs used to define each level tell a story of movement from the valuing of perceptual openness to greater cognitive closure. The generic concept of knowledge, skills and understanding of the HMI Framework of 1981 held firm. The level descriptions were not what had traditionally been thought of as assessment criteria. They were not thought of as indicators of quality and value, but outcomes of the musical teaching and learning. In this way the official curriculum was outcomes-centred rather than child-centred. The curriculum was conceived of not as a process which could be negotiated and developed through making and discovering, a reflexive journey in which pupil and teacher would move forward together in lively conversation, but as one dominated by an assessment structure focused on outcomes. In this way the culture of checking, auditing and general surveillance was extended and intensified.

Strategic Moves

By 2005 the Department for Education and Science had established a Strategy Unit with well rehearsed procedures that provided pedagogical templates in which classic models of curriculum planning and teaching and assessment were articulated in some detail, with always the behavioural objective deferring to Bloom's taxonomy and with outcomes explicitly declared. The Assessment for Learning revolution as tailored to target setting and to learners knowing ever more about their learning, how they were learning and how they might learn how to learn better was gathering momentum and becoming a part of the global marketing interchange of educational ideas.

National Strategies were now placed at the heart of the government's programme of school improvement. While strategies for English, mathematics and information and communication technology (ICT) were having some impact on the work of music teachers, the Secondary Strategy for Foundation subjects now placed music in the spotlight and with generic principles and practices with which to cohere. A 330-page pack of training materials accompanied by a video and CD were offered in support from the DfES. This was to be the precursor of a Strategy specifically created for music and in 2006–2007 this was piloted in a number of Local Education Authorities. In this a reformed view of how music should be taught to the 11 to 14 age range was established. This represented a response to a perceived lack of significant improvement in practice and to a general unresponsiveness to the curriculum set out in 1999. Attempts to move on to fresh ground where greater cultural understanding would be acquired through planning work around musical traditions, genres and styles, for example, had not been much in evidence. While there was common agreement about the musical processes children should experience, teachers' planning for progression was frequently weak as shown in a poor grasp of how national levels of attainment might be interpreted and used to ensure progression and raise standards.

Thus, the Strategy was launched setting out to provide a framework for progression in learning, inspired by the approach to achieving ever more sophisticated cognitive outcomes as set out in the National Curriculum Levels of Attainment. Pupil motivation and engagement were central concerns. The Strategy took on great legitimacy through the offices of the Department for Education and Skills and the now well established policy of strategy-making designed to support teachers and inform pedagogy, that once secret garden.

On Monday 16 April 2007 Circular 095/2007: National Strategy Music Programme for Key Stage 3 was dispatched by the DfES to all headteachers of secondary and special schools in England. The memo makes clear that:

> Full implementation of the materials should improve pupils' understanding of, and their engagement with music by enabling teachers to plan and deliver more effective lessons. Central to this planning will be an extension of rich musical experiences, more opportunity for expression and clearer individual targets for progression. The programme applies familiar National Strategy themes such as Assessment for Learning and specific aspects of pedagogy and practice in the context of music teaching. It has been described as the best CPD [Continuing Professional Development] that music teachers are likely to experience in their careers both specifically for music and in the way it integrates key improvements which are already a part of current whole-school initiatives.
>
> (Biggin 2007)

There was much here to attract the interest of headteachers and Local Education Authorities already responding to National Strategies. Music could nestle into the fold. Thus was launched an attempt to invigorate the working lives and practices of music teachers and to meld their work into the wider waves of school improvement. The moment was of some historical significance too, for while the Strategy was non-statutory, nevertheless, for the first time since the establishment of universal education in 1870, a detailed model of pedagogy for music was now available. The quiet yearnings of the past for a common way and by some for greater uniformity might now be assuaged. If music education had languished beside the other arts without a well formed pedagogy as Ross maintained, now came a strategy for music and the claim to have established one.

A Pedagogy for Music

Simon (1981) defines pedagogy as the 'act and discourse of teaching'. Alexander (2004) elaborates the notion of pedagogy as:

> The core acts of teaching (*task, activity, interaction* and *assessment*) [are] framed by *space, pupil organization, time* and *curriculum*, and by *routines, rules and*

rituals. [They are] given form, and [are] bounded temporally and conceptually, by the *lesson* or teaching session.

(Alexander 2004: 12)

In Alexander's view a pedagogy embodies explicit social values, the kind of relationships desired within a democracy, for example. In the case of music we might well wish to draw upon the ways in which teacher and pupil negotiate meanings together. We might want to recognize the social maturity of the pupils and ensure that there are opportunities for them to express needs. The lesson or teaching session might be thought of as a workshop, an event or an encounter where pupil impulse to create music and find aesthetic significance could be shaped and refined through the making process. Teaching might be thought of as an art, to some extent improvisatory, 'influenced by qualities and contingencies that are unpredicted ... [and] the ends it achieves are often created in process' (Eisner 1979: 153). The Strategy approached pedagogy in a different way.

Underpinning the Strategy was a central focus on developing musical understanding, understanding of musical conventions as they exist within musical traditions, genres and styles and as experienced through and referenced to musical activity. For some music teachers, but not for others, this represented a shift in curriculum practice where culturally undifferentiated musical activities concerned with uncontextualized elements of musical expression, musical techniques, musical devices and concepts led the way. The teaching of these in isolation it was thought now made little sense. Such things in the Strategy's terms had significance and meaning when taught within the context of a musical tradition, genre or style. Learning needed to have a context, a sense of time, place and social purpose and this involved understanding why the music engaged with existed.

There was a history to all this, only some of which by now will be clear. By the 1980s working with musical elements (sometimes called expressive elements), such as pitch, rhythm, timbre, texture, articulation, had become a common way of thinking about the curriculum. A topic on texture, for example, would look at a range of examples which might go across styles and involve composing, performing, and listening and appraising activities. In Paynter's *Music in the Secondary School Curriculum* of 1982, thinking about elements of expression is important and always elaborated into particulars. Melody, for example, opens up thinking about ornamentation, phrases of varying length and shape, repetition and sequence, unusual scalic shapes, modal inflections and so on. *Sound and Silence* of 1970 is well stocked with this kind of thinking that takes the maker into the deep structure of the subject. The composer Robert Orton shows this well in Paynter's 1982 book and reveals ways in which tempo and rhythm might be thought about in the context of evaluation and assessment.

Regular tempo is a feature of most music, and choice of tempo is one of the most fundamental creative decisions. It is possible, however, to establish tempo of events on a broad scale without a regular pulse; or to offset passages using regular pulse against 'aperiodic' sections. Turning to rhythm patterns on the small scale, these may show considerable subtlety, in lack of symmetry for instance. Yet we must not overlook rhythm on the large scale, the sense of drive forward, overall direction to a climax. In this sense rhythm is close to form.

(Orton 1982: 222)

For the composer, elements of expression become compositional craft, techniques, devices, procedures and Paynter's belief was that first hand experience of the ways in which elements combine was the most fundamental source of musical understanding, as significance was gained through the search for a sense of rightness and wholeness. Furthermore, it is the art of manipulating elements that forms the basis for progression and a focus for evaluating and assessing work. However, in the evolving practice of music teachers the idea of musical elements had frequently become a kind of 'catch all' planning mechanism. They had become musical concepts. Swanwick (1988) had raised the question 'concepts or features?' and pointed out the danger of working from and to concepts and losing the sense of 'encounter' that lay at the heart of the musical experience. For teachers and their text books rhythm, melody, timbre and so on were generalities that could shape the work covered for a half term block. The attraction lay in the universal nature of such elements enabling the drawing in of a wide variety of music. Children could be shown how rhythm was common to all and while some teachers avoided the equalizing out of cultural differences, this was by no means common. A constant criticism of teachers' work revolved around a lack of stylistic authenticity with elements of expression acting as a weak common denominator.

Elements of musical expression, musical skills, techniques, devices and procedures were the stuff of music and with movable and frequently interchangeable meanings depending whether it was the thinking as a composer, performer, listener-analyst or some other musical persona. Now, the Strategy made a case for traditions, genres and styles and their musical conventions to be the starting point from which elements and devices come to be identified, worked with and understood. By thinking in this way the curriculum had the potential to become 'culturally rich' and learning properly contextualized and in some sense more relevant and more meaningful. Students would be learning about the music of Indonesia, about Electronica, Canadian circus music or whatever. This approach was moving towards a recognition that music *is* in society and culture and this was in line with much philosophical debate within music education world wide. For example, David Elliot, the Canadian music educator, argued that 'music ought to be understood in relation to the meanings and values evidenced in actual music making and music listening in specific cultural contexts' (Elliot 1995: 14).

The Strategy was playing a part in securing the shift from music education as creative-aesthetic education to music education as cultural education in the cause of musical understanding. This approach assumed that all the world's music, indeed the music of every culture and sub-culture in every time and place, was worthy of inclusion in a music curriculum on its own terms. Its value would arise within the making of it in context. This conception of music education at once put considerable backbone into the curriculum. There was much content as well as much process. Curriculum making had been brought to order.

All Swans are White!

The Strategy was grounded in a precise definition of musical understanding. We saw through earlier enquiries the problematic nature of musical knowledge and understanding and the way in which Louis Arnaud Reid had helped to clarify thinking about the distinctive nature of knowledge and understanding in the arts. Reid's graphic example drawn from Yehudi Menuhin, for example, captured the idea of knowing and understanding as a thing embodied inside the creative act, a form of experience-knowledge and something akin to the inarticulacy of knowing a person, an understanding bodily felt, a matter of cognitive-feeling, tacit, intuitive and unmediated by language and conceptual thought, yet bounding in knowing, meaning and significance. In Chapter 5 *Cell 1* had shown appreciation of this too, as well as Tyson, Rachel, Brian and Morgan in their processes of 'making special'. This was the aesthetic core to artistic-musical understanding that attempted to capture the source of personal meaning, commitment, engagement, learning to discriminate and value, and achieve a sense of personhood and well-being. In the Strategy's terms musical understanding turns away from this kind of thinking with knowledge and understanding approximating to a form of propositional knowledge. Unit 1 of the Strategy proclaims that:

> This training promotes the view that the fundamental aim of music at Key Stage 3 is to develop pupils' musical understanding. It defines this essential understanding as an outcome which is the result of combining two areas of learning:
>
> * knowing about musical conventions, processes and devices
> * exploring a range of diverse musical styles, genres and traditions through practical music making.
>
> (DfES 2006)

By identifying this outcome as the main focus for learning, the unit strongly implies that although knowledge about music and involvement in practical experiences are critical, they should be seen as the means by which the main aim of musical understanding is enabled rather than being ends in themselves.

Thus, the practice of music or, if you prefer, the creative-performative act of making music, while contributing to understanding, is but a servant of musical understanding. It is a means to the achievement of understanding. The musical act in itself is not thought of as an act of musical understanding, or as an act involving cognitive feeling, fine-grained intuitive judgement and so on. The articulating of a musical phrase, the feeling for the space within and around a musical gesture in this view doesn't appear to constitute musical understanding. Nor the subtle giving and taking of time that marks mature musicianship and that might be considered to be a major indicator of progression in musical understanding. Practical music making requires the movement of the body and mind: perception and cognition are enjoined. Thought and feeling unite. That to be musical and understand music might involve feeling *and* thinking, the *body* as well as the mind, is not considered within the Strategy. This limitation is important to note for the Strategy's epistemological base will in due course lead to just what will be valued in the work of pupils, that is, what will be looked for, assessed, what will be thought worthy of valuing and evaluating.

Of course, there need to be many ways of conceptualizing musical understanding. But to what extent do these ways recognize the child as a meaning maker whose personal interests and concerns are respected? In the thinking of Bonnett, we saw earlier attention to the quality of transaction between teacher and pupil where meaning is allowed to arise rather than be imposed. Bonnett (1994) further suggests that if we are concerned that students develop the capacity to think poetically as well as think in a calculative way, the latter being the hallmark of much of school life, where categories and conventions are typically impressed on the learner, we need to expand our conception of what it is to understand. For Bonnett this would embrace:

- Rules and conventions
- Facts, evidence, data
- Knowledge of patterns, webs of explanations
- Compatibility with existing beliefs
- Appreciation of its underlying motive
- Empathy – ability to enter into
- Active involvement – sense of responding and responsibility
- Active sympathy – being able to positively relate to
- Personal experiences
- Being affected – having outlook transformed, sense of wonder or astonishment
- Felt relationship to own concerns

(Bonnett 1994: 142)

While the above are not intended as a hierarchy, the first three conform easily with the dominant conception of understanding. They are, to be sure, crucial and central to the growth of musical understanding and of course a helpful focus for assessment. However, the whole enterprise of music education may only take on a distinctive form and provide for significant value, meaning and purpose when the whole of Bonnett's list is invoked. In this way there can be an expectation of authentic engagement for the learner. The Strategy, in its necessarily bureaucratic and reductive style, provides a set of narrowing truths. There is no declared research base to propositions made and no internal possibility of falsification. In the Strategy's terms 'all swans are white' and this it seems is the way 'official knowledge' has to be.

This way of teacher development, working from deference to hard-earned autonomy, sits in vivid contrast to former curriculum development projects. The secondary Schools Council Project of the 1970s, as we recall, worked from a set of principles created by teachers and which in turn inspired teachers to construct their own philosophies of music education and to learn and develop through experiment and review. This change of approach is matched by the change in the governance and regulation of education, a move from professional autonomy to a 'constrained' and 'earned autonomy'.

For each of the Strategy's six units of study the teacher is presented with Key Messages and the teacher is asked to evaluate their current practice, so that in the case of Unit 1 there is an explicit focus on musical understanding, in Unit 2 on musical engagement through sequences of episodes that enable pupils to 'engage – learn – review', in Unit 3 on the development of creative teaching enabling pupils to use a wide variety of thinking skills and in Unit 4 on the ways that teachers can refine their practice so that there is greater clarity in expectation through the modelling of desirable musical outcomes and the ongoing process of learning how to learn. Unit 5 is concerned with challenge in music and Unit 6 with feedback in music. Finding these Key Messages comes as something of a relief after the denseness and quasi-theoretical obscurity of the study guides through which it is intended that the teacher as learner passes. However, clearly implied within the Strategy is the teacher's task of taking his/her students from implicit 'know how' to explicit 'know that' enabling a formal understanding of the subject in the context of practical music making. In this the pupil is a recipient of a top down managed curriculum. The adolescent's needs have been strongly inferred. In this fundamental respect it establishes a direction in sharp contrast to that of the Musical Futures project, the second current disturbing the idling river.

An Alternative Pedagogy

The task of the Key Stage 3 Strategy for Music was to bring order and coherence to classroom practice and to achieve common understandings amongst music teachers. It set out to achieve higher levels of musical engagement in school classrooms and finally meet the aspirations of those who had created a national curriculum for music. At the same time as the Strategy was being established a reformed version of the National Curriculum was in the making and while not having within its remit the determination of pedagogy, it was working in synergy with the official approach prescribed by the Strategy and at the same time responding to the freshly formed aims of the curriculum as a whole. These were simply stated.

The curriculum should enable all young people to become:

- *successful learners* who enjoy learning, make progress and achieve
- *confident individuals* who are able to live safe, healthy and fulfilling lives
- *responsible citizens* who make a positive contribution to society

(QCA 2008)

These aims were elaborated through attention to personal development as defined through the Every Child Matters initiative wanting children to be healthy and safe, able to enjoy and achieve, make a positive contribution and achieve economic well-being. Children's 'personal learning and thinking skills' as well as 'functional skills' are set out that will equip young people for the future. There are cross-curriculum dimensions thought of as 'unifying areas of learning' and this is linked to a website 'Respect for all'. A major dimension is 'identity and cultural diversity'. Concern for 'healthy lifestyles', 'community participation', 'enterprise', 'global dimension and sustainable development', 'technology and media', 'creativity and critical thinking' follow.

All this reminds us that school is charged with the responsibility for socializing young people into ways of being and thinking that are believed to be appropriate for their future roles in society. Moulding the social character is of fundamental interest to the state and its curriculum makers. The mechanisms for achieving this are seen in the statutory curriculum requirements, national strategies and the systems of monitoring the practice of these. If this is the case it is of great interest that in contrast to the ordering mechanism of the state there should come a potentially disordering mechanism sponsored by a charitable organization, the Paul Hamlyn Foundation, and quickly taken into the fold of the government's Education Innovations Unit. The Musical Futures website makes clear its claims to innovation. David Price, writing an introduction to the project tells how, in partnership with Youth Music and the DfES Innovations Unit, the project seeks

> … new and imaginative ways of engaging young people, aged 11–19, in music activities. Following a year of consultation in 2003, the Paul Hamlyn Foundation commissioned a number of research pathfinder projects (led by music services in Leeds, Nottingham and Hertfordshire) and research and development projects to realize a number of objectives:
>
> - To understand the factors affecting young people's commitment to, and sustained engagement in, musical participation;
> - To develop ways in which the diverse musical needs of young people can be met and their experience of music making enhanced;
> - To realize viable, sustainable and transferable models which can support a national strategy for music and young people;
> - To investigate, and make recommendations on, the most appropriate methods of mentoring and supporting young people's preferences and skills;

- To find ways of validating and (where appropriate) accrediting all forms of young people's musical experiences, including those undertaken without supervision;
- To facilitate support for music trainees, leaders, teachers and performers/ composers through the provision of development opportunities which highlight collaborative working practices.

(Price 2005: 1)

Following initial work with young people in Leeds, Nottingham and Hertfordshire there emerged two ways ahead to support the musical participation of young people. There was firstly a need to informalize the way music is often taught and secondly a need to provide for personalized opportunities in order to cater for individual needs.

In seeking out personalized opportunities there was immediately a potential synergy with the New Labour's 'personalization' and 'personalized learning' agenda. This 'big idea' had originated as an initiative setting out to customize public services such as health and education. The intention was to allow users of these services a more direct say in the way the service is designed, co-produced and co-delivered. Leadbeater (2005) proposes the first three steps as being intimate consultation, expanded choice and enhanced voice. He recognizes too that many currently use the term 'personalization' to mean a form of 'shallow personalization' where the user's needs are partially adapted to, while 'deep personalization' would mean giving users a far greater role and involve them in designing solutions to meet their particular needs. Whether 'shallow' or 'deep' there is scope for 'pupil voice' and 'choice'. While for most schools and their teachers personalization was accommodated as an enhanced form of differentiation where an element of choice might be added, Musical Futures boldly grasped the 'deep'.

In this the musical desires and ambitions of young people could be responded to and the teacher would be a facilitator. Unlike the Strategy for music, Musical Futures set about redefining the role of the teacher underpinned by key principles:

- Musical Futures places a high premium on informal learning – copying, playing by ear and self-expression;
- Students are strongly encouraged to play music that they're interested in (rather than a set of pre-determined works);
- Music learning is invariably through oral/aural means – students use forms of notation when they choose to, rather than as a 'text' to follow;
- Technique is introduced within the context of the piece being played, not as discipline in itself;
- Peer-learning, and student-led learning, are at the heart of Musical Futures;
- Music leaders learn alongside their students – they don't always have to be experts in the music being played by their students;

- Having started with music which students are motivated to learn, skilled teachers introduce less familiar musics, but within the teaching and learning strategies listed here.

(Price 2005)

Musical Futures offered a way ahead for music education that boldly broke through the school/not school divide, having its sights simply on the musical participation of young people in all those settings able to support this, including the school. This was in effect a major indictment of the meagre success of music as experienced in the school. Musical Futures at once challenged a vast array of orthodoxies, music educational schemes and ideologies. It was a far distance from stipulating definitions of 'musical understanding' and speaking of traditions, genres and styles, and had no immediate interest in the kind of progression set out in the National Curriculum. It was a socially-grounded movement encouraging the formation of musical collectives whether in classrooms or community. Most significantly it claimed to be meeting the expressed needs of young people. The only inferred need of young people was that they should be participants in musical activity. Its democractic credentials were impressive.

Celebration, not Alienation

The introduction of 'informal learning' in school finds release and fulfilment in the work of Lucy Green (1988, 2001, 2005). Green's seminal work *Music on Deaf Ears* is an investigation into:

> the nature of musical meaning as mediated by history and society and recognizes that commonsense understandings of music's value and meaning are ideologically blind to unconscious social processes accounting for their formation and maintainence ... Only when radical change is sought do ideologies become visible
>
> (Green 1988: 3).

Then and now were times of radical change. Writing in the afterglow of the reforms of the 1970s Green was able to challenge progressive music educational ideologies of the 1970s and 1980s, and to make an ongoing critique of dominant ideologies and how these worked against meaning being found through musical engagement in school. What was needed was a way of understanding social processes of meaning making that explained states of alienation and celebration. This recognized the vastly differing groups of meaning makers arising from class, ethnic and gender social identity construction, for example. In the 1988 study Green works with the case of Willis's biker-boys and hippies as an example of how music can become

A complete reflection and celebration of the self: of temporal experience through the relationship between consciousness and inherent meanings, and a belief in delineated meanings, moving with the self in time and across life experiences as one integral whole. When music is like this, it draws together our world: it celebrates us.

(Green 1988: 137)

Here is one way of explaining the sense of alienation felt by Martin in Chapter 4 and *Cell 1*'s celebratory moods in Chapter 5. For Willis the music of biker-boys and hippies is integral to their life style. Their music is how they live. Their life's tempo, its timbral grain, its lightness and heaviness of being, along with its nuanced corners, are all mirrored in their music's sonic properties and their inter-relationships experienced existentially, here and now, confirming their 'being-in-the-world', a celebration of self. It is the dialectical process of working towards the fusing of music's delineated and inherent meanings that achieves a full integration and authenticity of experience. This is precisely what Willis's hippies and bikers have achieved and are able to maintain as an ongoing process of self-realization. In a professorial lecture addressing the issue of musical meaning and experience in the classroom, Green argues that:

Many pupils are bound to have ambiguous experiences or, worse, 'alienated' experiences resulting from negativity towards both the inherent and the delineated meanings of much classroom music.

(Green 2005: 15)

Green's central mission is to bring popular music into the classroom in a way that is beyond a matter of content. It was not sufficient for teachers to work with popular music genres; attention needed to be paid to the ways of learning inherent to these genres. In this view, 'all kinds of music', that compelling phrase of John Paynter, had typically been mediated through a normative pedagogy, a 'school music' pedagogy legitimizing a dominant ideology. However, the characteristics of informal popular music learning lead to a new classroom pedagogy:

1. allowing learners to choose the music themselves;
2. learning by listening and copying recordings;
3. learning in friendship groups with minimum adult guidance;
4. learning in personal, often haphazard ways;
5. integrating listening, playing, singing, improvising and composing throughout the learning process.

(Green 2008: 10)

By achieving authenticity in the classroom there would arise personal autonomy and the awakening of the capacity to learn music independently and provide for life-long critical and practical engagement with it. In this way the school as an institution of musical education would be working positively for the majority if not all pupils.

The informal learning approach taken up by secondary schools, initially in Hertfordshire, involved self-regulated learning within a broad structure and within boundaries negotiated with their pupils. In reviewing what had been learned from the project, Green is able to analyse in fine-grained detail the learning processes of individual pupils. How learning was taking place in school had rarely, if ever, been exposed to such detailed analysis. In all this, and crucially, the power relationship between teacher and pupil was dramatically changed.

In Piaget's view, and this was a speculation and no more, the creation of more symmetrical relationships between teachers and students, typical of informal learning situations, would enable learning to be less superficial than one where the teacher managed the learning and where there was just too much pressure to accommodate the teacher's views (see Cole 2003). Here then was a sharp alternative to the Strategy. The Strategy is for the teacher to enact, and that may expect too much accommodation to the teacher's demand for formal knowledge and understanding, and particularly so as the Strategy's way of thinking about musical understanding had no stated interest in dispositional and existential knowledge that satisfied young people's interests and concerns. In contrast, the Musical Futures project, designed to allow the learner's mental and action schemas, or ways of knowing and understanding, to be fully acknowledged, and for assimilation of new experience and knowledge to take place, might with its subtle teacher-pupil interaction with teacher in the role of coach, be closer to creating musical learning in depth. In starting from a desire for expressive outcomes rather than objective-led outcomes, Musical Futures might also be capable of engaging young people at a more personally meaningful level. Here was a radical attempt not to revive the child-centred tradition but to replace it with an authentic source of meaning making and genuine fulfilment. Now there was no 'liberal-romanticism', no call to expressivist theories of art, no debate about education or training, or how imagination would be released, rather a full acknowledgement that children, and we might add 'freedom's children', may know best.

Needs, Pupil Voice and Personalization

The contrast between the official curriculum as represented by a national music strategy and the alternative offered by Musical Futures and the prospect of informal learning in the school, raised questions about the wants and needs of children and about the place of their voices in what is created for them. It sharply focuses questions surrounding our contemporary conceptions of childhood, ideas about children's place in society and their role in shaping and remaking the social order. The often made distinction between needs and wants makes for a helpful starting point.

In the Lamont et al. survey of 12- to 13-year-olds in 2003 (see above) a majority of students expressed an interest in learning to play the guitar and drums. Was this a want, a momentary desire or a genuinely expressed need? This is a complex question but one worth asking. Noddings (2005) argues that in setting up programmes of children's education much attention is paid to inferring what it is that children need. The new curriculum of 2008, for example, proposes that children should become 'successful learners', 'confident individuals' and 'responsible citizens' and proceeds to elaborate the personal qualities that will be needed if these aims are to be fulfilled. The school curriculum is an inferred curriculum. The state, society, the social order determines what is needed. However, what must by now appear obvious and in light of the advancement of the 'pupil voice' movement and the personalization of education, there will need to be some interplay between inferred and expressed needs if pupils are to be participants in their education … 'by ignoring expressed needs, we sacrifice opportunities to develop individual talents, intrinsic motivation, and the joys of learning' (Noddings 2005: 147).

Nodding's case rests on an ethical approach to education. Hers is an ethic of care (Noddings 2003b). This is concerned with relationships, and in educational settings this is most obviously about the relationship between teacher and pupil, pupil and pupil. In the teacher-pupil relationship the tension between 'expressed needs' and 'inferred needs' can be, and often is, as in the case of parent and child, very great. The interplay between 'expressed' and 'inferred' needs and the ways in which both are a matter of interpersonal understanding and negotiation takes us deep into an ethical view of music education. In the Hertfordshire informal music learning project teachers were immediately challenged to revise their role and to learn how to empathize and understand the needs that were being expressed by their pupils.

The Hertfordshire informal learning programme viewed children as having great agency, social maturity and the power of social insight and critique. It provided an image of school as a place where becoming was less important that being, where self-realization was a part of coming to know and understand music and where a deeper form of knowledge could be made. In the case of the informal learning initiative the teacher's regular role and asymmetrical relationships with pupils was challenged. In the depressing technicist language of the time, 'the power gradient was changed'. Time and space would be created to consider pupil needs. Green writes:

> The role of the teacher throughout the project was to establish ground rules for behaviour, set the task going at the start of each stage, then stand back and observe what pupils were doing. During this time teachers were asked to attempt to take on and empathize with pupils' perspectives and the goals that pupils set for themselves, then to begin to diagnose pupils' needs in relation to those goals. After, and only after, this period, they were to offer suggestions and act as 'musical models' through demonstration, so as to help pupils reach the goals that

they had set for themselves. Teachers told pupils that they would be available for help if required, but that they would not be instructing in the normal way.

(Green 2008: 24–5)

Attending to needs, those that might be inferred as well as those that might be expressed, requires an empathic setting, as *Cell 1* were seeking out and as Tyson, Brian, Rachel and Morgan insisted upon, one where there is openness to feelings being ironed out and voices listened to. Whereas the informal learning settings of Hertfordshire lent themselves to the building of empathic environments where the interplay between inferred and expressed needs could create productive learning, Laurence (2005, 2006, 2010) shows how this can work equally well through the formalities of the normal classroom providing that children's voices, their agency and interest in co-operative values are recognized. In fact, the matter of formal-informal learning here becomes irrelevant. In Laurence's case the goal is inclusion, mutual respect, overcoming hidden insecurities, forming a class as a social collective through the principles of musicking (Small 1998). In extending his work of the 1970s, Small maintains that the meaning of music resides in the act of articulating relationships and that 'participants not only learn about, but directly experience their concepts of how they relate, to other human beings and to the rest of the world' (Small 1999: 9). Here all involved work in continual dialogue and where the teacher has a legitimate role in working to elicit interests and concerns and becomes integral to the individual's and the group's making process. The work is one of artistic collaboration and dialogue. A dialogic education requires the avoidance of an authoritarian teacher-pupil model, and equally a *laissez faire* stand off one. The teacher in the role of educator has a responsibility to connect with the actual experiences of learners and to investigate what is of significance for them in their lives here and now (Freire 1993). Might this also be a foundational aspect of 'personalization', expecting the teacher, in Nodding's words, to be the 'one, caring and, second, enactor of specialized functions? As teacher, I am, first, one caring' (Noddings 2003b: 176).

Conclusion

In 2008 a new official curriculum was created for schools, their music teachers and their pupils to bring into being. In a speech launching the curriculum, Ken Boston, the head of the QCA, while assuring traditionalists of the curriculum's deference to British history and the English literature heritage, argues for innovation, and hints at new ways of covering the syllabus, and while not referring directly to the minds or voices of young people, moves quickly to the Assessment for Learning strategy as foundational to the idea of personalization within a global perspective.

> Across the Western world, the rate of improvement in educational attainment has slowed down in the past decade; in some countries it has reached a glass

ceiling, through which it cannot break. The traditional approach to covering the syllabus has been exhausted; it has delivered all it can; it will work no more.

Years of international research evidence have demonstrated that a new curriculum precisely along the lines of that now being introduced is the key to continued growth in educational performance for the individual, the school and the nation.

The foundation on which it is built can no longer be seriously questioned: the international jury came in years ago, and it is nationally important that we get on with it.

(Boston 2008)

As a whole, the speech is intended for a wide political constituency, embracing, for example, the neo-liberal cause and at the same time setting out to assuage reactions from cultural restorationists. Throughout the message is clear. Higher individual attainment will be achieved through the personalization of goals addressed through achievable tasks. Here is not even a shallow form of personalization, rather surface and entirely instrumental in character and part of the management of 'inputs and outputs'. The language of the market is appropriated and children are to be trained to be forever trainable (see Bernstein 2000). Appeals to the nation as a premier league player in the global education league become irresistible while the authority of incontestable and unattributed research knowledge acts as final legitimation.

Out of a crisis in confidence within music education marking the beginning of the new century came a flurry of initiatives prompted by government policy and the music education community's self-criticism. Public policy gave attention to the cultural and creative development of young people and their future entrepreneurial character as citizens. Music education, in whatever state of formality or informality, was recognized as a worthy project and to be supported in such a way that the potentials and talents of young people were released. Young lives were not to be wasted and music it was thought could play its part in preventing this. Music could work in the cause of social inclusion. Financially, strategically and structurally what was offered was not inconsiderable as efforts to re-master music educational provision gained pace. The Music Manifesto yielded high profile advocacy for the social, cultural and educational value of music and assisted in securing government funding. This led to a programme teaching primary aged children to 'sing up' and have access to learning a musical instrument, altogether a significant intervention. Curriculum revisions in 1999 and 2008 moved strongly in the direction of music education for culture and for musical understanding and were able to respond to the new curriculum's attention to pupils' understanding of identity and cultural diversity, led as it was by the government's concern for social cohesion and the power of culture to provide the missing social glue needed to make community. In this lay the potential to form a social-anthropological basis for music education.

Music in school at the secondary level experienced two sources of potential renewal, contrasted in ethos, yet both seeking greater pupil engagement, the one arising largely from the expressed needs of children, the other derived from children's needs inferred by curriculum makers. Together the questions of how much freedom to give to 'freedom's children', how much responsibility to bestow upon them in the name of full participation and the kinds of relationships characterizing music in the school were thrown into strong relief.

Did the Hertfordshire teachers learn greater empathy for their pupils in the same way that Tyson, Brian, Morgan and Rachel in Chapter 6 had learnt greater empathy for their teachers? If this had proved problematic for teachers it was believed to be less so for artists working in schools who, free from structural constraints, were able to reveal ways in which to trust children to have ideas and be creative (see Galton 2008). Musical Futures, Creative Partnerships and other forms of curriculum deregulation moved in sharp contrast to the templates offered by the Secondary Music Strategy, Ofsted, Examination Syllabuses and those disseminating the new curriculum of 2008. It was not so much an embarrassment of riches as a market place in which schools and their music teachers were required to choose how best to perform, for which audiences and for what purposes. The flagship Creative Partnership initiative, as Ross (2007) reported to a government select committee, was conceptually flawed in assuming that the arts were in some way privileged as sources of creativity, leading to the unrealistic expectation that the arts might transform the whole curriculum, when the prevailing orthodoxy of national curricula and school was not geared to playfulness, risk taking and creativity as 'an unquenchable desire for freedom' (Ross 2007: 4). At the same time 'freedom's children' were learning their own ways of taking risks and imaginative ways of making themselves that music in school might or might not be able to relate to. The need for music education to consider ways of consulting pupils enabling their participation was urgent, as was holding in tension the inferring and expression of their needs in such a way that would enable lively conversation and critique to flourish.

Chapter 8
Recapitulation and Retrieval

> It strikes me that schools are strange places. I have noticed how often teachers
> think that what they are doing is preparing students for the future, is providing
> them with the knowledge and the skills to equip them to deal with 'life'. I think
> we have to be a bit bolder and a bit more circumspect than that. I feel responsible
> for the students and the experiences that they are having right now – how are
> they doing? What's going to be interesting and possible? How are they dealing
> with one another? How independent do they feel they can be? What are they
> doing now? What does that mean? Where else could they go with this? What
> barriers are there? Do they look like they are enjoying themselves, properly? I
> don't presume to know what sorts of specific skills they are going to need in the
> future and I can only equip them (in a small way) to deal with 'life' as I know it
> and how it is at the moment.
>
> (Secondary school music teacher, email communication 2008)

If schools are strange places, then they can be no stranger than society itself, for
whose purpose they exist. Schools make citizens and children are now referred to
as 'learners'. Unlike the secondary school music teacher above there is a strong
desire to make 'learner-citizens' representing 'society in the making' (Rose 1990,
Arnot 2008). In this there is talk of making schools different so that they adapt to
a new world order where it is recognized that learning takes place in multiple and
diverse settings, where the school is but one agency amongst many others. There
is talk of 'institutional reconfigurations' and this in the context of a knowledge
economy where business, technologies and competitiveness require the nurture
and development of 'creativity, interpersonal skills and technical abilities, as well
as analytical intelligence' (Brown 2008: 27).

From this anxiety-laden drive for economic survival and race winning there
arise questions about the future, the future of music in school, its music teachers
and the relationship between the music teacher and the child. Who is the child's
teacher, who is the more knowledgeable other? And if music is in the school, what
is to be learnt, and why that, and for what purpose? If we are to find alternatives to
standardized curricula, to the prescription of outcomes, to standardized approaches
to assessment, to prescribed strategies; if we are to move beyond a fear of freedom,
a fear of failure in pupils and teachers, if we are to find alternatives to conventional
thought about progression in musical learning, to the homogenizing of ways of
knowing and understanding and the systematic downgrading of intuitive and
personal ways of knowing, we need to find fresh purpose for music education, a

music education that in a strong and positive sense is burdened by the self and that has interest in a way of knowing that recognizes the quest for self-realization, self-understanding and a productive, creative, critical and authentic orientation to the world. As I will show it is this that is required in our current state of late modernity if children are to survive the unstable and liquid nature of the society into which they are growing. But first a return to the beginning of the story told, recalling the story's episodic nature and always with an eye to discern sources of hope.

Releasing the Imagination

Rather like the secondary school music teacher above, Sybil Marshall was committed to addressing the present needs of children 'for the double notion of interest and treasure'. In retirement Sybil was able to look back on her Kingston days with gratitude, generously speaking of the great trust placed in her by her class and of her astonishment at their achievements realized through what appeared to be an effortless collaboration. It was the power of the arts above all else that Sybil could see enabled her children to symbolize, to make sense, to comprehend fully and to be fully educated. Sybil was soon to realize that she was not alone in seeing children as artists with artistic imaginations. There were, as she put it in her 1993 appearance on the radio programme *Desert Island Discs* and recalling her 'experiment in education' of the 1950s, 'the greats … you know … Herbert Read, Marion Richardson and so on'. And once enrolled on David Holbrook's English Literature evening classes held at Basingbourne Village College she was hearing about Holbrook's work with those he thought of as the rejected, the lowest stream of pupils in the same place. His books *English for Maturity* and *English for the Rejected*, published in 1961 and 1964 respectively, were particularly influential in opening up a space in which to see young people as imaginative makers and creators. In doing this Holbrook saw the tensions between the subject of study and the personhood of the learner. He was all too aware of the dangers of a misconceived child-centred progressive education. Reflecting on earlier writing and addressing criticism he writes:

> I had come to distrust the self who made such sweeping statements about the beneficial relationship between English work and personal growth, yet on the other hand I wasn't prepared to give ground to those who wished to cling on to beliefs that the English teacher's work had nothing to do with personality, but with a subject or 'structure'.
>
> (Holbrook 1961: ix)

For Holbrook there was a matter of preserving the dignity of children through a liberal education calling for a humanizing relationship between the teacher and pupil, always resisting the purely functional and narrowly vocational. Acquaintance with Sybil Marshall we imagine would have been mutually educative and inspiring, and here Holbrook tacitly acknowledges her work and others like her while lamenting the secondary school's submission to the world.

> ... primary schools have demonstrated that at the centre of education there needs to be that pleasure which propagates sympathy and is the basis of civilization: the pleasure of organizing experience in art. The primary school concentrates on the development of beings: the secondary schools have to turn their attention to pupils as workers, intellectuals and technologists. A minority are groomed for the best places and academic achievements; his civilization is left to take care of itself. Our education begins by being one thing and ends by being another: the result is too often the inarticulate scientist, the illiterate workman, the immature being.
>
> (Holbrook 1961: 19)

As well as the belief that children need cultural sources of succour, to develop positive attitudes to life, and develop human sympathy (ibid.), there is the issue of social justice and the idea of a liberal education in the arts for all. The challenge for child-centred progressive educators was the delicate holding together of the freedom to make, create, express and to self-express, with the literature, art and music of the past and present, while at the same time remaining loyal to the structure of the subject, its disciplines and conventions. Of this Holbrook is acutely aware as he questions Herbert Read's idea of 'spontaneous making', his acknowledged commitment to 'anarchy' as a political creed and disregard for conventions. Conventions provide the link with the world outside, to tradition providing sufficient control to enable what may well come to appear to be spontaneous (Holbrook 1961: 114). What seems now so remarkable about the teaching of Holbrook, so vividly communicated through his books, is his engagement with his pupils' 'lived experience'. He is concerned that they make sense of their lives here and now, that they see their existence more plainly as he elicits stories of the stark dullness of their lives animated only by their expression of phantasy, suggesting modest hopes and desires.

Two years after the publication of *English for the Rejected* in the 1966 March/April volume of the journal *Music in Education*, and in amongst articles on 'Music and Secondary School Boys', 'The Teaching of Music in Sixteenth Century England' and an analysis of Benjamin Britten's War Requiem, Roger Eames writes an account of 'A man and his music at York'. In three short paragraphs Eames tells of Wilfred Mellers, 'musician, musicologist and lecturer' now head of the Music Faculty at the University of York. In particular there is news of the Faculty's undergraduate syllabus and the three courses offered. One includes composition; another combines music with English and a third brings together music with education. On this course students go into schools engaging in 'Creative Experiment' lessons and, in preparation for work in senior schools, students 'will also be taught to improvise so that they and their pupils may express themselves through Improvisation and by the children writing their own popular songs' (Eames 1966: 83). This was fertile ground for the imagination of another musician, composer, musicologist and lecturer to work on. John Paynter had been moving forward with a good deal of practical thinking about how children could be taught to compose music.

> It was largely pragmatic: 'I have 30 or more pupils in this class; how can I get them to work directly with sounds to create complete pieces of music?' I do recall reflecting upon the way I myself worked as a composer: thinking about the kind of piece I wanted to make; imagining the overall sound of the piece – how it would begin and end; and then – perhaps at the piano – trying out fragments of melodic, harmonic, or textual material; returning to mental 'imaging', little by little defining and confirming significant details. I suppose that, whenever I introduced a 'composing' task to a class that had divided into small groups, I must have been drawing upon this kind of thinking: 'Here is an idea; talk about possibilities for music; choose instruments (or use your voices); make some sounds; talk together about the sounds and how you can combine them; where is the piece "going"? Remember that you are making *music*, not sound effects!' And so on. As time went on, I refined the techniques ...
>
> (Paynter written communication 2008)

Paynter was convinced that for music in the school curriculum to be recognized as having educational value it would need to give up its commitment to what amounted to little more than a form of musical training. Undue emphasis on training acted to defer and close down possibilities opened up by the child's imagination. Working with what the child had to offer would enable music to join the arts and share in a common identity. It would provide a liberal education.

> For me the general notion of a 'liberal education' was derived largely from my much earlier reading of Jean-Jacques Rousseau's *Émile*. In the mid-eighteenth century he was advocating a style of education that would allow children to develop as individuals able to form independent judgements; and in that context, his view of musical education is especially interesting: '... to understand music, it is not sufficient to be able to play or sing; we must learn to compose ... or we shall never be masters of the science'.
>
> (Rousseau 1763: 222 in Paynter written communication 2008)

In all this the teacher's authority was softened. The teacher listened attentively to the musical thinking of those learning, as teacher and pupil took part in a shared process of making as a creative conversation out of which new problems and possibilities would emerge. It was this idea of the teacher as co-artist that proved so difficult to transmit to music teachers as they took up the idea of children as composers rather than children as composers alongside teachers as teachers of composition. The role required was far more subtle than abstract definitions and theoretical constructs could encapsulate: teacher as enabler, facilitator, midwife and so on could never capture the dynamic of this communal-making process in which the teacher's mind was that of a composer continually imagining and being in a state of alertness, discerning potential relationships emerging as productive 'coincidences' in the journey to finding form, towards what felt right, complete and whole.

While Paynter was placing composing at the centre of his own teaching so Malcolm Ross was placing children's writing centre stage in his classroom and surrounding it with the voice of Milton, the poetry of Ted Hughes, popular song and Shakespeare dramatized. Ross, in drawing on Winnicott's notion of 'the good enough mother' was able to develop, following the work of Witkin, the idea of the teacher as playfully responsive as opposed to the teacher as obdurately reactive, and the idea of expressive as opposed to impressive learning. The 'Arts and the Adolescent' project set about making the arts in school times of 'lived experience', times of freedom to be and to connect out of school life within school life and where abstractions were kept at bay. The adolescent had a whole life, a life of feeling that was with them in and out of school.

> And that was the way to get kids connected and allowing for a kind of hunger for work, for school work. Because the kids could sense the connection with their own lives, their own questions, their own feeling, their own culture … visual art teachers seemed to have no difficulty in embracing youth culture, not in a paternalistic way but connecting it up with new art that was going on in galleries. Going into art departments in large comprehensive schools was to enter a culture apart. Here were teachers making coffee, brewing up, kids sitting around. These were often disorderly schools, 'no goes', yet inside the art room and studio doors were being made all kinds of sound objects, huge projects, installations and so on. Now go to the music department and you know … poor old music, where was it?
>
> (Ross interview 2008)

Well, music was following behind, and beyond the seminal work of Paynter, the 1970s were a decade of experiment within music education directly challenging the past. Simpson's conservationist's view was in line with the emerging political new right arguing for the restoration of discipline, authority and standards. Disorderly youth and disorderly schools needed order, the order provided by:

> … schooling, as it has evolved, stands for reason, order, objective thought, precision and sustained application – in other words, for the denial and rechannelling of our raw reactions to our experiences.
>
> (Simpson 1970: 85)

Music educators of the past had found ways of taming and training the musical impulse and of bringing order and structure to learning and of making it sequential and progressive and based on sound psychological and musical principles. Witkin and Ross, in their visits to secondary school music rooms, found much order but little enthusiasm or mutual understanding. Music teachers did not want raw reactions. But in Ross and Witkin's terms, raw reactions were to be expected, understood and easily channelled, and made into knowing responses and intelligible feelings. That is what the arts did in response to the adolescent state. It was what adolescents themselves did in response to their state. This was that part of the adolescent that need not be denied. The great divide between reason and emotion, between order and chaos, civilized life and all against all which Zygmunt Bauman came to see as the trade mark of modernity was brought to the surface. Reason was equated with a moral order underwriting a civilized order and this would mean that 'impulse, predispositions, passions would need to be stifled, that is unless they were passions for order' (Bauman 1994: 4). In the culture debate emerging in the 1970s no less than a moral order was at stake. The potential for creating a wide chasm separating subjective intelligent feeling from objective rational thought and an education that on the one hand could all too easily be stigmatized as little more than therapy and on the other as feeding the passionless mind was considerable. In this it was easy to align order with tradition and a particular form of music.

Holbrook's 'working on the child's inner world' sounded dangerous stuff but the 'inner world' *was* part of the 'whole child', and while the 'whole child' made a typical case for the analytic philosopher to expose as meaningless, according to those speaking on behalf of the child, there could be no phantasy or imagination without the 'inner world' of the 'whole child'. The expectation was that teachers would enjoy helping children to say what it was they wanted to say and that teachers would be sensitive enough to know that children needed to be given creative-imaginal spaces where they would be free to explore their private worlds. But this required sensitive, knowing teachers. Holbrook's descriptions of his work with the children he taught in the lowest stream of the secondary modern school attest to such sensitivity and a remarkable humanity at work.

However, in the view of social liberators, such humanity disguised the power of Western European ideologies that privileged particular cultural forms and social practices. In the case of music, for example, notation stood in the way of meeting with the rawness of the music experience that pop music offered. This was the view of Vulliamy and Shepherd. For Swanwick, ideology, dominant ideology, hegemonic discourse and privileging practices were matters to rise above. In Swanwick's view we are 'symbol-takers' and 'symbol-makers' engaged in cultural histories and their renewal with healthy tensions between past and present, and understanding this could lift eyes higher (Swanwick 1992b). And this taking and making goes on in 'the space in between', in between the individual and the collective, for this is where music exists (Swanwick 1979, 1999). For Swanwick the child-centred progressives along with the social liberators and cultural conservatives were missing the point of music's transcendent work as a great symbolic form, a 'form of human discourse as old as the human race' (Swanwick 1997). 'Inner worlds' and the politics of lived culture could easily become distractions.

The Mood of the Music Changes

In an epilogue to the July edition of the *British Journal of Music Education* 1989 entitled 'The Challenge of Creativity', Paynter reminds readers of the progress made by music education during the past 25 years. He writes:

> [Music education] *is* closer to the centre of educational thinking – we have seen to that; but are there now more words than actions? ... How do we achieve a healthy two-way flow between properly detached exchange of ideas and lively classroom practice?
>
> (Paynter 1989: 236)

Paynter is asking: where now are the innovative music teachers? Are we in danger of creating little more than a community of fine words? Paynter saw only too clearly the end of a cycle. The age of teacher autonomy, freedom to think differently, to innovate and to question was coming to a close as a centralized curriculum required that learning be a linear and predictable process, involving the submission to non-negotiable standards. For the teacher as artist-composer the world was turning on its dark side. And beyond the reasonableness of the programmes of study devised for music in the National Curriculum, there came the age of bureaucratic state intervention, surveillance, a culture of auditing and the de-professionalization of teachers. The validity of teachers' ethical views of their calling was overridden; the legitimacy of the teacher as a source of professional knowledge was rejected. Teacher autonomy was now conditional and something to be earned. In being de-professionalized teachers could now be re-professionalized.

Clearly, those making a National Curriculum for music were presented with great challenges and for all their noble efforts it was a greater political force that came to control the process of curriculum making and the character of music in school and teachers' ways of working. The old theory-practice divide had been significantly healed with music endorsed as an essentially practical subject in which composing held equal status alongside performing, with a supportive place for critique and appraisal. While Shepherd and Vulliamy (1994) showed how political ambition, ideology and intervention by the conservationist political right had created unintended consequences, the bureaucratic mechanisms arising from the making of a National Curriculum did their work in creating 'new era values'.

As the 1990s proceeded Sybil Marshall entered her eighties maintaining her love of life and the telling of stories. Between 1993 and 1999 a final nest of five fenland novels was produced. Her daughter Pru, like Jill, a member of the Kingston schoolroom of the 1950s, was moving towards the end of her own career as a primary school teacher and twice headteacher. Pru tells of the time of the 1990 'new era' values.

> I welcomed the National Curriculum which I thought was very good. It gave a helpful structure. But in those first days of the National Curriculum you could

interpret that structure just however you fancied. For me there was music, always art and creative stuff, working in groups and all that. But things had been changing. Topic work was now frowned upon, for example. For me it was very successful. The topic would have something which would captivate the interest of everybody. The fact that children sometimes went off at tangents never bothered me. If somebody got interested in some aspect of a story because you happened to mention the Pole Star or whatever, then that was a bonus and you let that child go and find out what they could about it and then you drew them back in again.

Oh, the topic webs that we did were wonderful things. And I think to some degree they may be coming back. Now they seem to be saying, 'it's all very well separating everything out but where are the links between English and music and music and history?'

I had two Ofsted inspections. We came out as a good school both times. In one they said that I didn't share my enthusiasm enough with my staff. I'm not quite sure how much more I could have done. I ran my school in a non-hierarchical way. As far as I was concerned I was just one of the team. Yes, the buck finally rested with me and I always had to have the right answer in the right kind of fashion to convince inspectors that I knew what I was doing and that the school knew what it was going to do. But there was no pecking order. And I think I was quite proud of that. I laboured that too much with my Inspector who seemed to think, 'I don't see how this can work. If you're the head you should be telling, you should be kicking butt'. I didn't need to, any more than my mother did.

How different Ofsted inspections were to meeting with the old fashioned council advisor of the 1960s and 1970s. They were wonderful, and HMI, they were so efficient. They were on your side. If you had a difficult child they took you to one side after the lesson and they enquired about the history of that child and what you could tell them about why the child was behaving in the peculiar way that they were. And what kind of strategies you had to deal with this disruption. They were just delighted that you knew the reasons and that you were trying to do something about it. The fact that at that moment in that lesson you weren't 100 per cent successful was understood. They would have hardly expected it to be, because they were realists. I am very much against inspections and very much against that Chief Inspector Chris Woodhead. I think he did irreparable damage to the morale of teachers which is lower now than I can ever remember it being. This shouldn't be. Teachers should go into the profession because they want to do it and because they can do it. To be squashed at every possibility by somebody up there at the top, this hierarchical thing again … who does he think he is?

(Interview 2008)

Chris Woodhead had been Head of the National Curriculum Council and of the Schools Curriculum and Assessment Authority before moving to be Chief Inspector of Schools in 1994 and remaining there until 2000, by which time the New Labour government had produced a 'cultural turn', 'based on a distinctive combination of cultural, economic and social themes' while maintaining and extending the culture of performativity (Buckingham and Jones 2001: 1). The political ambition was potent: culture and creativity in the knowledge economy seeking social inclusion and productive civic activity. Buckingham and Jones point out that

> In this new discourse, the terms in which earlier generations of progressives depicted the relationship between education and industry are turned about. No longer is the liberatory potential of the one contrasted with the calculating rationality of the other; and no longer does 'culture' offer a vantage point from which to comment and make judgements on economic processes. On the contrary – discursively, at least – the reverse is now true: the language of creative practice and personal development is more a feature of contemporary business rhetoric than it is of an education system dominated at all levels by centrally and narrowly established performance indicators and norms.
>
> (Buckingham and Jones 2001: 5)

The arts were becoming coextensive with the idea of 'business innovation' and this we find in the most recent official definitions of school curricula. The bringing together of enterprise, vocational and creative education was an obvious neo-liberalization of the education system and there was no shortage of enthusiastic advocates spinning and glossing music education as a commodity. Raymond Williams's three conceptions of education as socialization, specialist training and cultural enhancement could become as one where an education was conceived of as being for the entrepreneurial learner-citizen, now at the same time the producer and consumer of culture with the emphasis on consumer.

The Commodification of Music Education

In a secondary school's Autumn Newsletter 2007, in striving to improve its test scores, the school's community of staff, students and parents are encouraged to take advantage of an e-learning resource branded as SAM Learning and described as a market leader with 60 per cent of all English state secondary schools as subscribers. The newsletter tells that:

> SAM Learning offers a good way to learn, a new and better way of absorbing information and they can work at their own pace, which helps all pupils whatever their ability.
>
> (Aldworth Science College Newsletter 2007: 18)

It is a case of 'absorbing information' rather than coming to know or understand, and the language of a marketing orientation promoting this product from the company, set up in 1994, is striking.

> The program is *research proven*. More than four years of independent research involving more than 300,000 students demonstrates the positive, proven relationship between the use of SAM Learning and consistent improvement in students' performance on high-stakes tests in the UK ... The company mission is to help raise achievement in schools by providing high value services that reduce workload for teachers and administrators while empowering students to take responsibility for their own learning and improve their performance on high-stakes tests.
>
> (SAM Learning 2008)

In another school, one of the newly formed Academies seeking to raise the achievement of pupils in areas of traditionally low achievement, there is investment in human relationships and the implementation of a 'Zero to Hero' programme. This is a whole package of personal and social education. Such packages proliferate in the conviction that this is the way to improvement and higher achievement. In all this the child is continually assessed, labelled and packaged as a unit of production and the school customized to the measures of achievement publicly declared. As schools become consumers of educational improvement packages so the curriculum itself opens up to commercial interest.

In the *Education Guardian* of 29 January 2008 is set out a scheme of work crossing subject boundaries seeking to 'extend pupils' interest in music to look at the massive changes taking place in the industry' (Kneen 2008). By 'the industry' is meant the global music industry. The starting point for the learning is the case of the music corporation EMI and its radical response to changing market circumstances in the music industry. The article argues that:

> The music industry is a great topical choice for the classroom. Teachers can hand the mantle of expertise to their students, allowing them to bring their knowledge, experience and opinions to bear on the subject, while the teaching simultaneously develops their understanding and skills. It is relevant to music and ICT, of course, as well as other areas such as English and maths.
>
> (ibid.)

The work is adaptable to all ages between seven and 16 and especially citizenship education. It represents well the notion of the new flexible curriculum that champions fluidity between subject disciplines and the need for relevance and topicality. It exemplifies the notion of being prepared for the world of the future and for economic competence and economic well-being (QCA 2007). Education thus becomes obsessively future-orientated and increasingly bounded by the principles of the market. It was now time to trust what the market had to offer and to move the balance between producer-consumer to consumer and consumption.

In Bauman's 'liquid modernity' citizens learn to consume and commodify themselves as a means of survival. Thus, it is not so much that music is a commodity but that music forms a part of the shifting identities of the consumer.

In this way the consumer is commodified with music used to sustain membership of the 'style pack', to keep abreast and ahead of it and to avoid alienation and the terrifying prospect of social exclusion that threatens (Baumann 2007). I need to be a 'guitar hero'. Identity is no longer a given but had become a task, 'a compulsive and obligatory self-determination' (Bauman 2008: xv). Not identity but freedom is a given as children 'practise a seeking, experimenting morality that ties together things that seem to be mutually exclusive: egoism and altruism, self-realization and active compassion' (Beck and Beck-Gernsheim 2008). In this view we have to accept children as members of the 'me' generation, and as an inevitable product of democratic evolution and the source of new values. Freedom has arrived and children have the self-reflexive capability to shape their own education. And they do this beyond school and in ways unimaginable to former generations of young people. The case of Jack makes this clear.

Freedom's Children

Jack aged nine has been well cared for. Singing came quickly and he was early into composing spontaneous songs: 'Let's go to the fair', 'Crash down the door', performed to gatherings of family and friends were memorable moments. With the help of his mother's video recorder Jack produced his first pop album at the age of five. Now at nine Jack plays the clarinet and guitar. The clarinet is learnt in school and there are times out of school when he can play along with his granddad's folk guitar. 'When the Saints' is performed with gusto, Jack strolling around the family living room as if a member of a Dixie Jazz Band. He likes to perform, calls for an audience. In school assembly, the formal clarinet pieces being learned for the first grade examination are performed with more solemnity, but still with intensity and enthusiasm. At Cubs, Jack gains a music badge to sew on his jumper for his performance. In school he learns the clarinet alongside a boy from a different class. Little by little they encourage each other and develop subtle performance routines, where for example, elbows are raised to emphasize a gestural point in the music.

Jack's musical times form part of '… the child's overflowing activity spread[ing] aboard. He feels, if we may say so, strong enough to give life to all about him' (Rousseau 1993: 39). Jack plays games too: football in a local team, more games played at Cub night; and there is 'Guitar Hero' the digital game for his playstation where Jack can attempt to hit the notes on the accompanying guitar and score points. 'Guitar Hero' enables Jack to meet new musical genres, as does 'Singstar', another digital game where Jack sings along with pop artists from the last 50 years and accumulates points for accuracy of pitch and rhythm. 'What good songs are there?', he asks himself before typing in the artist's name and selecting his new musical companion with a song to be memorized and danced to. Most recently 'High School Musical 1, 2 and 3' and X Factor have been popular sources of learning although a preference for American Rhythm and Blues artists is leading the way. Jack is learning to be a chooser, a consumer of what there is on offer and finding values to live by, making himself, seeking out spaces of his own and learning to write his own biography. Jack's self-determination on Bauman's reading is a necessary part of his growing into the instability of living with a 'not given' democratic order and 'not given' values. And Madeleine Arnot points out:

> In this country Freedom's Children will experience difficulty in being directed from above or being forced into particular identities or types of commitment, preferring their own self-organization and political action that is focused on different activities rather than on participation in a given democratic order.
>
> (Arnot 2008)

It is this conception of the child as an active agent, socially adroit and reflexively making identity that the pupil voice movement sought to recognize as both structurally transformative and personally empowering. The school was challenged to catch up with the child as it were. There would of course be the 'perils of popularity' and inevitable appropriation of the idea by government, its policy makers and mentors – school managers along with their imaginary and real puppeteers, the school inspectors. Schools would typically respond by creating a 'pupil voice' structure centred on a representative school council, and a generic approach calling for written impersonal evaluations and surveys, while some, and perhaps a small minority, would seek a fuller and more fully democratic style. Pupil voice of course would draw in a deceptive apparatus that sustained benevolently authoritarian structures. We saw the empowerment of Tyson, Rachel, Brian and Morgan in Chapter 6 and their capacity to use freedom productively as something that came to be patronized by their school, left to take the form of a gently repressive tolerance rather than a case to be learnt from and listened to. In the informal learning offered by Musical Futures teachers were challenged to see learning music and their pupils differently, and for pupils to see school and music in school differently. Here lay the possibility of open transactions between pupil and teacher and the sensitive balancing of expressed and inferred needs. However, as Green (2008) points out, there was a major difference from the attempts to meet with the child's lived experience in the child-centred progressive movement of the 1970s and 1980s. Now the music was selected by the child and there could be an expectation of celebration rather than alienation. However, might not Musical Futures, despite its radical prospectus, be in danger of becoming one more package to be consumed and exported? Do we know any longer what music education is for and whether it can have an ethical purpose?

From Nihilism to Ethical Considerations

Bowman (2005) writing from North America about a legitimation crisis within music education argues that music education has slipped into a state of nihilism, having little or no regard to purpose, intention or value. It has no ethical basis or emancipatory awareness. It is simply a compliant agent of instrumental rationality content to distribute and circulate the packages that are offered for consumption thus sustaining the efficient running of the system. In Britain we are just beginning to understand how this is too: there is the loss of critical attention to public policy, to local and individual school policy with its many initiatives and innovations delivered and consumed at an ever increasing rate. Perhaps there has never been so much advocacy for a music education and so little attention to purpose, aims and values. Bowman defines advocacy as:

> ... promising the world, without asking about the circumstances under which its promises might be realized, or acknowledging their contingency. It invests all its energies and resources rhetorically and politically, treating musical value as self-evident.
>
> (Bowman 2005: 30–31)

Advocacy becomes a marketing exercise as claims and further claims for the efficacy of a music education begin to rival the presentation of all that is consumable. Statements declaring the importance of music in the curriculum of 1999 and 2008 take the form of advocacy, building one attractive claim upon another. They form neither justification nor rationale. They are promises that excite and placate but are unlikely to be realized. It is the principles of the market that provide the morality and standards by which the good life can be made and justified. This is the neo-liberal way and is easily linked to the notion of globalization and the free movement of labour, investment, markets and the marketing of ideas including educational ideas (see Ball 2007; Woodford 2009). Thus the 'not good enough' culture arises within a culture of 'performance' and the measurement of outcomes in relationship to inputs. Education, and with it music education, is to be viewed as operating as a system and like any other system it needs to be seen as running efficiently and in a fully accountable manner serving the nation's economic competitiveness. In a neo-liberal age education is to be thought of instrumentally and as a utility. Lyotard (1984) wrote of this idea of justification by performance as 'performativity' and later to be defined by Ball as:

> ... a technology, a culture and mode of regulation, or even a system of terror in Lyotard's words, that employs judgements, comparisons and displays as means of control, attrition and change.
>
> (Ball 2004: 144)

For Ball performativity carried with it corruptions, inauthenticities and fabrications as the techniques of performance became embedded in the professional practice of teachers and their schools.

The ethics of competition and performance are very different from the older ethics of professional judgement and co-operation ... There is 'the possibility of the triumphant self' of becoming a new kind of professional or of entry into the ever expanding ranks of the executors of quality. We learn that we can become more than we were and be better than others – we can be 'outstanding', 'successful', 'above average'.

(Ball 2003: 218–19)

How to teach an 'outstanding lesson', a 'never fail lesson', and how to be an 'outstanding teacher' are the lures of the moment. How now does a secondary school music teacher respond to a detailed specialist Ofsted inspection of his department and its work when the judgement reached is 'good'. The music teacher's headteacher receives this news as 'not good enough', the teacher's work will need to become 'outstanding'. What if the teacher, after much soul-searching decides that he knows he is good at what he does, and needs no other to testify to this? Why would he want to be 'outstanding'? What if the teacher renewed his efforts to clarify his vision for his school and its music, unwilling to become a compliant agent of 'performativity' and a drift into nihilism? What if this teacher carried on caring for his students and their music with personal integrity intact? There would be a risk. The teacher might now be viewed as being less able to contribute to the policy making of the school than in the past. The risk would be to become mis-recognized. His gain would be personal integrity and authenticity. This example of what might be thought of by some as an act of disobedience represents for Fromm (1984, 2003) the exercise of the humanistic conscience where we hear our own voice. It is the proper expression of self-interest not of social-adjustment. Fromm is drawing on the Aristotelian tradition of virtue ethics, extended by Spinoza and developed in the early Marx. Here ideals are set out for what a fully developed life might be like. For Fromm this requires making sense of our own existence and discerning how reason, love and productive work reveal possibilities for greater human solidarity. In this view the growth of a humanistic conscience allows productive, creative fulfilment in relation to others, belonging and the exercise of non-instrumental reason. Viewed as an existential imperative common to all, an orientation is offered at variance with the demands of a society over-driven by material wants and an economic structure that in the case of modern times is concerned with humans as consumers and their self-formation as commodities. An ethical self-realization becomes the necessary humanistic goal in the face of the social order.

Paulo Freire (1993) is working with Fromm's 'having' and 'being' distinction when he speaks of 'banking' knowledge as opposed to a dialogic form of knowing which engages with the learner's imminent personal, social and political interests and concerns. In Fromm's view the education system is functional. It trains people to have more knowledge, to become bankers of knowledge. So, schools provide their students with 'knowledge packages' that as a minimum will enable them to function in the workplace and beyond in order to gain feelings of self-worth and social prestige. In Fromm's terms rational authority is found in a form of ethics that supports those aspects of human nature needed for human flourishing, fullness of being and self-understanding: non-exploiting love, reason and productive work (Wilde 2004).

For the music educator therefore the question of values clarification arises. What is it that we hold to? In answering this question I propose three ethical demands. Firstly, we recognize the curiosity and creative potential that lives within the child's and the teacher's impulse to make music; secondly, we recognize the playful-dialogic quality of the relationship made in the classroom in the nurture of curiosity, creativity and imagination; and thirdly, we recognize the role played by the clarification of values in the growth of the child's and the teacher's critical awareness and use of 'mental skills'. Here are three ethical demands for a music education. All three address the question of *how* we teach while the third goes much further and challenges *what* it is that we teach and *why*. It is the 'what' and 'why' that must be our starting place.

The example of the 'not good enough' teacher above shows the teacher finding an ethical position out of ambivalence and likewise it will be the teacher's students who will need to find authenticity out of value confusions, moral ambivalence and the absence of rules and duty that determine the right course of action. Bauman clarifies:

> The assertions (mutually contradictory, yet stated all too often with the same force of conviction) 'Humans are essentially good, and they only have to be assisted to act according to their nature', and 'Humans are essentially bad, and they must be prevented from acting on their impulses', are both wrong. In fact, humans are morally ambivalent: ambivalence resides at the heart of the 'primary scene' of human face-to-face. All subsequent social arrangements – the power-assisted institutions as well as the rationally articulated and pondered rules and duties – deploy that ambivalence as their building material while doing their best to cleanse it from its original sin of being an ambivalence. The latter efforts are either ineffective or result in exacerbating the evil they wish to disarm. Given the primary structure of human togetherness, a non-ambivalent morality is an existential impossibility.
>
> (Bauman 1992: 10)

In *The Ethical Demand* Løgstrup works from a belief in the 'spontaneous concern for the other' (Løgstrup 1997). This is an unconditional commitment. There is no bargain involved. There is no seeking out of reciprocity, no social contract. The ethical demand, all the more challenging because of its silence, arises out of mutual dependency. The 'other' is my responsibility and I am alone in accepting it. It demands that I trust the children I am teaching and that while I differ in years and experience I share the same challenge of resolving the moral ambivalences of living and learning to flourish. Thus, the relationship is a matter of dialogue where there is an expectation, though logically impossible, of symmetry from the start.

Face to face, teacher-pupil, pupil-pupil, the primary structure of human togetherness is the existential condition about which we have no choice and it is for this reason that a music education is in need of, and cannot avoid, an existential underpinning. Witkin's concern for children's sense of 'existing in the world' (1974) and Ross's notion of 'participating in the world and changing it' (1989) is the language of the existentialist. For the existentialist the notion of authenticity is crucial and the idea of 'authentic self-expression' is a necessary goal. Thus, children and their teachers together learn that they can be true to their feelings. Learning this is likely to be arduous. Bonnett writing in the light of Heidegger's thought:

> ... the essence of human being is not so much that we are rational, symbol users, etc. (though we are these things to a greater or lesser extent), but that we are mortal, meaning by this that we live in an awareness of the fact that we ourselves will die, though we usually try to cover this awareness over. And the real problem for each of us then, the problem that provides the contexts for all our choices and understanding, is not what is the meaning of life where we look outside ourselves (e.g. where we look to religion or science) for the answer; it is: what meaning will I give to my life?
>
> (Bonnett 1994: 106)

The search to give meaning to actions is an inherent part of the child's reason for being and the ultimate source of their motivation in all parts of the curriculum. Realizing one's musical mind through 'authentic self-expressive acts' provides for meaning. For example, children who are ill at ease performing in a half-engaged manner, trying to guess and satisfy the mind of the teacher or somebody else, are rejecting the opportunity to act authentically. Their work is meaningless. Ultimately, as Abbs points out:

> The student has to be the protagonist of his or her own learning. This means that in the teaching of any intellectual or artistic discipline there must be open structures – gaps for the unknown, gaps for reflection, gaps for revision, gaps for contemplation, gaps for questions, gaps for the imagination, gaps for Socratic *elenchus*, gaps which constantly invite, provoke, unsettle and support the deep self-involvement of the student.
>
> (Abbs 2003: 15)

Tending to What We Teach and Why We Teach It

The publication *Curriculum Matters 4* marked a significant step in the process of defining the music curriculum. It provided official sanction for the idea of a culturally diverse curriculum '... *what* music is taught is only slightly more important than the *way* it is taught ...' (DES 1985b: 2; see also p. 169 below), and with one of the seven curriculum aims to 'develop an awareness of musical traditions and developments in a variety of cultures and societies' (ibid.: 3). The culture debate was in the process of being accommodated. The question of which traditions, cultures and societies and how various these might be left the problem of 'whose music' and 'whose musical values' were worth engaging with largely untouched. In the years elapsing between this official document marking out the ground on which a National Curriculum for music could be built, the cultural drift of later modernity was at work and in due course could be seen to resolve the matter. For now the fluidity of cultural forms, values and individual identities created a freedom to choose.

So, the danger of music education easily slipping into a state of nihilism, having little or no regard to purpose, intention or value is present. It loses an ethical basis and emancipatory awareness. In this situation the questions of what we teach and why we teach it quickly become redundant for these questions require attention to and examination of means and ends, to the clarification of values, the re-evaluation of these values, authenticity, commitment and personal responsibility. The problem is now not about cultural hierarchies. These have melted away. For an ethical return we will need to work once more with Williams's notion of the ordinariness of culture but now its capacity to reveal extraordinariness. That is, to properly engage with people, their musical interactions, their ways of being musical, the social circumstances in which their music is made and under what conditions and for what purpose. This includes attention to oppressions, resistances, triumphs, alienations, celebrations, matters of human interest, to the various forms of embodied aesthetic significance, the ways of coming to know in the making of music and in the discourse surrounding its making. The ubiquitous inclusion of the Blues as a topic of classroom music makes a good case. Why teach the Blues? Is it because:

- a harmonic progression can be introduced?
- improvisation skill can be developed?
- 'Hanging in the breeze' can be listened to, the music signalling everybody to stand at the end of the evening at the New York Blues Club?
- a Blues 'feel' can be had?
- the school's most experienced Blues musician can lead the work?
- students can learn about Blue notes?
- students can feel the Blues through their voice?
- it is useful preparation for writing cadences?
- a song can be written about the people-trafficking read about in the local newspaper?

It is at this point that we face up to the beliefs and values we hold or more likely are ambivalent about. In what ways will we together address human interest and concern through music? A music teacher responds:

I think that music gives you the opportunity to stand in someone else's shoes and to feel some of what they might feel. My top reason for teaching the Blues would be to get a feel for it – but that feel is about the human spirit dealing with horrible circumstances – those blue notes are sadness, they're also African and they're 'blue' against Western chords and none of this would have happened without particular circumstances ...

(Email correspondence 2008)

This response reveals a human interest that provides the possibility of teaching with a critical edge and with emancipatory awareness. Thinking of the harmonic progression of the Blues in hegemonic terms with melodic inflection arising as resistance creates a challenging value dissonance and a powerful social metaphor to work with. The Blues become worth teaching. We need to imagine many more reasons for teaching the Blues and to do this we must remain curious, politically engaged and ambivalent.

Tending to Playful-dialogic Encounter

Eighteen girls aged 11 to 16 are gathered in the large rehearsal room in their school's music department. With double basses in one corner and orchestral percussion in another they have come to take part in a project that will take them out of school, beyond their immediate city environs to the Barbican Concert Hall where they will hear the Fifth Symphony of Gustav Mahler in two days' time. They have in common a commitment to playing an orchestral instrument and this they bring with them to the beginning of the day where they meet animateur Hannah, who will lead them during the day and in their pre-concert performance at the London Barbican in two days' time.

They form a circle, and following introductions, Hannah creates a movement-sound sequence figuratively faithful to motives from the symphony's first movement, the 'Trauermarsch'. The musical material transmitted is Mahler's. There are 15 minutes of intensive working where Hannah gives and the girls give back, where Hannah insists through repetition that all get it. The transaction is already playful. Like catching balls moving fast between all within the circle, the girls catch melodic fragments as well as rhythmic ones. 'You really need to get hold of this material, this is very important.' Now with a voice of enchantment and mystery Hannah reveals Mahler's use of the song 'Der Tambourg'sell', a song about one of Mahler's ill-fated 'children', a drummer boy condemned to execution and his long walk to death, the 'trauermarsch'. The girls want to know what it is that the boy has done that deserves such a fate. However, this is to remain a mystery for the time being. The work proceeds until groups have created their own 'trauermarschen'. In the minds of the girls live the drummer boy and his fate and the musical ideas and feelings that in some sense are now theirs as well as

Mahler's. The girls remain curious, always asking questions of their teacher and each other.

There is unlikely to be creativity without curiosity and it is an ethical demand on teachers to be curious about their students, their interests and concerns and for the teachers themselves to remain curious, fuelled by their own interests and concerns. Together teacher and pupil will be curious about what will be created and what Mahler has created. A class of 12- to 13-year-olds in a different place, and with curiosity in abeyance, will need to remember where to sit for their weekly music lesson for it is their first music lesson after the Easter holiday. Kate and Lee have coloured their hair and they are still in love. The teacher plays the music of Puccini while the class finds their places. The teacher calls for correct places and firmly insists on a number of moves. A minute of insisting with his intentions follows. Some pupils tacitly disagree with the teacher's judgements about their places and a mood of resentment grows.

Teacher:	Don't pull faces … Abi to the front. A few Easter eggs have made us forget. I don't want to do a life skills lesson. I want to do a music lesson. What kind of music is it? My mother-in-law is an opera singer and when she comes to stay …

The story takes five minutes and includes the teacher singing Ring-a-Ring-a-Roses in operatic style. The class like stories and are happy with the teacher's open and often rhetorical 'I wonder' style.

Teacher:	Do you like this music?
Pupil 1:	Opera is for old people.
Teacher:	Ah! But Chester likes it.
Pupil 2:	Boring; can't hear the words; all the same; la, la, la; we don't understand it.
Teacher:	I know what you mean – different language; Italian, German.
Pupil 3:	Jamaican.
Teacher:	Listen to a bit more. What's the most striking thing?
Pupil 4:	Starts low gets high.
Teacher:	Yes, it uses a lot more notes than my pop song

(*demonstrates*). Listen to the different moods.

(*Motorcycle magazine is taken from Tyson.*)

Why am I teaching you opera? We are going to sing and play an opera. Fair deal? Have I convinced you about opera yet? No. We need to hear more. No. Listen. Remind me not to be a salesman.

Carl Orff's 'Carmina Burana', not technically an opera, but grist to the music teacher's mill, is played as the teacher leaves the room closing the door behind him. In a moment he reappears with upper body pressed in a grotesque form against the window of the classroom door. Will, an extremely passive pupil, becomes a little animated. The teacher enters the room as a hideous creature crawling the floor only to rise in terror in the faces of selected pupils.

Morgan:	Sir, could you do that again?
Teacher:	I didn't see anybody miserable when I did it.
Pupil 5:	That was OK that one.
Teacher:	Why?
Pupil 6:	People like scary stuff. It was the shock effect.
Teacher:	Focus. All the instruments at once. It's like it's building up tension; evil chant; like Lord of the Rings; it's in a primitive language. (*Head movements from boys.*) (*Various*) OK, how do you move to it? What will happen when the music changes? (*Class responds with upper body movement.*) Have I turned you on to opera yet? One more piece.

Puccini's 'Nessun Dorma' is played. Ah! Pizza advert and Chester tells of the 1990 World Cup in Italy when this music was used. Chester prides himself on this kind of knowledge and is an expert on the flags of the world's nations. During this sequence of teaching there are a number of discrete vocal experimentations underway from pupils and the teacher acknowledges these without stopping the flow of his teaching. Now the climax of the lesson arrives.

Teacher:	We will listen to the music again and who can sing the last line when I stop the music?

Three hands go up. Chester is selected. The music is played and Chester stands and sings from the heart. Tears come to my eyes and I recall the teacher speaking of tears coming to his eyes in lessons too. The class is impressed by Chester. He is famous. 'Nessun Dorma' is Chester's song and he likes this. In Year 7 Chester was teased about his size and truanted.

For the teacher this lesson was a game he loves to play, 'a game of don't like it – do like it. A game of enticement'. Following the lesson at lunchtime Shane explains:

> We like teachers who play with us. I hear a lot of opera at home. My gran has it on all the time. Sometimes there is an opera singer in the Centre on Saturdays. I sit on the bench and listen, pretend to be having a rest. Chester is a good opera singer. I never knew he could do it. I am looking forward to doing this opera.

Being playful involves yielding to those with whom we play, letting it be known that we are 'allowed to', that now we are free from necessity, and in a place where our questions will be addressed.

From Playful-dialogue to Critique

'Why teach the Blues?' is a question to be asked of our pupils as they contribute to the planning of their learning. In making a 'trauermarsch' the class learn to compose music through a persistent dialogue with teacher and with each other. In the case of teaching opera playful teaching leads in due course to a conversation about the street children of Calcutta as the teacher discovers that here is a topic the class are fascinated by in another lesson. The lives of the street children provide the narrative for the class to make and explore musical drama. They are eager to imagine living alone on busy city streets, frightened and hungry, and hunted by the police. In reflecting on the lessons the teacher writes:

> In many ways these lessons were not lessons at all but a structured extension of their home/playground lives. Engendering creative empathy within a task environment which tries to avoid the often threatening strictures of the school classroom, students were empowered by the proximity to their own learning and experiences and thus all students were engaged, motivated and enabled to achieve highly.

This view speaks of an intense level of student commitment where the quality of what arose and the communal valuing of this proved to be some distance from what can be contained within National Curriculum levels and criteria. We should note that here the project undertaken and the musical events emerging, far from responding to the students' declared wants, nevertheless connect with what had come to be of interest, concern and relevance. The interplay of inferred and expressed needs underscores the dialogue that makes meaning and purpose. The class had expressed a need to better understand the plight of the street children of Calcutta; their teacher worked with this while inferring a great many musical needs besides. Conversation and dialogue disturb the distinction between formality and informality.

In thinking about why we might teach the Blues, a Mahler Symphony, the street children of Calcutta as a music drama, we are asking questions that challenge. Of course, challenging questions are likely only to be partially heard and poorly answered. Then we must probe further until the question asked demands thinking that reorders reality and allows for a better understanding of where we stand and the ambiguities of our value position. Curiosity, playfulness of mind and body in human transactions allowing for conversation and dialogue feed this process. All this is critique. There is emancipatory awareness thought of as not an unusual matter but one depending on a particular kind of relationship between the teacher and pupil where there is a tending to mutual ignorance. In this way we emerge from educational encounters distinctly less ignorant and wanting to know and understand more. There is much more to this than the acquisition of instrumental and vocal skill, although of course this is important. Skills, knowledge and understanding, considered ethically, are imminent to the life of the learner, the teacher and the music that is to be known.

Final Words

Because there has never been an agreement about the purpose of the English education system, education itself remains a contested concept and the site of a struggle for democracy. Our children are educated in what is called a liberal democracy and there has been a long tradition of seeking to make their education liberal, in some sense liberating, broadening, with horizons expanded. There would be a going 'beyond the present and particular' enabling awareness, self-understanding and critique. But, as Fromm noted in commenting on the progress of liberal education, there is a persistent recourse to the employment of authoritarian structures, with power and authority disguised contributing to the formation of the non-productive social character (Fromm 2004). And now childhood is constructed in a way that gives the voices of young people space, notionally at least, as their capacity to know much about the social world and to shape it is recognized. Young people's search for autonomy, seen as a freedom to choose, develop self-reflexivity, individualize, become self-managers and artists of their own existence, finds a response from those who administer and monitor the music curriculum in sponsoring that which personalizes learning and shapes the learner-citizen.

The child-centred progressive educators emerging from the 1950s were moved by a different idea. This was the enlightenment idea of allowing children to develop as individuals and to be free to form independent judgements. In this lay an ethic of concern for each child's way of understanding ... 'a *clear* space is created that allows and even calls each person to articulate his or her own values and beliefs' (Doddington and Hilton 2007: 89). In music it was believed that this would be achieved through a liberalization of the classroom, allowing music to be made in the way that art was made, as plays and poems were made. Make, come to know, critique and understand. This was not a 'having more' but a 'being and becoming more'. The child was an artist and her uniqueness was mirrored in the novelty of her artistic creations. In a century of extremes this was a near golden age, a time of 'breaking out' when innovative teachers, enthusiastic Local Authority Education Officers and their advisors along with the impulsion of the Schools Council worked to forge new curricula for schools that took account of democratic ideals. However, the movement was interrupted by a call to account as a new economic order slid into being, Hobsbawm's landslide into an unstable international state, an age of crisis. As globalization progressed, national identity and social cohesion came under threat and music education as a form of cultural education began to take shape in collusion with government social policy. But by now artistic culture as well as cultures in general had become liquid and unstable. Cultures were no longer clearly defined wholes. Identities were fragile and while 'complaints about the decline of musical taste' were largely a thing of the past, music still represented 'at once the immediate manifestation of impulse and the locus of its taming' (Adorno 2004: 29). An ethical meeting of pupil and teacher was urgently needed.

Bibliography

Abbs, P. (2003) *Against the Flow. Education, the arts and postmodern culture.* London: Routledge Falmer.

Adorno, T. (2004) On the fetish character in music and the regression of listening, in *The Culture Industry: Selected Essays on Mass Culture*, edited by J.M. Bernstein. London: Routledge.

Aldworth Science College Newsletter (2007) SAM Learning. Aldworth Science College.

Alexander, R. (1995) *Versions of Primary Education.* London: Routledge.

— (2004) Still no pedagogy? Principle, pragmatism and compliance in primary education. *Cambridge Journal of Education*, 34(1), 7–33.

— (2008) *Essays on Pedagogy.* London: Routledge.

Arnold, M. (1869) *Culture and Anarchy: An Essay in Social and Political Criticism.* London: John Murray.

Arnot, M. (2008) *Educating the Gendered Citizen.* London: Routledge.

Aspin, D. (1982) Assessment and education in the arts, in *The Aesthetic Imperative*, edited by M. Ross. Oxford: Pergamon.

Ball, S. (2003) The teacher's soul and the terrors of performativity. *Journal of Education Policy*, 18(2), 215–28.

— (2004) Performativities and fabrications in the education economy: towards the performative society, in *The Routledge Reader in Sociology of Education*, edited by S. Ball. London: Routledge Falmer.

— (2007) *Education PLC: Understanding Private Sector Participation in Public Sector Education.* London: Routledge.

— (2008) *The Education Debate.* Bristol: Policy Press.

Bauman, Z. (1992) *Postmodern Ethics.* Oxford: Blackwell Publishing.

— (1994) *Alone Again: Ethics After Uncertainty.* London: Demos.

— (2007) *Consuming Life.* Cambridge: Polity Press.

— (2008) Foreword: Individually, Together, in *Individualization* by Beck, U. and Beck-Gernsheim, E. London: Sage.

BBC (1951) *Broadcasts to Schools: Singing Together – Rhythm and Melody.* Broadcasts to Schools, Spring Term.

— (1993) *Radio 4: Desert Island Discs.* 11 November.

Beck, J. (1996) Nation, curriculum and identity in conservative cultural analysis: a critical commentary. *Cambridge Journal of Education*, 26(2), 171–98.

— (1998) *Morality and Citizenship Education.* London: Cassell.

Beck, U. and Beck-Gernsheim, E. (2008) *Individualization.* London: Sage.

Bentley, A. (1975) *Music in Education: A Point of View.* Slough: NFER.

Bernstein, B. (1971) *Class, Codes and Control, Vol. 1*. London: Routledge and Kegan Paul.

— (1995) *Pedagogy, Symbolic Control and Identity*. London: Taylor and Francis.

— (2000) *Pedagogy, symbolic control and Identity: Theory, Research, Critique* (revised edition). Lanham, Maryland: Rowman and Littlefield Publishers Inc.

— and Davies, B. (1969) in *Perspectives on Plowden* by R.S. Peters. London: Routledge and Kegan Paul.

Biggin, T. (2007) Circular 095/2007: National Strategy Music Programme for Key Stage 3. 16 April. DfES.

Blacking, J. (1973) *How Musical is Man?* London: Faber and Faber.

— (1985) Verses Gradus Novos as Parnassum Musicum: Exemplum Africanum, in *Becoming Human through Music*, edited by D.P. McAllester. Reston, Va: Music Educators National Conference 1985.

— (1995) *Music, Culture and Experience. Selected Papers of John Blacking*, edited by R. Byron. Chicago: The University of Chicago Press.

Blunkett, D. (1999) Foreword to NACCE (1999) *All Our Futures: Creativity, Culture and Cultural Education*. London: DfEE/DCMS.

Board of Education (1927) *Handbook of Suggestions for Teachers*. London: HMSO.

Boethius (2002) The principle of music, an introduction, in *Music Education. Source Readings from Ancient Greece to Today*, edited by M. Mark. London: Routledge.

Bonnett, M. (1994) *Children's Thinking: Promoting Understanding in the Primary School*. London: Cassell.

— (1996) 'New' era values and the teacher-pupil relationship as a form of the poetic. *British Journal of Educational Studies*, 44(1), 27–41.

Boston, K. (2008) Curriculum for the Twenty First Century. Speech at the launch of the new secondary curriculum. [Online]. Available at: http://www.qca.org.uk/qca_12423.aspx. [accessed: 10 September 2008].

Bowman, W. (2005) Music education in Nihilistic Times, in *Music Education for the New Millenium: Theory and Practice for Music Teaching and Learning*, edited by D.K. Lines. Oxford: Blackwell Publishing.

Bray, D. (2000) *Teaching Music in the Secondary School*. London: Heinneman.

Brown, G. (2008) We'll use our schools to break down class barriers. *The Observer*, 10 February, 13.

Brown, M. and Precious, N. (1968) *The Integrated Day in the Primary School*. London: Ward Lock Educational.

Buckingham, D. and Jones, K. (2001) New Labour's cultural turn: some tensions in contemporary educational policy. *Journal of Education Policy*, 1, 1–14.

Callaghan, J. (1976) Towards a national debate: speech by Prime Minister James Callaghan at the foundation stone-laying ceremony at Ruskin College, Oxford on October 18. *Education Guardian* [online]. Available at http://education.guardian.co.uk/thegreatdebate/story/0,574645,00.html [accessed: 16 April 2009].

Cambridgeshire Council of Music Education (1933) *Music in the Community: The Cambridgeshire Report on the Teaching of Music*. Cambridge: Cambridge University Press.

Carr, W. and Hartnett, A. (1997) *Education and the Struggle for Democracy: The Politics of Educational Ideas*. Buckingham: Open University Press.

Cassell's New Popular Educator (circa 1880) *A Complete Cyclopedia of Educational Knowledge. Vol. 1*. London: Cassell and Company.

Central Advisory Council for Education (England) (1963) *Half our Futures (The Newsom Report)*. London: HMSO.

— (1967) *Children and their Primary Schools (The Plowden Report)*. London: HMSO.

Cole, M. (2003) *Cultural Psychology: A Once and Future Discipline*. London: Harvard University Press.

Cooke, P. (1978) Music learning in traditional societies, in *Folk Music in School*, edited by P. Leach and R. Palmer. Cambridge: Cambridge University Press.

Cox, G. (1993) *A History of Music Education in England 1872–1928*. Aldershot: Scholar Press.

— (2002) *Living Music in Schools 1923–1999: Studies in the History of Music Education in England*. Aldershot: Ashgate Press.

Creative Partnerships National Website [Online]. Available at http://www.creative-partnerships.com [accessed 22 October 2009].

Crick, B. (1999) The presuppositions of citizenship education. *Journal of Philosophy of Education*, 33, 337–52.

— (2002) *Democracy*. Oxford: Oxford University Press.

Cunningham, P. (1988) *Curriculum Change in the Primary School*. London: The Falmer Press.

Dearden, R.F., Hirst, P. and Peters, R.S. (1972) *Education and the Development of Reason*. London: Routledge and Kegan Paul.

Dearing, R. (1994) *The National Curriculum and its Assessment: Final Report*. London: School Curriculum and Assessment Authority.

DES (1980) *A Framework for the School Curriculum. Proposals for Consultation by the Secretaries of State for Education and Science and for Wales*. London: HMSO.

— (1985a) *The Curriculum 5 to 16: Curriculum Matters 2*. London: HMSO.

— (1985b) *Music from 5 to 16: Curriculum Matters 4*. London: HMSO.

— (1985c) *GCSE Criteria*. London: HMSO.

— (1987) *The National Curriculum 5–16*. A Consultative Document. London: HMSO.

— (1988) *Education Reform Act (ERA)*. London: HMSO.

— (1991a) Music Working Group: Interim Report. London: DES.

— (1991b) *Music 5–14*. London: DES.

— (1992) *Music in the National Curriculum (England)*. London: DES.

DfEE (1999) *The National Curriculum for England*. DfEE: London.

DfES (2006) National Strategy Music Programme *Foundation subjects: KS3 music*. [Online]. Available at http://www3.hants.gov.uk/music [accessed: 19 May 2009].

Dewey, J. (1958) *Experience and Nature*. New York: Dover Publications Inc.

— (1971) *Experience and Education*. London: Collier-MacMillan.

Dissanayake, E. (1999) *Homo Aestheticus. Where art comes from and why*. London: University of Washington Press.

Doddington, C. and Hilton, M. (2007) *Child-Centred Education: Reviving the Creative Tradition*. London: Sage Publications.

Eagleton, T. (1990) *The Ideology of the Aesthetic*. Oxford: Basil Blackwell.

Eames, R. (1966) A man and his music at York. *Music in Education*, March/April 318, 83.

Eisner, E. (1979) *The Education Imagination*. New York: Macmillan Publishing.

Elliot, D. (1995) *Music Matters*. Oxford: Oxford University Press.

ESRC Network Project (2003) *Consulting Pupils About Teaching and Learning. University of Cambridge Faculty of Education*. [Online]. Available at: http://www.educ.cam.ac.uk [accessed: 28 May 2004].

Finney, J. (1980) From Prima to Secunda Prattica: from darkness to light. Discussion paper, Richard Aldworth Community School, Basingstoke.

— (2000) Curriculum Stagnation: the case of singing in the English National Curriculum. *Music Education Research*, 2(2), 203–11.

— (2002) Music education as aesthetic education: a rethink. *British Journal of Music Education*, 19(2), 119–34.

Freire, P. (1993) *Pedagogy of the Oppressed*. Harmondsworth: Penguin Books.

Fromm, E. (1941/2007) *Fear of Freedom*. London: Routledge Classics.

— (1979) *The Sane Society*. London: Routledge and Kegan Paul.

— (1984) *On Disobedience and other Essays*. London: Routledge and Kegan Paul.

— (2003) *Man for Himself: An Enquiry into the Psychology of Ethics*. London: Routledge Classics.

— (2004) *To Have or to Be?* London: Continuum.

Galton, M. (2008) Creative practitioners in schools and classrooms. Final Report of the Project: The Pedagogy of Creative Practitioners in Schools. University of Cambridge.

Gammon, V. (1999) National curricula and the ethnic in music. *Critical Musicology* [Online]. Available at http://www.leeds.ac.uk/music/Info/CMJ/articles/1999/01/01 [accessed: 22 May 2009].

Green, L. (1988) *Music on Deaf Ears: Musical Meaning, Ideology and Education*. Manchester and New York: Manchester University Press.

— (2001) *How Popular Musicians Learn: A Way Ahead for Music Education*. London: Ashgate.

— (2005) Meaning, autonomy and authenticity in the music classroom. Professorial Lecture. Institute of Education, University of London.

— (2008) *Music, Informal Learning and the School: A New Classroom Pedagogy.* Aldershot: Ashgate.

Harland, J., Kinder, K., Lord, P., Stott, A., Shagen, I. and Haynes, J. (2000) *Arts Education in Secondary Schools: Effects and Effectiveness.* Slough: NFER.

Harre, R. (1983) *Personal Being.* Oxford: Blackwell.

Hartley, D. (2007) Personalisation: the emerging 'revised' code of education? *Oxford Review of Education*, 33(5), 629–42.

— (2009). Personalisation: the nostalgic revival of child-centred education? *Journal of Policy Study*, 24(4), 423–34.

Harvey, D. (2005) *A Brief History of Neo-liberalism.* New York: Oxford University Press.

Hewitt, A. (2008) Book review: Bernarr Rainbow with Gordon Cox, music in educational thought and practice. *Psychology of Music,* 36(1), 129–32.

Hickman, R. (2005) *Why We Make Art and Why it is Taught.* Bristol: Intellect Books.

Hirst, P. (1972) Liberal education and the nature of knowledge, in *Education and the Development of Reason*, edited by R.F. Dearden, P. Hirst and R. Peters. London: Routledge and Kegan Paul.

HMSO (1956) Music in schools. *Ministry of Education Pamphlet No. 27.* London: HMSO.

Hobsbawm, E. (1994) *Age of Extremes. The Short Twentieth Century 1914–1991.* London: Michael Joseph.

Holbrook, D. (1964) *English for the Rejected. Training Literacy in Lower Streams of the Secondary School.* Cambridge: Cambridge University Press.

— (1961) *English for Maturity.* Cambridge: Cambridge University Press.

Holmes, E. (1911) *What is and What Might Be. A Study of Education in General and Elementary Education in Particular.* London: Constable and Co.

ILEA (1973) Obscured horizons: music in schools. August.

Jorgenson, E. (2003) *Transforming Music Education.* Bloomington and Indianapolis: Indiana University Press.

Kingsley, C. (circa 1910) *Hereward the Wake.* T. Nelson and Sons.

Kneen, J. (2008) The sound of revolution. *Education Guardian*, 29 January, 7.

Kynaston, D. The Festival of Britain – a model of today's South Bank or an awful warning. Speech delivered 3 May 1951 on the steps of St Paul's Cathedral. *The Telegraph* [online]. Available at http://www.telegraph.co.uk/culture/music/3665398 [accessed 15 March 2009].

Lamont, A., Hargreaves, D.J., Marshall, N. and Tarrant, M. (2003) Young people's music in and out of school. *British Journal of Music Education*, 20(3), 229–42.

Langer, S. (1979) *Form and Feeling.* London: Routledge and Kegan Paul.

Lauder, H., Brown, P., Dillabough, J. and Halsey, A.H. (2006) *Education, Globalisation and Social Change.* Oxford: Oxford University Press.

Laurence, F. (2005) Music and empathy: a study of the possible development, through certain ways of 'musicking', of children's empathic abilities, responses, motivation and behaviour within a primary school context. A thesis submitted for the degree of Doctor of Philosophy to the School of Education, University of Birmingham, February.

Laurence, F. (2006) *Making space for Toby: Musicking and Empathic Experience and Inclusion in the Classroom.* Matlock: National Association of Music Educators (magazine issue 19).

— (2010) Listening to children: voice, agency and ownership in school musicking, in *Sociology and Music Education*, edited by R. Wright. Farnham: Ashgate.

Lawrence-Lightfoot, S. (1997) *The Art and Science of Portraiture*. San Francisco: Jossey-Bass.

Leadbeater, C. (2005) The future of public services: personalised learning, in *Schools of Tomorrow: Personalising Education*. OECD Publishing.

Løgstrup, K.J. (1997) *The Ethical Demand*. London: University of Notre Dame Press.

Lyotard, F. (1984) *The Postmodern Condition: A Report on Knowledge*. Minneapolis: University of Minnesota Press and University of Manchester Press.

Marcuse, H. (1987) *Eros and Civilisation*. London: Ark Paperbacks.

Marshall, S. (1963) *An Experiment in Education*. Cambridge: Cambridge University Press.

— (1968) *Adventure in Creative Education*. London: Pergamon Press.

— (1971) Sybil Marshall favours a return to learning in tranquillity and less misunderstood 'activity'. *Times Education Supplement*, 2 July.

— (1976) Language – Arts? *Education 3–13*, 4(1), 26–9.

— (1995) *A Pride of Tigers*. London: Penguin Books.

Maslow, A. (1973) What is a Taoist teacher, in *Facts and Feelings in the Classroom*, edited by L.J. Rubin. London: Ward Lock Educational.

Moore, R. (2004) *Education and Society: Issues and Explanations in the Sociology of Education*. Cambridge: Polity Press.

Music in Education (1977) MANNA Conference – 1: the future of class music. July/August.

NACCE (1999) *All Our Futures: Creativity, Culture and Cultural Education*. London: DfEE/DCMS.

Noddings, N. (2003a) *Happiness and Education*. Cambridge: Cambridge University Press.

— (2003b) *Caring: A Feminist Approach to Ethics and Moral Education*. London: University of California Press.

— (2005) Identifying and responding to needs in education. *Cambridge Journal of Education*, 35(2), 147–59.

North, A.C., Hargreaves, D.J. and O'Neil, S.A. (2000) The importance of music to adolescents. *British Journal of Educational Psychology*, 70, 255–72.

North West Regional Curriculum Development Project (1974) *Creative Music Making and the Young School Leaver*. London: Blackie and Smith.

Oakshott, M. (1972) Education: the engagement and its frustration, in *A Critique of Current Educational Aims*, edited by R.F. Dearden, P.H. Hirst and R.S. Peters. London: Routledge and Kegan Paul.

Ofsted (2009) Making more of music. An evaluation of music in schools 2005/08.

Orton, R. (1982) Assessment: a composer's view, in *Music in the Secondary School Curriculum*, edited by J. Paynter. Cambridge: Cambridge University Press.

Paynter, J. (1982) *Music in the Secondary School Curriculum. Trends and Developments in Classroom Teaching*. Cambridge: Cambridge University Press.

— (1989) The Challenge of creativity. *British Journal of Music Education*, 6(2), 235–7.

— (1992) *Sound and Structure*. Cambridge: Cambridge University Press.

— (1995) Working on one's inner world, in *Powers of Being: David Holbrook and His Work*, edited by E. Webb. London: Associated University Press.

— (1997) The form of finality: a context for music education. *British Journal of Music Education*, 14(1), 5–21.

— (2000) Making progress with composing. *British Journal of Music Education,* 17, 5–31.

— and Aston, P. (1970) *Sound and Silence: Classroom Projects in Creative Music*. Cambridge: Cambridge University Press.

Peters, R. (1969) *Perspectives on Plowden*. London: Routledge and Kegan Paul.

Pitts, S. (2000) *A Century of Change in Music Education: Historical Perspectives on Contemporary Practice in British Secondary School Music*. Aldershot: Ashgate.

Plato (1982) *The Laws*. London: Penguin Books.

— (1988) *The Republic*. Oxford: Clarendon Press.

Plummeridge, C. (1996) Curriculum development and the problem of control, in *Music Education: Trends and Issues*, edited by C. Plummeridge. London, Institute of Education: University of London, 27–40.

Popper, K. (1972) *Objective Knowledge*. Oxford: Clarendon Press.

Pratt, G. and Stephens, J. (1995) *Teaching Music in the National Curriculum*. London: Heinemann.

Preston, H. (1986) *Assessment and Progression in Music Education*. Music Advisors' National Association (MANA).

Price, D. (2005) Musical Futures, an emerging vision. Paul Hamlyn Foundation. [Online]. Available at http://www.musicalfutures.org.uk/c/first+edition [accessed: 24 November 2009].

Pring, R. (2004) *Philosophy of Education: Aims, Theory, Common Sense and Research*. London: Continuum.

QCA (2007) *National Curriculum: Cross-curriculum Dimensions*. [Online]. Available at: http://curriculum.qca.org.uk/cross-curriculum-dimensions/index. aspx [accessed: 5 September 2009].

— (2008) *Curriculum for the Twenty First Century* [Online]. Available at: http:// curriculum.qca.org.uk/subjects/index.aspex [accessed: 5 February 2008].

Rainbow, B (1989) *Music in Educational Thought and Practice. A Survey from 800 BC.* Aberystwyth: Borthius.

— with Cox, G. (2006) *Music in Educational Thought and Practice.* Woodbridge: The Boydell Press.

Read, H. (1958) *Education through Art.* London: Faber and Faber.

Reid, L.A. (1979) Foreword in *A Basis for Music Education* by K. Swanwick. London: NFER Publishing Company.

— (1980) Meaning in the arts, in *The Arts and Personal Growth*, edited by M. Ross. Oxford: Pergamon Press.

— (1983) Aesthetic knowledge, in *The Arts: A Way of Knowing*, edited by M. Ross. Oxford: Pergamon Press.

— (1986) *Ways of Knowing and Understanding.* London: Heinemann Educational Books.

Rice, T. (1985) Music learned but not taught: the Bulgarian case, in *Becoming Human Through Music*, edited by D.P. McAlister. Reston: MENC.

Rose, N. (1990) *Governing the Soul: The shaping of the private self.* London: Routledge.

Ross, M. (1975) *Arts and the Adolescent.* Schools Council Working Paper 54. London: Evans/Metheun Educational.

— (1978) *The Creative Arts.* London: Heinemann Educational Books.

— (1980) *The Arts and Personal Growth.* Oxford: Pergamon Press.

— (1981) Hard Core: The predicament of the arts in curriculum issues in *Arts Education Volume 2: The Aesthetic Imperative, Relevance and Responsibility*, edited by M. Ross. Oxford: Pergamon Press.

— (1984) *The Aesthetic Impulse.* London: Pergamon Press.

— (1989) The last twenty five years: the arts in education, 1963–1988, in *The Claims of Feeling: Readings in Aesthetic Education*, edited by M. Ross. London: The Falmer Press.

— (1995) What's wrong with school music? *British Journal of Music Education*, 12(3), 185–201.

— (2007) Memorandum submitted to the United Kingdom Parliament Education and Skills Select Committee. Hansard Archives.

—., Radnor, H., Mitchell, S. and Bierton, C. (1993) *Assessing and Achievement in the Arts.* Buckingham: Open University.

Rousseau, J.J. (1763) *Emilius*; or *A Treatise of Education.* First English Edition Vol. 1, 222 *et seq.* Edinburgh 1763.

— (1993) *Emile*, translated by Barbara Foley. London: Dent.

Rudduck, J. (2002) *The Pupil Voice.* Talk given to East Anglian Researchers in Music Education Seminar, November 30.

— (2004a) Pupil voice is here to stay! QCA futures. QCA. [Also available at http://www.qca.org.uk/futures/].

— (2004b) *The Challenge of Year 8.* Cambridge: Pearson.

— and Fielding, M. (2006) Student voice and the perils of popularity. *Educational Review.* 58(2), 219–231.

— and McIntyre, D. (2007) *Improving Learning through Consulting Pupils*. Abingdon: Routledge.

Sadie, S. (ed.) (1994) *The Grove Concise Dictionary of Music*. London: MacMillan.

SAM Learning [Online]. Available at: https://www.samlearning.com [accessed: 30 January 2008].

Sarson, S. (1990) *The Predictable Failure of Educational Reform*. San Francisco: Josey-Bass.

Schools Council *Enquiry 1* (1968) *Young School Leavers*. London: HMSO.

Schools Council (1971) *Music and the Young School Leaver: Problems and Opportunities*. Working Paper 35. London: Evans/Metheun.

Scott, M. (1943) *Beethoven*. London: J.M. Dent and Sons.

Scottish Education Department (1995) *Junior Secondary Education*. Edinburgh: HMSO.

Shepherd, J. and Vulliamy, G. (1994) The struggle for culture: a sociological case study of the development of a national music curriculum. *British Journal of Sociology of Education*, 15(1), 27–40.

Simon, B. (1981) Why no pedagogy in England?, in *Education in the Eighties: the central issues*, edited by B. Simon and W. Taylor. London: Batsford, 124–45.

— (1991) *Education and the Social Order 1940–1990*. London: Lawrence and Wishart.

Simpson, K. (1970) Music in schools: the problems of teaching, in *Black Paper 3*, edited by C.B. Cox and A.E. Dyson. London: Critical Quarterly.

— (1975) *Some Great Music Educators*. London: Novello.

Sloboda, J. (2001) Emotion, functionality and the everyday experience of music: where does music education fit? *Music Education Research*, 3(2), 243–53.

Small, C. (1977) *Music-Society-Education*. London: John Cader.

— (1998) *Musicking: The Meanings of Performing and Listening*. Hanover, NH: Wesleyan University Press.

— (1999) Musicking – the meanings of performing and listening. *Music Education Research*, 1(1), 9–21.

Smith, C. (1999) Foreword to NACCE (1999) All Our Futures: Creativity, Culture and Cultural Education. London: DfEE/DCMS.

Swanwick, K. (1979) *A Basis for Music Education*. London: NFER Publishing Company.

— (1988) *Music, Mind and Education*. London: Routledge.

— (1992a) Open peer commentary: musical knowledge: the saga of music in the National Curriculum. *Psychology of Music and Music Education*, 20(2), 162–79.

— (1992b) *Music Education and the National Curriculum*. London: Tufnell Press.

— (1994) *Musical Knowledge, Intuition and Analysis*. London: Routledge.

— (1997) Editorial. *British Journal of Music Education*, 14, 3–4.

— (1999) *Teaching Music Musically*. London: Routledge.

— and Lawson, D. (1999) 'Authentic' music and its effect on the attitudes of secondary school students. *Music Education Research*, 1(1), 47–60.

— and Tillman, J. (1986) The sequence of musical development: a study of children's composition. *British Journal of Music Education*, 3(3), 305–39.

Taylor, C. (2007) *A Secular Age*. London: Harvard University Press.

Taylor, D. (1979) *Music Now*. London: Oxford University Press.

Vulliamy, G. (1975) Music education: some critical comments. *Journal of Curriculum Studies*, (7), 18–25.

— (1977) Music as a case study in the 'new sociology of education', in *Whose Music? A sociology of musical languages*, edited by J. Shepherd et al. London: Latimer.

— (1978) Culture clash and school music: a sociological analysis, in *Sociological Interpretations of Schooling and Classrooms: a reappraisal*, edited by L. Barton and R. Meighan. Driffield: Nafferton Books.

Weinstock, A. (1976) I blame the teachers. *Times Education Supplement*, 23 January.

Wilde, L. (2004) *Erich Fromm and the Quest for Solidarity*. New York: Palgrave Macmillan.

Williams, R. (1961) *The Long Revolution*. London: Penguin Books.

— (1963) *Culture and Society 1750–1950*. Harmondsworth: Penguin Books.

Willis, P. (1978) *Profane Culture*. London: Routledge and Kegan Paul.

— (1990) *Moving Culture: An Enquiry into the Cultural Activities of Young People*. London: Calouste Gulbenkian Foundation.

—., Jones, S., Cannan, J. and Hurd, G. (1990) *Common Culture. Symbolic Work at Play in the Everyday Cultures of the Young*. Milton Keynes: Open University Press.

Winnicott, D. (1985) *The Child, the Family and the Outside World*. London: Penguin Books.

— (1987) *The Maturational Process and the Facilitating Environment*. London: Hogarth Press.

Witkin, R. (1974) *The Intelligence of Feeling*. London: Heinemann.

— (1989) Expressivist theories of arts education, in *The Claims of Feeling: Readings in Aesthetic Education*, edited by M. Ross. London: The Falmer Press.

Woodford, P. (2005) *Democracy and Music Education: Liberalism, Ethics, and the Politics of Practice*. Bloomington: Indiana University Press.

— (2009) Two political models for music education and their implications for practice, in *Sound Progress: exploring musical development*, edited by A. Lamont and H. Coll. Matlock: National Association of Music Educators.

Wyness, M. (2000) *Contesting Childhood*. London: The Falmer Press.

Young, M.F.K. (1971) *Knowledge and Control*. London: Collier-Macmillan.

Glossary

Arts and the Adolescent Project 1968–72
A Schools Council Project undertaking radical research into ways of bringing together the in and out of school involvement in the arts of young people, and exploring the relationship between each of the arts and between the arts and other subjects in the curriculum (see also Schools Council).

Black Papers
A series of five pamphlets on education published between 1969 and 1977, edited by C.B. Cox and A.E. Dyson, opposed to the excesses of progressive education. The first two, 'Fight for Education' and 'Crises in Education' coincided with the student revolts of 1968 to 1970. The writers were concerned with the threat to standards, order and discipline and in their view this threat was no better exemplified than by the introduction of 'comprehensive education'.

Board of Education
Established in 1899 to oversee matters relating to Education in England and Wales and replaced by the Ministry of Education in 1944. The Board provided teachers with suggestions and guidance.

Central Advisory Council for Education (England)
Established by the Butler Act of 1944 as the advisory body with responsibility to inform the government minister on relevant matters relating to the theory and practice of education. The body was little referred to after the Plowden Report and officially abolished in 1986.

Certificate of Secondary Education (CSE)
A system of examinations introduced in 1965 in England and Wales, mainly for pupils in secondary modern schools (and later some of those in comprehensive schools) to improve their educational and employment prospects. The CSE was replaced in 1986 by the GCSE (see below).

Colleges of Education
Places of teacher training and education in England established in 1965 and replacing the former Teacher Training Colleges.

Comprehensive School
A school that does not select on the basis of academic achievement or aptitude, coming into being from the late 1940s to the late 1970s.

Creative Music and the Young School Leaver 1966–74
A teacher-led project responding to the Newsom Report and seeking to make music education accessible to the secondary school pupil of average or below average ability. The project was supported by Local Education Authorities in the North West of England. The project devised strategies for creative music making to be implemented and evaluated by teachers.

Creative Partnerships
The New Labour government's flagship creative learning programme bringing together schools and creative professionals including artists, performers, architects, multi-media developers and scientists. The programme was designed to help young people perform well at school and also in the workplace and wider society.

Department for Culture, Media and Sport (DCMS)
Government department established by New Labour in 1997 to promote cultural activity, and linked to the nation's creative and innovating potential.

Department for Education and Science (DES)
Redesignation in 1964 of the former Ministry of Education.

Department for Education (DfE)
Re-designation in 1993 of the former DES.

Department for Education and Employment (DfEE)
Re-designation in 1996 of the enlarged DfE which assumed responsibility for employment in addition to education.

Department of Education and Skills (DfES)
Re-designation in 2005 of the enlarged and reorganized DfEE and since redesignated as the DfCSF: the Department for Children, Schools and Families.

Desert Island Discs
A BBC radio programme created by Roy Plomley in 1942. It has a simple format: an invited guest chooses the eight records they would take with them to a desert island.

Economic and Social Research Council (ESRC)
The government funded council supporting research and training in social and economic issues including significant research in education.

Education Reform Act (ERA) 1988
The Education Act establishing a National Curriculum for England and Wales, a system of national testing and leading to a new framework of inspection (see also Ofsted).

Eleven plus examination (11+)
An examination administered by Local Education Authorities to pupils in their final year of primary education and governing admission to secondary school. The examination was instituted in the Butler Education Act of 1944 as part of the tripartite system which selected pupils for grammar, secondary modern or technical schools.

General Certificate of Education (GCE)
School examinations in England and Wales that replaced the School Certificate and the Higher School Certificate in 1951: available at Ordinary (O) and Advanced (A) level.

General Certificate of Secondary Education (GCSE)
An examination system introduced in 1986 to provide a single method of assessment for all pupils aged 16 (replacing O level and CSE examinations) and first examined in 1988. Typically, students who are entered sit five or more GCSE subjects, which are assessed by written papers and coursework. In the case of music at least 60 per cent of assessment is of performance and composition.

Grammar School
The selective tier of the tripartite system of state education (see Eleven plus examination). Grammar schools were considerably reduced in number by the introduction of comprehensive education.

Hadow Reports
Comprising six reports published between 1923 and 1933. The 1926 and 1932 reports explicitly encouraged teachers to adopt a more progressive curriculum.

Her/His Majesty's Inspectorate of Schools (HMI)
The first HMIs were appointed in 1840 and then, as in subsequent times, were essentially concerned with the improvement of education (see also Ofsted).

Inner London Education Authority (ILEA)
The education authority responsible for the education of children in boroughs comprising central London, and in existence from 1965 to 1990.

Local Authorities (LAs) and Local Education Authorities (LEAs)
Administrative authorities (LAs) originally created by the Balfour Education Act (1902) to provide elementary and secondary education in defined geographical areas (originally counties and county boroughs). Within this arrangement LEAs were vested with authority over the administration and development of local education policies in response to central government policies.

Ministry of Education
Set up by the 1944 Education Act replacing the Central Board of Education.

Music Advisors' National Association (MANA)
An association of Local Education Authority Music Advisors in existence from 1947 to 1996. In the early years of the organization the term 'organizer' was common before 'advisor' became the norm and latterly 'inspector'.

Musical Futures
A radical approach offering new and imaginative ways of engaging young people aged 11 to 19 in musical activities, and working with models of successful informal music-making practices in evidence beyond school. Musical Futures is funded by the Paul Hamlyn Foundation.

National Advisory Committee on Creativity and Cultural Education (NACCE)
The committee established in 1998 by the Secretary of State for Education, David Blunkett and Secretary of State for Culture, Media and Sport, Chris Smith, commissioned to recommend on the cultural and creative development of young people.

National Curriculum Council (NCC)
The agency established by the 1988 Education Reform Act to oversee the detailed planning and implementation of the National Curriculum. The NCC was replaced by the School Curriculum and Assessment Authority (SCAA) in 1993 and in 1998 by the Qualifications and Assessment Authority (QCA).

National Curriculum Music Working Group
The group was set up in 1990 by the Secretaries of State for England and Wales, to advise on attainment targets and programmes of study for music in the National Curriculum.

National Strategy for Music
Following the establishment of the government's National Strategy Unit in 2005, and concerned with the teaching of literacy and numeracy, a strategy was designed specifically for music for ages 11–14 in 2007 and disseminated across England chiefly through Local Education Authorities.

Newsom Report
The Newsom Report *Half our Futures* (1963) formed the report that led to the raising of the school leaving age from 15 to 16. The report made specific recommendations that a purposeful education be provided for those pupils who found the later years of secondary schooling unrewarding. In this the arts were recognized as playing a significant part.

Office for Standards in Education (Ofsted)

Ofsted was brought into being by the 1992 Education Act and the Schools Inspection Regulations of 1993. It replaced the school inspection functions previously performed by Her Majesty's Inspectorate of Schools (HMI). As a non-ministerial department of government, Ofsted is less independent than was Her Majesty's Inspectorate.

Organization for Economic Co-operation and Development (OECD)

An organization of 30 member countries committed to democratic government and the market economy that publishes, among other things, statistical research related to economic development, education and technical change.

Plowden Report

A review of primary education commissioned in 1963 by the Minister of Education, Sir Edward Boyle and published in 1967.

Primary School

The first stage of schooling typically for children aged 5 to 11.

Programme(s) of Study (POS)

Each Core and Foundation subject of the National Curriculum for England has its statutory prescribed content specified in a Programme of Study: there are separate Programmes of Study for each of the four Key Stages within the National Curriculum.

Qualifications and Curriculum Authority (QCA)

The government agency established under the provisions of the 1998 Education Act, with powers to propose, consult upon, and prescribe revisions and amendments to the National Curriculum and other government initiatives and the areas of curriculum and assessment in schools. The QCA replaced SCAA (the School Curriculum and Assessment Authority). The QCA has published an abundance of advisory and exemplar materials to assist schools and teachers in the implementation of the National Curriculum. In 2009 the QCA was renamed the QCDA: Qualifications and Curriculum Development Authority.

Schools Council

The body formed in 1964 and abolished in 1984 which gave responsibility to teachers and teachers' organizations to develop the curriculum and have greater responsibility for the ordering of public examinations. Over 150 curriculum research and development projects were sponsored by the council and a large number of reports, teachers' guides and materials were produced.

Schools Council *Enquiry I*: *Young School Leavers*
This report published in 1968 revealing that music in secondary schools was rated as useless and boring by large numbers of the teenagers who were questioned.

Schools Council *Working Paper 35: Music and the Young School Leaver*
This report published in 1971 tackled issues raised by the Schools Council *Enquiry I*. The sentence 'a great deal of cherished and time-honoured methods will have to be discarded as irrelevant to the contemporary situation' (ibid: 30) is characteristic of the report's recommendations.

Schools Council Music Project: Music in the Secondary School Curriculum
An innovating and reformist teacher-led curriculum project directed by John Paynter from 1973 to 1980 that provided creative and imaginative ways of working with the whole secondary age and ability range. Thus providing 'music for the majority'.

Secondary Modern School
A type of secondary school established in the Butler Act of 1994 within the tripartite system. It was designed for the majority of students and provided learning in basic subjects and training in simple practical skills.

Secondary School
The second stage of schooling typically for those aged 11 to 16/18.

Technical School
A type of school established in the Butler Act of 1944 within the tripartite system for those secondary aged students who showed aptitude in mechanical and scientific subjects.

Times Educational Supplement (TES)
A weekly publication reporting and commenting on topical issues in education, first published in 1910.

Index